G000040062

Watch Your Language!

TEACHERS!

SUPPORT MATERIAL

For your support material check our website at www.gillmacmillan.ie

Support material is available to teachers only within a secure area of this website.

Support material for this book consists of suggested solutions to exercises in the book.

To access support material for **Watch Your Language!** second edition:

1. Go to www.gillmacmilllan.ie
2. Click on the 'logon' button and enter your username and password. (If you do not already have a username and password you must register. To do this click the 'register' button and complete the online registration form. Your username and password will then be sent to you by email.)
3. Click on the link 'Support Material'.
4. Select the title **Watch Your Language!** second edition.

Watch Your Language!

Second Edition

Grammar, Punctuation, Spelling, Vocabulary

Mary Ó Maolmhuire

Gill & Macmillan

Gill & Macmillan
Hume Avenue
Park West
Dublin 12
with associated companies throughout the world
www.gillmacmillan.ie

© Mary Ó Maolmhuire, 1999, 2004

978 07171 3716 9

Artwork p.151 © Kate Walsh 2004

Picture research: Image Select International Ltd.

Design and print origination in Ireland by Metaphor

The paper used in this book is made from the wood pulp of managed forests. For every tree felled, at least one tree is planted, thereby renewing natural resources.

All rights reserved.

No part of this publication may be copied, reproduced or transmitted in any form or by any means without written permission of the publishers or else under the terms of any licence permitting limited copying issued by the Irish Copyright Licensing Agency.

Picture Credits

For permission to reproduce photographs and other material, the author and publisher gratefully acknowledge the following:

www.inpho.ie: 1 bottom row left, 1 bottom row right, 13 top, 138, 252

www.photos.com: 1 top left, 1 top row second from left, 1 bottom row second from right, 90 top row left and right, 90 bottom row left and right, 100, 239

Topham Picturepoint: 1 top row second from right, 1 top row right, 5 all, 10, 11, 13 third from top, 13 bottom, 36, 47, 88, 89, 189, 203 both, 204, 216, 217, 246, 249 top

Other photographs: 1 bottom row second from left © Kieran Clancy; 13 second from top © courtesy of An Post; 48 © Tony Hardacre; 51 © Spectrum Colour Library; 59, 61 © Ann Ronan Picture Library; 137 © Collins Photo Agency; 187 top courtesy of The Griffin Group; 187 bottom courtesy of Sinnott Hotels; 250 © Image Select

Cartoon: 200 © Brick/The Irish Times

Promotional material: 12, 37, 90 top row centre, 90 bottom row centre

The author and publishers have made every effort to trace all copyright holders, but if any has been inadvertently overlooked we would be pleased to make the necessary arrangements at the first opportunity.

Contents

Watch Your Language!

Introduction

The limits of my language mean the limits of my world.

Ludvig Wittgenstein

Correct and imaginative use of language is essential for good English. Yet many students experience difficulties in grammar, punctuation, spelling and vocabulary. They are generally very careless with punctuation, for example. They appear to know the rules but don't apply them in practice. Similarly, spelling is often a hit-or-miss affair, even though there are rules governing spelling, as there are for most things.

When our students write well, we say their language is 'colourful', 'vivid' or 'descriptive'. Yet, this kind of writing is rare, and as teachers we are constantly frustrated by our students' lack of vocabulary and needless and boring repetition. With grammar, too, we assume that our students are familiar with structures, tenses, parts of speech, etc. Yet, their written work often displays an ignorance of the basic rules and practices of good English.

This book comprises ten units, all of which (with the exception of Unit 10) contain four sections: grammar, punctuation, spelling and vocabulary. The book concentrates on the most important areas of language, and exercises them thoroughly. Actual explanations of grammatical elements, for example, are kept simple and to a minimum. The emphasis is on the word 'practice'. There are opportunities for oral class warm-ups and games, pair and groupwork activities, as well as lots of written work for the individual student. There is also a key for the teacher on the Gill & Macmillan website www.gillmacmillan.ie.

In grammar, punctuation and vocabulary, the exercises are progressive, in Stages 1 to 3. Students are encouraged to complete the exercises within a certain time limit. Stage 1 is broadly aimed at First and Second Year students. Stage 2 provides more challenging work, and Stage 3 exercises, although related directly to the Junior Cert. Higher and Ordinary level exam, may also be used with a Transition Year group or Senior classes.

Each section within a unit is complete within itself, but may be used in conjunction with the other three. Personally, I feel that at least one period a week should be devoted to developing language skills. Alternatively, a module of language work, spanning a half-term, for example, could work well. However, even if time is a real constraint, this book contains many exercises that students may tackle themselves, without direction from the teacher.

It is my firm belief that as students exercise their language skills, both orally and in writing, they will become aware, not only of how English works, but also of the practical benefits of expressing themselves clearly and precisely. At the same time, the 'Words at Work' sections, with their creative and functional writing exercises, will enlarge students' vocabulary, encourage them to explore words and their meanings, and to exercise their imaginations.

Acquiring good language and communication skills will, of course, also provide a sound basis for Senior English work. Indeed, in the new English syllabus for Leaving Cert., the Department of Education and Science emphasises the importance of language skills:

'At both levels a competence in the accurate and appropriate use of language will be a fundamental requirement. All students will be expected to be assiduous in their attention to paragraphing, syntax, spelling and punctuation.'

I am convinced that exercising the language itself will result in a more confident and creative use of English by students. It will, of course, also enhance their performance in state exams. More importantly, however, they will be acquiring skills for life.

Mary Ó Maolmhuire

Unit 1

Grappling with Grammar

Nouns

Question What is a noun?

Answer A noun is the name of:

- a person
- a thing
- a place
- a quality or emotion.

The word 'noun' comes from the Latin word 'nomen', meaning name.
There are **four** kinds of nouns:

common   student, chips, car, cat

proper   Bart Simpson, Paris, Heinz Beans, August

abstract   speed, energy, love, happiness

collective   a **class** of students, a **flock** of sheep, a **bunch** of grapes, a **team** of footballers.

Stage 1

Classroom activities, teacher directed, oral and written

A. Common nouns

These nouns are 'common' to many persons, places and things. See examples given above.

Exercise 1. Make a list of **ten** common-noun objects in your classroom in under one minute. Start with the word 'chair'.

Exercise 2. Ask the student beside you to list ten objects he/she has in his/her school **locker** in under one minute. Listen very carefully! Then, **write down** as many as you can remember in under one minute also. He/she will time you and will check to see if you have them all.

Exercise 3. Swop roles. This time you tell him/her ten objects you have in your bedroom at home. Your neighbour must write these down in under one minute as before. Then you check his/her list. The one who has remembered the most **common-noun objects** wins!

B. Proper nouns

These words **name** a particular person, place or thing. They are always written with a capital letter. See examples given above.

Exercise 1. Write down the **first names only** of ten people in your class in ninety seconds.

Exercise 2. Ask your neighbour to name five brand-name food or household items in under thirty seconds. You must write these down from memory in under thirty seconds also. Your neighbour will check to see if you have them all.

Exercise 3. Swop roles. This time you ask him/her to name five sport or fashion brand labels in under thirty seconds. You must write them down from memory also. Your neighbour will check to see if you have them all.

C. Abstract nouns

These are the names of **qualities** or **emotions**. They are things we cannot see or touch but which we feel. See examples given above.

Exercise 1. In pairs, write out a list of ten **emotions** in under two minutes. Your teacher will time you. Begin with the word 'love'.

Exercise 2. Your teacher will now ask one student from each pair to call out their list. The other student-pairs in the class will compare these with their own abstract nouns, and add to them any **new** ones they hear. At the end of this exercise you should have at least twenty abstract nouns each.

Exercise 3. Underline the **abstract nouns only** in this list:

  happiness, restaurant, monster, guilt, humour, library, patience, beauty, stadium, scissors, disappointment, Germany, bicycle, sympathy, garden, friendship, wisdom, Tuesday, pride, youth

D. Collective nouns

These refer to a **collection** or group of people, animals or things. See examples given above.

Exercise 1. Which collective noun would you use in the following phrases, instead of 'a lot'? The first letter of the word is given to you, as is the number of letters per word. You may work in pairs. Time limit: five minutes.

1. a c**rowd** of people (5)
2. a f**lee** of ships (5)
3. a h**erd** of cattle (4)
4. a s**tring** of beads (6)
5. a g**ang** of thieves (4)

6. a l**itter** of pups (6)
7. a b**and** of musicians (4)
8. a f**lock** of birds (5)
9. a h**ive** of bees (4)
10. a c**ollection** of stamps (10)

Exercise 2. Match these collective nouns to the **common nouns** we usually associate with them.

(Example) A pack of _____ : **wolves** or **cards**

1. a shoal of _____
2. a bunch of _____
3. a plague of _____
4. a clump of _____
5. a set of _____
6. a board of _____

Compare your answers with the student next to you. Remember there may be more than one common noun for each collective noun! Add any different ones to your own list. Time limit: five minutes.

Exercise 3. Write five sentences of your own with the following collective nouns. Remember that you can use them with a number of different common nouns.

(Example) pack: The story he told me was a pack of **lies**!
       or
       A pack of **hungry dogs** ran through a field of sheep.

1. bunch
2. litter
3. flock
4. pack
5. collection

Watch Your Language!

Stage 2

A. Common nouns

Exercise 1. What is the common noun for someone who . . . ?

1. treats sick people
2. writes for a newspaper
3. investigates crime
4. rides horses in a race
5. flies aeroplanes
6. designs buildings
7. studies the stars
8. paints pictures
9. cooks for a living
10. lends books

Exercise 2.

1. Write one common noun for each letter of the alphabet. Use your dictionary if you get stuck.

> **Example**   A = apple, animal.

Try to complete the exercise in twelve minutes – thirty seconds per word!

2. Using each of the twenty-six common nouns on your list, write a short continuous piece, in prose or dialogue, in which each word is used just once. (100–120 words)

Exercise 3.

1. Study the pictures of twenty common household items (and pets!) below for three minutes. Your teacher will time you.
2. Cover the page.
3. Write out as many of these twenty common objects from memory as you can in under five minutes. (Remember to write them all with a **small** letter!) The student who remembers the most items wins!

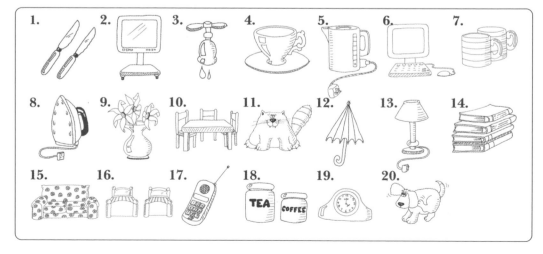

B. Proper nouns

Exercise 1.   Underline all the proper nouns in the following passage:

Roddy Doyle was born in Dublin in 1958. He taught English and Geography at Greendale Community School, Kilbarrack, in north Dublin. His first play, *Brownbread*, was produced in Dublin in 1987. His first novel, *The Commitments*, was published in 1988, and made into a film by Alan Parker. His second novel, *The Snapper*, was published in 1990. *The Van* was shortlisted for the Booker Prize in 1991, and *Paddy Clarke Ha Ha Ha* actually won it in 1993.

Exercise 2.   Answer the following questions with proper nouns. (Don't forget those **capital** letters!)

1. Which is your favourite football team?
2. What is their home ground called?
3. Name three teams they have played this season.
4. What is the name of their manager?
5. Who is their best player?
6. Which is your favourite group or band?
7. What are the full names of the members of the group or band?
8. What nationality are they?
9. What is the name of their latest album?
10. Which is your favourite track?

Exercise 3.

1. Here are some stars from the world of TV, music and film. Who are they? You must give their full names.

2. Choose one star and write a brief profile of his/her life and career, using as many proper nouns as possible. (100–120 words)

C. Abstract nouns

Exercise 1. Give the abstract nouns corresponding to the following adjectives:

> **Example**   mad – madness

1. sane	6. cruel
2. shy	7. beautiful
3. gentle	8. proud
4. passionate	9. energetic
5. wise	10. real

Exercise 2. Write one sentence for each of these ten abstract nouns that clearly illustrates its meaning.

> **Example**   It's **madness** to go out without a coat in that rain!

Exercise 3. Fill in the gaps in the following passage with a suitable abstract noun from the list below. The number of letters is indicated in each case.

humour, excitement, generosity, madness, patience, sanity, caution, guilt, truth, happiness

Christmas is a time of unrivalled _____ (7) as far as shopping is concerned. In the _____ (10) of the days leading up to the big event, we all lose our _____ (6) and spend, spend, spend. No one seems to feel the least _____ (5) at the prospect of having an enormous overdraft in the New Year, and even the most crotchety neighbour appears to have a sense of _____ (6). 'It's all for the kids,' we say. The smiles on their faces when they open their presents on Christmas morning are worth every penny. We have no _____ (8) with those who say we should exercise _____ (7). The _____ (5) of the matter is, Christmas is the one time of the year when everyone, even the least fortunate, experiences a little _____ (9). And after Christmas, we can always rely on the _____ (10) of our friendly bank manager, can't we?

D. Collective nouns

Exercise 1. Fill in the blanks in the following sentences with a suitable collective noun from the list below:

nest, suite, hum, board, litter, bunch, swarm, ray, bouquet, hordes, block, chain, canteen, wad, pile

1. The board of directors decided to go ahead and build a twenty-storey block of flats and a chain of shops.
2. When Denis and Aileen got married, they got a nest of tables from Gran, and a canteen of cutlery from Uncle John.

3. When really famous bands visit Dublin, they don't just book a room in a hotel, they book a ~~suite~~ of rooms. *suite*

4. A _ray_ of sunlight lit up the corner of her drab room.

5. What a lovely _litter_ of puppies!

6. The film star took a _wad_ of notes from his wallet, and tipped the waiter €100.

7. It was easy to speak privately in the restaurant as the _hum_ of conversation from those around us completely drowned out our words.

8. _(stream)_ of tourists visit our town every year, especially Americans.

9. He was a romantic. He brought her a _bouquet_ of flowers, a _bunch_ of grapes, and a huge _pile_ of magazines when she was ill.

10. She was badly stung by a _swarm_ of bees while on holiday in Spain.

Exercise 2. Write out these sentences, choosing the most suitable collective noun from those in brackets:

1. The bus slowed down behind a (party, herd, clump) of cattle.

2. On Valentine's Day, Tom bought a huge (packet, bunch, bundle) of flowers for his girlfriend.

3. Mum has bought a new (case, set, pack) of luggage for her holidays.

4. Gran says that she will leave me her antique (collection, group, chest) of drawers.

5. Sally, our dog, had her (pile, litter, stack) of pups in the garage.

Exercise 3. Write a sentence of your own for each of the two words you rejected from the sentences in Exercise 2.

> (**Example**)   1. The soldier hid behind a clump of trees.

Stage 3

The Exam; Personal writing

This photograph is taken from the Junior Cert. Higher level, Paper 1, 2002.

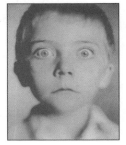

1. What emotion is the boy experiencing in this picture? Make a short list of abstract nouns that might suitably express his feelings at this moment.

2. Write a composition inspired by this picture.

Punctuation Please!

Capital Letters and Full Stops C and •

Question When do we use capital letters?

Answer
1. For names of:
   - people (Mary, Paul, Bono)
   - countries (Ireland, France, USA)
   - cities (Dublin, Cork, Paris)
   - rivers (Slaney, Liffey, Amazon)
   - months, days (March, Friday)
   - brand names (Cadbury's, Kelloggs, Nescafé)
   - books, films (*The Hobbit*, *Star Wars*)
   - football teams (Manchester United, Shamrock Rovers).
2. For the **first** word in direct speech: 'Get up now!' roared Mum.
3. At the **beginning** of a sentence: We hate Monday mornings.

Question When do we use full stops?

Answer
1. When we want to mark the **end** of a **sentence**: 'Before you meet your handsome prince, you have to kiss a lot of frogs.'
2. After **initials**: M. C. Moore, J. K. Rowling.
3. After words that have been **abbreviated** (shortened): Mon. Feb. St. Dr.

Question   Why do we use full stops?

 Answer   1.   Full stops help the reader to **make sense** of what we are writing.

2.   Full stops show that we have **finished** a point we have been making.

3.   Full stops allow the reader to **pause** for a moment, in order to **think about** what we've just written.

Stage 1

Exercise 1.

Capital letters

1.   Odd Man Out! In each of the following groups, only two words should start with a capital letter. Write these down. Do not write down the other words.

   a.   thomas, woman, boy, jennifer, man

   b.   galway, country, australia, place, land

   c.   atlantic, sea, river, alps, mountain

   d.   hour, spring, october, month, april

   e.   irish, language, buddhism, religion, church

   f.   energy, peter, angry, woman, london

   g.   pupils, spain, cautious, austria, city

   h.   canada, pepper, liffey, science, week

   i.   mother, america, rupert, cheese, ocean

   j.   madrid, county, vegetable, bicycle, raleigh

2.   Now write ten sentences of your own, which must include the two capital-letter words from each group.

Example   Thomas and Jennifer are engaged.

Exercise 2.

Full stops

1.   **In pairs**, write one **amusing** sentence with a full stop at the end. (Time limit: ninety seconds)

2.   One student from each pair then reads their sentence out loud to the whole class.

3.   Students must write down all the sentences they hear, **highlighting** the full stop at the end in each case.

4.   'Today is Saturday. This is Sara's/Tom's favourite day . . .' Continue the story for eight more sentences. Each sentence must begin with a capital letter and end with a full stop. It should also include one other capital-letter word. Try to write a **complete** story (a mini-saga) within the ten-sentence exercise.

Watch Your Language!

Exercise 3.

Abbreviations

1. Write out the following with **full stops** and **capital letters**:

mr s t murphy	st anthony	dr b ryan
td	man united	usa
rte	gaa	merrion sq
park ave	o'connell st	ms g gibbs
taney rd	sr agnes	mrs p tancred
la law	o j simpson	b b king
madison ave	d j carey	

2. Write the following in **abbreviated** form:

County Galway	Reverend Smith	Lansdowne Road
Professor Martin	Parnell Square	County Cork
General Michael Collins	Automobile Association	Patrick Street
Mister Sean Browne	Federal Bureau of Investigation	County Cavan
Doctor Sheila Conlon	General Post Office	Teachta Dála
Saint Brigid's Church	Prime Minister	Bachelor of Arts
Bachelor of Science	Bachelor of Commerce	

Stage 2

Exercise 1. Rewrite the following sentences with **capital letters** where necessary and full stops at the end. Don't rush it! Write carefully.

1. the film starts at eight o'clock
2. my pen-friend lives in paris
3. i read an article about atomic kitten in bliss magazine
4. the most common surname in the world is chang
5. birds sing
6. a young italian boy wrote 500 letters to his girlfriend but she married the postman
7. school is boring but so is the telly sometimes
8. when i really concentrate i can do this
9. i bet man united will win this weekend
10. friday is my favourite day of the week

Exercise 2.

Classroom exercise, in pairs

1. a. Choose a partner.
   b. Within a time limit of ten minutes, write nine sentences, beginning with a sentence of just two words, then one with three words, then four, and so on until you get to sentence number nine which, of course, should have ten words in it! Remember those **capital letters** at the beginning and **full stops** at the end of each sentence.
2. Exchange your sentences with another pair of students from the class, and check theirs for **capital letters** and **full stops**. Award two marks per sentence for correct punctuation, making a total of eighteen marks in all.

Exercise 3.

Capital letter quiz

This may be used as an individual exercise for class or homework, or as a table quiz in class, with a time limit set by the teacher of perhaps 20–25 minutes. Remember! All the answers must be written with a **capital letter**!

1. Write down the names of all six characters in the TV series *Friends*.
2. Which team won the English FA Cup Final in 2003?
3. What are the capital cities of France, Spain, Italy and Germany?
4. Name all the members of the Simpson family.
5. Which chocolate company sponsors *Coronation Street*?
6. Name five major supermarket chains in Ireland.
7. Write the titles of five books that have been made into films.
8. Which month has the smallest number of days?
9. Which county won the All-Ireland Hurling Final in 2003?
10. Complete the following advertising slogans:
    a. '_____ is good for you.'
    b. 'A _____ a day helps you work, rest and play.'
    c. 'Because you're _____ ___.'
11. Who won a silver medal for Ireland in the 2000 Olympics?
12. Which female actress starred in the TV series *Buffy the Vampire Slayer*?
13. Write the first names of all five members of the group Westlife.
14. Name five brand labels of sports gear.

15. In which major cities would you find the following?
    a. The Eiffel Tower
    b. The Vatican
    c. The Empire State Building
    d. Oxford Street
    e. Old Trafford
16. Name five mountain ranges in Europe.
17. Complete each of the following statements with a word beginning with a capital letter:
    a. '____ that door!'
    b. '____ till your father gets home!'
    c. '____ me up, Scottie.'
    d. '____, Romeo, wherefore art thou, Romeo?'
    e. '____ up, Doc?'
18. Name five TV series with one-word titles.
19. Name five animal characters from books, magazines, cartoons or films.
20. On which day of the week do you usually do the following?
    a. Go to the cinema
    b. Go to a disco
    c. Go to church
    d. Eat pancakes
    e. Pig out!

Stage 3

The Exam; Media studies

Exercise 1.

Here are some television highlights from *The Irish Times Magazine*. I have removed all the **capital letters and full stop.** Can you replace them?

1. fantasy: buffy – the last ever episode, sky one, 8 p m

    after seven seasons of kicking vampire butt, buffy (sarah michelle gellar) is finally hanging up her stake, but not before she leads her band of slayers into the hellmouth for a final cataclysmic battle against the forces of evil go, buffy!

    The Irish Times Magazine, 7 June 2003

2. sport: heineken cup rugby, n2, 7 30 p m

live coverage of round five of heineken cup rugby action from donnybrook in dublin where leinster's scoring machine brian o'driscoll will be hoping to make a dent in welsh outsiders swansea with commentary by jim sherwin and tony ward

The Irish Times Magazine, 4 January 2003

3. comedy: fear an phoist, tg4, 9 30 p m

this is described as a mr bean meets charlie chaplin, but with a touch of walter mitty the description certainly fits our local fear an phoist who, apart from his oversized uniform, looks fairly normal, but appearances can be deceiving

The Irish Times Magazine, 4 January 2003

4. harry mania: j k rowling: the interview, bbc2, 7 30 p m

with less than 48 hours to go to the publishing event of the year, the arrival of *harry potter and the order of the phoenix* in bookshops worldwide, the promotional rollercoaster continues harry creator j k rowling talks to jeremy paxman in this primetime special

The Irish Times Magazine, 14 June 2003

5. music: imagine . . . the hip hop generation, bbc1, 10 35 p m

hip hop today has become synonymous with youth culture, and this documentary explores why britain's kids have become the hip hop generation and asks what is it about rap music and the street language of african-america that has britain's youth enthralled presented by alan yentob, the programme begins on detroit's eight mile road, the current hip hop capital of the world, and travels from new york and south central la to brixton and buckinghamshire interviews include eminem, ms dynamite, chuck d and the roots

The Irish Times Magazine, 21 June 2003

Exercise 2. Can you write a 'Television Highlights' style article of your own?
Include the following:

1. The name of the programme, channel and time of transmission.
2. The actor(s)/presenter(s) involved in the programme.
3. A brief summary of what it's about. (50–70 words)
4. The reason(s) why you, the critic, would recommend this programme to the viewer. (50–70 words)

The Exam; Fiction

Exercise 3.

Here is the opening extract from the Fiction section, Junior Cert. Higher level, Paper 2, 2003. I have removed all the **full stops** and **capital letters** , but the other punctuation is correct.

1. Write the extract into your copy (without looking at the exam paper, of course!), putting in full stops and capital letters where you feel they are appropriate.
2. Having completed this task, consult the exam paper (or ask your teacher) in order to check how correct your punctuation is.

Background to the extract:

Anthony Cross has a holiday job as a porter in Spitalfields market in London.

wednesday was not going well for anthony cross his day had begun at 4 a m , and it was now nearly nine it had been drizzling steadily since the first grey shadows of dawn had crept over the city, and the lanes and alleyways around spitalfields market were glistening with rain and vegetable refuse the great steel barn of the fruit market echoed with the shouts of porters, the whinings of forklift trucks, the crashing of crates and the tramp of feet

while anthony hauled crates and tallied sacks of onions, mr mant, his boss, would emerge regularly from the cracked wooden den that he called his office and shuffle across to the café with his little stainless steel teapot there it would be filled, and mr mant, small and dark and bent and unwashed, would make his way back to the office with his tea and doughnut he never offered to share his tea with anthony

How Do You Spell . . .?

Spelling Rules OK! Plurals

Rule 1

Most words just add 's' to make the plural:

word – words	book – books
teacher – teachers	parent – parents

Exercise 1. Write the plurals of the following nouns:

1. friend _friends_
2. student _students._
3. brother _brothers_
4. sister _sisters_
5. chocolate _chocolates_

6. burger _burgers_
7. star _stars_
8. film _films_
9. pet _pets_
10. dog _dogs_

Exercise 2. Now write a short paragraph (50–70 words) **connecting** all of the above words in some way and using them in the plural only. Begin like this: 'John/Sheila Ryan had lots of **friends** . . .'

Rule 2

Words ending in a vowel (a, e, i, o, u) **and** 'o' add 's' also:

radio – radios   video – videos   stereo – stereos

Exercise 1. Write one sentence for each of the above words, using the plural form of the word only in each case.

Exercise 2. 'Why do people watch horror videos?' Write a paragraph of 100–120 words which attempts to answer this question, using the plural form of the word **at all times**.

Rule 3

But! Words ending in a consonant (all other twenty-one letters of the alphabet – b, c, d, f, g . . .) **and** 'o' add '**es**' in the plural:

hero – heroes   potato – potatoes

Exercise 1. Here are six words ending in a consonant and 'o':

hero, echo, motto, potato, tomato, volcano

Fill in the blanks in the following sentences with the plural form of a word from the list above:

1. 'Don't worry. Be happy' and 'Smile and the world smiles with you' are good _mottoes_ for life.
2. The actor was so bad, the audience threw rotten _tomatoes_ at him.
3. There are _echoes_ of her childhood on every page.
4. _volcanoes_ are common in Italy.
5. Hercules and Andromeda were _heroes_ in ancient Greece.
6. Tommy Murphy eats a ton of _potatoes_ with his dinner!

Exceptions: Watch out for these!

solo – solos   piano – pianos   halo – halos

Exercise 2. Write one **question-style** sentence for each of the words in Exercise 1 **and** the three exceptions, using the plural form of the word only.

> **Example**   Do they really have two pianos in their house?
>   Are there any volcanoes in Ireland?

Rule 4

Words ending in a consonant **and** 'y' change the 'y' to 'i' **and** add 'es':

baby – babies lorry – lorries

Exercise 1. Write the following words in the plural:

1. country _countries_
2. secretary _secretaries_
3. hurry _hurries_
4. study _studies_
5. try _tries_
6. spy _spies_
7. lady _ladies_
8. ferry _ferries_
9. opportunity _opportunities_
10. penny _pennies_

Exercise 2. Write a short piece of **dialogue** (100–150 words) in which each of these words is used once only, in the **plural**. Begin like this:

Tom: You want to visit other countries? Why?

Mary: Because I . . .

Rule 5

Words ending in a vowel **and** 'y' keep the 'y' and add 's':

play – plays boy – boys

Exercise 1. Write the following words in the plural:

1. chimney _chimneys_
2. tray _trays_
3. holiday _holidays_
4. day _days_
5. key _keys_
6. valley _valleys_
7. toy _toys_
8. trolley _trolleys_
9. monkey _monkeys_
10. storey _storeys._

Exercise 2. Write one **negative** sentence for each of these words, using the plural form.

> **Example** I haven't seen Siobhan for **days**.

Rule 6

Most words ending in 'f' or 'fe' drop the 'f' or 'fe' and add 'ves':

half – halves wife – wives loaf – loaves

Exercise 1. Write the plurals of these words:

1. thief _thieves_
2. yourself _yourselves_
3. calf _calves_
4. leaf _leaves_
5. scarf _scarves_
6. wolf _wolves_
7. life _lives_

Exceptions: Watch out for the following words ending in 'f'. They add 's' in the plural:

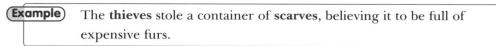

chief	chiefs
handkerchief	handkerchiefs
cliff	cliffs
cuff	cuffs
belief	beliefs

Learn these!

Exercise 2. Write six sentences in which **two** of the words from Exercise 1 or the exceptions are used in each sentence in the **plural** form only.

> **(Example)** The **thieves** stole a container of **scarves**, believing it to be full of expensive furs.

Rule 7

Words ending in 's', 'x', 'z', 'ch', 'sh' or 'ss' add 'es' in the plural:

bus	bus**es**
fox	fox**es**
waltz	waltz**es**
ben**ch**	ben**ch**es
bru**sh**	bru**sh**es
class	class**es**

Exercise 1. Write the following words in the plural:

1. dish _dishes_
2. glass _glasses_
3. six _sixes_
4. watch _watches._

Exercise 2. Answer the following questions with a complete sentence, using a suitable word from either the Rule 7 list, **or** Exercise 1 words in the **plural form** only.

1. What sort of food do you like to cook?
2. Doesn't Tony wear contact lenses?
3. Are trains the only means of transport in your area?
4. Which dances were most popular at the turn of the century?
5. What did you buy for the garden?
6. Which numbers are difficult to throw on a dice?
7. What are the Swiss famous for?
8. Which animals are often hunted for their tails?
9. What do artists and house painters have in common?
10. What do many schools run at night time during the winter?

Rule 8

Some words **do not change** at all in the plural:

- fish words – salmon, herring, trout, cod, ray
- the following – deer, sheep, aircraft, series, species, buffalo, giraffe, pheasant, swine.

Exercise 1. Write one **negative** sentence for each of the fourteen words above, using the plural form only.

> (Example) Some species of animals are not respected by man.

Exercise 2. Choose ten of the fourteen words above and write a sentence for each that **disagrees** with the negative statement made in Exercise 1, as in a debate.

> (Example) I believe that man has a healthy respect for all species of animals.

Rule 9

Some words have **no singular form**. They can only be used in the plural:

shorts	jeans
measles	scissors
police	cattle
belongings	dregs
outskirts	pliers

Exercise 1. Fill in the blanks in the following sentences with a word from the list above which is used only in its **plural** form.

1. When cutting out a pattern, you need a sharp _scissors_
2. Sheila knew she wouldn't get the nail out without a _pliers_
3. Tom will only wear Levi _jeans_
4. Uncle Peter looks really funny in _shorts_, because his legs are so skinny.
5. She gathered up all her _belongings_ in a black sack, and trudged off down the street.
6. The _police_ arrested him at six o'clock.
7. Mr. Ryan's _cattle_ strayed onto the main road, and two were killed.
8. Poor Susan! She picked up the _measles_ from her little brother.
9. The old man stared into the _dregs_ of his drink, wishing the glass were full again.
10. There is a large graveyard on the _outskirts_ of the village.

Functional writing

Exercise 2.

'Teenagers are snobs. They will only buy designer jeans.'

You have been asked to debate this topic in the next issue of the school newsletter. Write an article of about 200 words either for or against the motion, including words that can only be used in their **plural form**, where possible.

Rule 10

Some words **change quite a lot** in the plural. We call these irregular plurals. They don't appear to follow any rule, but you will be familiar with many of them already:

foot – feet   man – men   mouse – mice

Exercise 1.   Write the plural of the following words:

1. child ___children___
2. tooth ___teeth___
3. woman ___women___
4. louse ___lice___
5. goose ___geese___
6. ox ___oxen___

Personal writing, dialogue

Exercise 2.

Pat: What's wrong with those children at all?

Mary: Oh, that's right, blame me! – or your mother. If you ask me, nobody listens to the women in this house, anyway.

Continue the dialogue between Pat and Mary, using the words given in Rule 10 and Exercise 1 just once each.

Summary – Plurals

Rule 1..   Most words add 's' in the plural (student – students).

Rule 2.   Words ending in a vowel **and** 'o' add 's' too (video – videos).

Rule 3.   Words ending in a consonant **and** 'o' add 'es' (hero – heroes).

Rule 4.   Words ending in a consonant **and** 'y' change the 'y' to 'i' and add 'es' (baby – babies).

Rule 5.   Words ending in a vowel **and** 'y' keep the 'y' and add 's' (play – plays).

Rule 6.   Most words ending in 'f' or 'fe' drop the 'f' or 'fe' and add 'ves' (wife – wives).

Rule 7.   Words ending in 's', 'x', 'z', 'ch', 'sh' or 'ss' add 'es' (bus – buses, fox – foxes).

Rule 8.   Some words **don't change** at all (salmon, deer, sheep).

Rule 9.   Some words have **no singular form** (jeans, scissors).

Rule 10.   Some words are **totally irregular!** (foot – feet, man – men).

And finally . . . test yourself!   A 'mixed bag' exercise.

Re-read and study **all the rules** before you attempt this last exercise, as your knowledge of the rules is being tested here. Your teacher will set a time limit of fifteen minutes for this task.

Good luck!

Write the plural of each of the following words:

1. loaf _loaves_
2. piano _pianos_
3. pony _ponies_
4. pheasant _pheasants_
5. bus _buses_
6. giraffe _giraffes_
7. chief _chiefs_
8. valley _valleys_
9. ox _oxen_
10. potato _potatoes_
11. fact _facts_
12. baby _babies_
13. church _churches_
14. child _children_
15. wife _wives_
16. light _lights_
17. factory _factories_
18. tax _taxes_
19. buffalo _buffaloes_
20. chocolate _chocolates_
21. holiday _holidays_
22. boss _bosses_
23. soprano _sopranos_
24. mystery _mysteries_
25. waltz _waltzes_
26. salmon _salmon_
27. cuff _cuffs_
28. country _countries_
29. play _plays_
30. radio _radios_

3/30   100%
/30   100%

Words at Work

Word Formation

Stage 1

Let's begin by forming some new words from those you already know. For example, if we take the word 'ash', and add the word 'tray' to it, we get a new word – **ashtray**. These kinds of words are called **compounds**.

Exercise 1. Now you do it. Combine each word from list A with a suitable word from list B in order to form a new word. Write them out as a list, under C.

A	B	C
ash	tray	**ashtray**
book	ache	_____
door	box	_____
tape	room	_____
night	paper	_____
tooth	recorder	_____
match	step	_____
post	room	_____
dining	man	_____
wall	shop	_____
bed	club	_____

Exercise 2.

Classroom activity; in pairs

Here are some more words you know, but this time you must think of your own 'partner' or combining words to add to them to make one new word. There may be more than one possibility in some cases. Your teacher will time you. Try to complete the exercise in ten minutes.

1. pick
2. flash
3. hitch
4. house
5. dark
6. light
7. brief
8. gold
9. school
10. camera

Exercise 3. Now write one sentence of your own for **each** of the new compound words you've made in Exercises 1 and 2.

All of the examples in Exercises 1 and 2 are compound nouns, that is, made up of two nouns; for example, bedroom = two nouns, **bed** and **room**.

We can also make **compound adjectives**, for example **curly-haired**, **long-playing**; and **compound verbs**, for example **break through**, **go ahead**.

Compounds are sometimes written:

- as one word – bedroom,
- as two words – living room, or
- with a hyphen between – curly-haired.

If in doubt check it out in your dictionary! (See also exercises on hyphenated words in Unit 7 – Punctuation Please!)

Stage 2

Exercise 1. Combine the words in the following list with the words in the list below to make **compound nouns and adjectives.** Use your dictionary to check if the compound is one word, two words or hyphenated.

1. stark	2. science	3. driving	4. hot	5. broad
6. dog	7. good	8. head	9. flat	10. well
11. snack	12. self	13. spot	14. petrol	15. letter
16. dish	17. cross	18. prime	19. old	20. ice

footed, blooded, ache, minded, naked, cream, looking, tired, known,
roads, fashioned, fiction, licence, service, bar, head, cloth, station,
minister, light

Exercise 2.

In pairs

1. How many words can you think of that could combine with the following keywords to form a completely new word? Try to come up with at least two per keyword. Remember your related word might come before or after the keyword. Time limit: ten minutes.

> (**Example**) sand; new words: quick**sand**, **sand**castle

a.	sea	f.	post
b.	wind	g.	under
c.	sand	h.	up
d.	water	i.	light
e.	out	j.	back

2. Now practise using your new words by writing one sentence per new keyword.

Exercise 3. Here are some examples of **compound verbs.** (These are also called phrasal verbs.) Note that each is a combination of a verb and a preposition, for example 'write' (verb) **and** 'off' (preposition).

1.	to write off	9.	to look out
2.	to bring in	10.	to send up
3.	to give up	11.	to tip off
4.	to break through	12.	to hold up
5.	to get away	13.	to turn up
6.	to go ahead	14.	to come across
7.	to take over	15.	to run off
8.	to get on		

Now, complete each of the following sentences with a suitable compound verb from the list above. Only ten are needed for this exercise. Make any necessary changes to the spelling.

1. John ____ ____ the car last weekend.
2. Mum is always promising to ____ ____ smoking.
3. Miss Ryan will ____ ____ from Mr. Murphy next month.
4. You have to ____ ____ for pickpockets in the city centre.
5. Poor Tom! His best friend ____ ____ with his girlfriend.
6. The storeman ____ ____ the police in return for a fat reward.
7. The council are ____ ____ with their plan to cut down the trees.
8. The thieves ____ ____ with €10,000 in banknotes.
9. Dad ____ ____ some very old books when he was clearing out the attic.
10. The school draw ____ ____ over €1,000 for charity.

Stage 3

Another useful way of forming new words is to start with a particular part of speech, for example a **noun**, and add to it its related **adjectives, adverb and verb**. These are often referred to as 'word families'.

Example	Noun	Adjective	Adverb	Verb
	student	studious	studiously	study

Exercise 1.

1. Complete the following table:

Noun	Adjective	Adverb	Verb
obedience	_____	_____	_____
_____	imaginative	_____	_____
_____	_____	_____	describe
success	_____	successfully	_____
_____	_____	_____	recognise
_____	thoughtful	_____	_____
laziness	_____	_____	_____
_____	frightening	_____	_____
_____	_____	_____	invent
care	_____	carefully	_____

2. Write sentences using:
   a. 'success' as an **adjective**
   b. 'describe' as a **noun**
   c. 'frightening' as a **verb**
   d. 'imaginative' as a **noun**
   e. 'recognise' as an **adverb**

Exercise 2. Rewrite the words in the right hand column so that they fit suitably into the blank spaces in each of the following sentences. Be careful with the spelling.

> **Example** The manager's signature was at the bottom of the letter. SIGN
> The chair looked hard, but in fact was very comfortable. COMFORT

1. Only recently have people realised what a _____ situation
   the world is in.   DANGER

2. We have known for a long time that we live in a world where
   nuclear war is a _____.   POSSIBLE

3. Such a war could be started _____, just by someone pushing
   the wrong button.   ACCIDENT

4. But we are _____ by more immediate dangers.   THREAT

5. We have only recently realised that the world's resources, such as
   coal and oil, are _____.   EXHAUST

6. Population is increasing at a _____ rate, particularly in those
   countries that can support such populations least efficiently.   DRAMA

7. Millions face _____, but things will almost certainly get worse. STARVE

8. We have hardly started to learn how to use the world's resources
   in an _____ way.   ECONOMIC

9. It is possible that we have realised the _____ of such products
   as coal and oil too late.   SCARCE

10. Yet we still continue to be too _____ with our unnecessary
    use of petrol, electricity and food, as if no danger existed.   WASTE

The Exam; Functional writing

Exercise 3.

(Junior Cert. Ordinary level, 2003)

Look at the picture. You are a resident in this locality and you are upset by the dumping of all this rubbish. Write a letter to your local county council or corporation. In it, you should:

- describe the problem
- state your annoyance
- make suggestions for dealing with the situation.

N.B.! Be aware of the work you've covered in this unit on **nouns, capital letters and full stops, plurals** in spelling and **compound words**. Use as many of these words as possible, and watch that punctuation and spelling!

Litter Blackspot

Unit 2

Grappling with Grammar

Pronouns

Question What is a pronoun?

Answer A **pronoun** is a word which **replaces a noun** in a sentence. 'Pro' comes from the Latin word meaning 'for', so a pronoun **stands for**, or takes the place of, a noun. Without them your writing can be very repetitive.

Example Imagine your name is Siobhan Ryan, and you asked your mother for €10. Without **pronouns**, this is how the story might read.

Siobhan Ryan went to Siobhan Ryan's mother. Siobhan Ryan asked Siobhan Ryan's mother if Siobhan Ryan's mother could give Siobhan Ryan €10 for a school concert. Siobhan Ryan's mother sighed, took out Siobhan Ryan's mother's purse, and handed the €10 to Siobhan Ryan.

Phew! Here is the same situation, **with pronouns**.

Siobhan went to **her** mother and asked **her** if **she** could give **her** €10 for a school concert. **Her** mother sighed, took out **her** purse, and handed **her** €10.

Much better, isn't it?

In this unit, we will be exercising:
- **personal** pronouns (I, me, myself, etc.)
- **possessive** pronouns (mine, yours, etc.)
- **relative** pronouns (who, which, that).

Stage 1

Personal pronouns

When a pronoun replaces a noun which names **a person** or **persons**, it is called a **personal pronoun**:

I	me	myself
you	you	yourself
he	him	himself
she	her	herself
it	it	itself
we	us	ourselves
you	you	yourselves
they	them	themselves

Exercise 1. Circle the pronouns in the sentences below:

1. Mary did her homework all by herself.
2. Peter was delighted when he won the cash.
3. Sheila didn't like the dress, so she gave it to Rita.
4. I got up late this morning.
5. Between you and me, I didn't understand a word.
6. Our aunt Jackie came to see us last summer.
7. 'The twins don't like them,' she said, referring to the mushy peas.
8. He told them to keep the cup so they took it home with them.
9. They never really liked us – just the money.
10. 'I don't fancy her!' he said. 'You fancy her yourself!'

Exercise 2. In the following sentences, which **nouns** do the **pronouns in bold** refer to?

1. Jack was carrying the vase into the living room. At the door, **he** dropped **it**.
2. 'Watch **yourself**, Tom. **You're** going to get hurt,' shouted Peter.
3. When the cat saw Sarah with the milk, **it** purred, and followed **her** into the kitchen.
4. These flowers are from John, Teresa. **He** told me to give **them** to **you**.
5. Tracy and Orla are quite capable of doing this work by **themselves**.
6. The little boy ran away from his mum. We found **him** and brought **him** back to **her**.
7. My grandad bought me a pair of runners and **he** gave **them** to me for Christmas.
8. 'Yes, we are very proud of **ourselves**,' said Tom and Simon.
9. The old man walloped the thief with **his** umbrella, much to **his** surprise.
10. The teacher corrected Barbara's work, and praised **her** for **it**.

Watch Your Language!

Exercise 3.

1. Write ten sentences of your own, like those in Exercise 2, in which it is easy to identify the **noun** to which the **pronoun** refers.

2. **Don't** underline the pronouns.

3. Exchange your copy with your neighbour, and ask **him/her** to identify all the **pronouns** used, and to say which **noun** or nouns they refer to, in your sentences.

Stage 2

Possessive pronouns

The possessive pronouns are: **mine, yours, his, hers, ours, yours, theirs**. We use these to replace a **noun** and a **possessive adjective** in a sentence. In **dialogue** especially, it avoids boring repetition.

> **Example**   'That's **my** bag!'
> 'No, it's not. It's **mine**!'

Exercise 1.   In the list below, replace the possessive adjective and noun in each case with a **possessive pronoun**, as shown in the first example.

That's **my bag**.	That's **mine**.
That's **your car**.	That's _yours_
That's **his book**.	That's _his_.
That's **her problem**.	That's _hers_
That's **its bone**.	That's _his_.*
That's **our secret**.	That's _ours_
That's **your child**.	That's _yours_
That's **their house**.	That's _theirs_

* If the **gender** of the owner of the bone is unknown, you may use either 'his' or 'hers'.

Exercise 2.   Rewrite the following piece of dialogue by **replacing** the possessive adjectives and nouns in bold with a **possessive** pronoun.

Steven: Is that **my shirt** you're wearing?

Helen: No, of course not. It's **my shirt**. I never wear **your shirts**. You're always going on about them. It's boring.

Steven: Oh really?! And what about Stan's shirts then? You like **his shirts**, don't you? You're always borrowing them.

Helen: That's true, but **his shirts** are nicer than **your shirts**. That's why I wear Stan's shirts.

Steven:	Right! Well, that's it then. I'll have to start wearing Tina's shirts then, won't I?! I like **Tina's shirts**. They're very nice.
Helen:	Fine. We'll all swop! **Our shirts** for **Stanley and Tina's shirts**. What do you think?
Steven:	Oh, I don't know!! **Your shirts! My shirts! Tina's shirts! Stan's shirts**! It's all too ridiculous for words!
Helen:	You started it.

Exercise 3.

1. Write a description of yourself, in five sentences, using the pronouns **I, me** and **mine**.

2. Write a similar piece on any famous person – sports star, film star, singer, etc. – using the pronouns **he, him, his** or **she, her, hers**.

3. Discuss the good and bad points of some characters from your favourite TV soap, book or film, using the pronouns **they, them** and **theirs**. (70–100 words max.)

Stage 3

Relative pronouns

The relative pronouns are: **who, that, which, whose, where**. As the name suggests, they **relate** to a particular **noun** in a sentence.

1. **Who** refers to **people only**, and to the **subject** of the sentence, i.e. the **person** who is doing the **action**.

(**Example**)   The woman **who** won the car couldn't drive.

In this sentence the woman is the **subject**. The pronoun relates to her.

2. **That** refers to both **people** and **things**, and to either the **subject** or the **object** in a sentence.

(**Example**)   She's the woman (subject) **that** won the car.
        or
        He's driving the car (object) **that** the woman won.

3. **Which** refers to **things only**, and to either the **subject** or the **object** in a sentence.

(**Example**)   This is a scheme (subject) **which** should work.
        or
        These are problems (object) **which** you must solve.

4. **Whose** is a **possessive** relative pronoun. It refers to people, things and animals. It denotes possession or ownership.

Watch Your Language!

(Example) a. She's the girl **whose** brother is a millionaire. ('Whose' refers to the girl.)
  b. **Whose** book is this? ('Whose' refers to the **owner** of the book.)
  c. That's the horse **whose** leg was broken. ('Whose' refers to the horse.)

5. **Where** is actually a relative **adverb**, used to talk about places.

(Example) That's the town **where** I was born.

Note: You can **leave out** the relative pronouns **which, who** and **that** when they relate to the **object** in the sentence.

(Example) Those are the problems (which) you must solve. (In this sentence 'problems' is the object.)
  or
  She's the woman (whom) I met last week. (In this sentence 'woman' is object.)
  or
  She's the woman (that) lost her dog. ('Woman' is also the object here.)

Now let's practise these various types of relative pronouns.

Exercise 1. Combine the following **pairs of sentences** to form **one sentence**, by replacing the word in bold with a suitable relative pronoun.

(Example) I'd like to buy runners. **They** will match my new jeans.
  I'd like to buy runners **which/that** will match my new jeans.

1. This is my brother. *who* **He** lives in Cork.
2. I went to see the house. *which* **They** lived in ~~it~~ when they were first married.
3. This is the boss. *who* **He** founded the company.
4. What we really need is a canteen. *that* **It** would cater for all our students.
5. That's the hospital. She was born **there**.
6. The writer is Bryan MacMahon. *who* **He** wrote *The Master*.
7. *Friends* is a TV series about six people. *that* **They** live in New York.
8. John knows the family. *whose* **Their** house was burnt down.
9. Did you lose the ring? *that* I gave **it** to you on your birthday!
10. That's the guy! *whose* **His** brother stole my car.

Exercise 2.

Writing dialogue

Fill in the blanks in the following piece of dialogue, with a suitable relative pronoun in each case.

Denis: It's like a ghost town these days _____ everyone sleeps and nothing much happens.

Mary: It wasn't always like this, though, was it? Do you remember that guy _____ came home from the States and started a shirt factory on Patrick's Street?

Denis: Oh yeh! He was the fella _____ was going to make us all rich, _____ shirts were going to be worn all over the known world, from Passage East to Timbuctoo! Yeh. I remember him. It didn't last, but.

Mary: Yeh. Two years in _____ we all had loads of money and blew it on holidays, _____ at least the sun was guaranteed, not like here.

Denis: Yeh. And do you remember when there was that raffle for a Merc, and Paddy Redmond (_____ son was a right waster) crashed it into the front wall of his house the very first week _____ he had it!

Mary: Right enough, he did! But sure, who in their right mind would give a car like that to a fella _____ couldn't drive?! _____ fault was that, I wonder?

Denis: Don't ask me. I only know that Paddy was the one _____ won it. The son drove it back to the garage _____ it had been bought, and the front wing (_____ had been badly dented) cost about a thousand to repair! Can you believe it? A thousand euros! . . .

The drama continues

Now **continue** the dialogue between Denis and Mary for another ten lines, using each of the relative pronouns **who, that, which, whose** and **where, twice** each.

The Exam; Personal writing

Exercise 3.

Read the following passage carefully and underline or highlight **all the pronouns**.

On Sunday mornings you see them everywhere. They seem to come out of nowhere. Sometimes, in twos and threes, sometimes in groups, with a leader. They always wear bright gaudy colours and seem to advertise themselves. You almost expect them to run over to you promoting some new product for washing. They run on footpaths, on roads, on grass, in parks, on concrete, anywhere. They even dodge in and out and between cars, risking life and limb. They are . . . yes, the joggers!

Some are tall and athletic and have a suntan no matter what season of the year it is. Some are short and stumpy and not just a little overweight. Their faces always look the same – convulsed. A dangerous shade of red flashes like a neon light behind the permanently trickling drops of sweat. Inside the body their hearts are pounding, possibly at a dangerous rate. Do they ever look joyous? No, they look as if they are in constant agony.

When they reach a traffic light they are at their most curious. They are frustrated because their rhythm has been interrupted, so they stamp up and down as if throwing a tantrum, and glare at the cars and drivers speeding by. Sometimes I smile out at them but this is a risky business. They stamp even faster and breathe more furiously. On cold mornings their breathing is for all the world like a dragon breathing fire and hatred.

Once the light changes they hop, skip and jump a little before 'taking off' horizontally once more. And off they go, pounding the earth with their rubber soles and short socks. Do they ever feel as ridiculous as they look? And where in God's name are they going in such a hurry? Usually round and round in circles!

Now, write a prose composition on any **one** of the following titles:

● Sunday drivers   ● Football fanatics   ● Sales fever.

N.B.! Remember to use the three different types of pronoun (personal, possessive and relative) in order to avoid the kind of **repetition** outlined in the Siobhan Ryan story at the beginning of this unit.

And finally . . . a problem pronoun!

Should you say 'Sarah and **I**' or 'Sarah and **me**'?

Look at these two sentences.

a. Sarah and I ate six doughnuts each.

In this sentence, Sarah and I are the subject of the sentence. They are performing the action (ate). I is correct in this case.

b. Sean gave the €10 to Sarah and **me**, to share.

In this sentence, **Sean** is the subject, performing the action (gave), and **Sarah and me** are the **objects**. Therefore, **me** is correct in this case.

So . . .   **I** for **subject**, and

me for **object**, is the rule.

Exercise 4.   Fill in the correct word – **I** or **me** – in the following sentences, according to which is correct in the situation. Remember, **I** for subject, **me** for object.

1. Tom and ___ went to the cinema.
2. Philip and ___ bought popcorn.
3. Donna gave Tom and ___ two tickets for the disco.

4. Mum and ___ went shopping for jeans.
5. Dad gave ___ some money.
6. My friends and ___ went to Paris on a school trip last Easter.
7. The coach driver told Tom and ___ to sit down and stop singing.
8. Brian sent a Valentine card to both Trudy and ___.
9. Trudy and ___ hate Brian. He's a nerd.
10. The class and ___ are getting really good at this 'pronoun' business!

Punctuation Please!

Commas ,

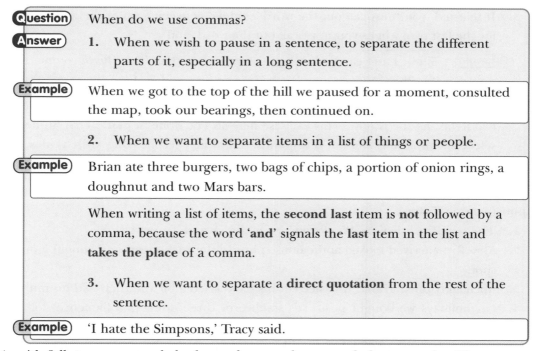

Question When do we use commas?

Answer
1. When we wish to pause in a sentence, to separate the different parts of it, especially in a long sentence.

Example When we got to the top of the hill we paused for a moment, consulted the map, took our bearings, then continued on.

2. When we want to separate items in a list of things or people.

Example Brian ate three burgers, two bags of chips, a portion of onion rings, a doughnut and two Mars bars.

When writing a list of items, the **second last** item is **not** followed by a comma, because the word '**and**' signals the **last** item in the list and **takes the place** of a comma.

3. When we want to separate a **direct quotation** from the rest of the sentence.

Example 'I hate the Simpsons,' Tracy said.

As with full stops, commas help the reader to make sense of what you write. The comma is a **short pause** but an important one, particularly in a long sentence. Commas are **sharper** and **clearer** in a sentence than a succession of 'ands'!

Watch Your Language!

Stage 1

Exercise 1.

Classroom exercise, oral, teacher directed

1. Within a time limit of thirty seconds, you will be asked to call out a list of **five items**, under one of the following headings:

   - Food
   - Sports
   - Careers
   - TV programmes
   - Films

   - Book titles
   - Pet hates
   - Favourite music groups
   - Weekend activities
   - Holiday destinations

2. Your teacher will choose the topic, and select students at random.

3. If selected, you must call out the word 'comma' between each of the items, except for the last two, where you must call out the word 'and'.

> **Example** Films: Last year I saw *Gangs of New York* comma *Phone Booth* comma *The Transporter* comma *Catch Me if You Can* and *8 Mile*.

If a student fails to say 'comma', he/she is out! If he/she says comma between the last two items, he/she is out! (This exercise may also be done **in pairs**. First Student A selects the topic and Student B responds. After thirty seconds they **switch roles**, and Student B selects the topic.)

Exercise 2. **Rewrite** these sentences, putting in the necessary commas. All the other punctuation is correct.

1. The semi-finalists were Wexford Cork Limerick and Tipperary.

2. Mrs. Ryan arrived looked at the house phoned the auctioneers and bought it on the spot.

3. Michael tripped grazed his knee cut his hand cried a bit and then told his mum.

4. On holidays we bought postcards sombreros three donkeys a flamenco doll and indigestion tablets.

5. Sam hopped skipped and jumped his way through the dancing competition.

6. 'I'd like an answer today please Jane' Miss Furlong sighed.

7. My friend who is tall handsome intelligent and rich is taking me to Paris at Easter.

8. 'I'm going home now' said James grabbing his teddy bear.

9. Sandra loves *Eastenders Coronation Street Will and Grace* and *Friends*.

10. Shamrock Rovers Finn Harps Bohemians and Cork City are all Irish soccer teams.

Exercise 3. Terry is very excited. He has just been picked for the school football team, and he has written a letter to his friend, Dave, in Cork, telling him all about it. However, in his haste, he has forgotten to put in any **full stops, capital letters or commas**! Can you **rewrite** this letter, so that it is clearer and makes more **sense**?

35 meadow avenue

thurles

co tipp

20 january 2004

hi dave

guess what? i finally did it got picked for the first team it's brilliant it's what i've always wanted i trained every monday wednesday saturday and sunday all last term during the christmas holidays too i can't believe they picked me and not loopy les from 3b he's a real headcase cheeks the teachers fakes absence notes chats up every babe in the school who'll listen to him he's sick i tell you i can't wait to try on the new team kit it's cool red black gray with a yellow stripe the women love it anne carroll says she'll come and see me play bring a few mates can't wait god! is that the time? have to go mate must train do sit-ups press-ups laps around the field you name it o'neill can do it!

see you at the finals in naas

take care be cool

terry

Stage 2

Look at this sentence:

Mr. Gorman, the principal, is sick today.

We use a comma between **nouns in apposition**, that is, where there are **two nouns** in a sentence, and they both refer to the **same person** or the **same thing**. In the above sentence, 'Mr. Gorman' is a noun, and 'principal' is a noun that tells us more about 'Mr. Gorman'. Here are some more examples:

1. Sonia O'Sullivan, the Olympic silver **medallist,** is Irish.
2. I was talking to my **neighbour, Mrs. Feeney**, about her dog.
3. **Dublin**, the **capital** of Ireland, is a popular European destination.

Watch Your Language!

Exercise 1. Now, you do it with the following sentences. Insert commas where they are needed.

1. Brigid's class went to Paris with their teacher Miss Greene.
2. John McDonald my sister's boyfriend buys her chocolates every weekend.
3. Doing homework even when it's necessary is a real pain.
4. Charlotte who was very nervous never said a word to him.
5. Two girls who were smoking in the loos got us all into trouble.
6. Man. United are happy with their manager Alex Ferguson.
7. A free taken by Donna Graham struck a tree in Mr. Lyons's garden bounced off the cat and smashed his living-room window.
8. The plane took off rose a few hundred feet in the air and then nose-dived into the ground.
9. The film *Titanic* which cost $200 million to make was a huge success at the box office.
10. Commas when used properly make our writing much easier to read.

Exercise 2. Can you **complete** the following sentences using your **own** nouns in apposition and inserting commas in the correct places? The first comma is supplied for you.

> **Example** Tom Jones, . . .
>
> Tom Jones, the Welsh singer, performs on the track 'Perfect Day'.

1. *Eastenders*, . . .
2. Limerick, . . .
3. Eminem, . . .
4. Seamus Heaney, . . .
5. William Shakespeare, . . .
6. The Eiffel Tower, . . .
7. Bart Simpson, . . .
8. Brian Kerr, . . .
9. The Special Olympics 2003, . . .
10. Colin Farrell, . . .

Exercise 3. Read the following sentence:

'We're going to Wicklow,' said Tom.

This is an example of the use of the comma when we want to separate **direct speech**, or **quotation**, from the rest of the sentence.

Can you fill in the **blanks** in the following sentences with a word of your own choice? And remember to put in the **comma**, as in the example above.

1. 'I would love to go to _____' said Gemma.
2. 'We are going on holiday in ____' said Mary.
3. 'The new shopping centre is _____' said Sean.
4. 'I love my teddy bear and my teddy bear loves _____' said Garfield.
5. 'I always have to do the _____' grumbled Eric.
6. 'Make sure you're wearing your _____' warned the policeman.
7. 'Eat your _____' said Gran.

8. 'I have found the ideal _____' announced Jane.
9. 'That's it. I'm nearly _____' said Bob.
10. 'I'm getting really good at _____' said Peter.

Stage 3

Exercise 1. Here is an extract from a newspaper article about the cast of the award-winning TV series *Friends*. I have removed all the **commas** and **full stops**. Can you **replace** them? Use a red biro for clarity. Try to complete this task in under ten minutes.

They own six of the most recognised and best marketed faces in the world Every week 30 million viewers tune in to see what their television *Friends* are doing while millions more buy the T-shirts calendars cappucchino mugs and even cook books

But although Jennifer Aniston David Schwimmer Matthew Perry Matt LeBlanc Lisa Kudrow and Courteney Cox discover in every episode that a friend in need is a friend indeed a Friend in the movies has proved a different ball game altogether

Translating their television stardom into box office success has proved problematic and at times almost embarrassing – note LeBlanc playing straightman sidekick to a chimp in his first movie outing *Ed*

Now Jennifer Aniston she of the infamous hairdo has made her first attempts at actually carrying a movie on her name and her name alone

Having chosen to start small with supporting roles in *She's The One* and *'Til There Was You* Aniston opted for *Picture Perfect* a romantic comedy which hopes to match the surprise hit factor of *While You Were Sleeping*

Carrying it on her shoulders – with or without the much copied Rachel 'do' resting on them – is a brave move Her leading man is the little known Jake Mohn and she is even taking the risk of moving away from the kooky screen persona of the dizzy waitress to play a hard-nosed ambitious girl so intent upon success she invents a fiancé to enhance her career chances

She is aware however that her *Friends* success isn't a cast-iron guarantee to big screen fame

'Every movie I have done except for *Perfect Picture* I have had to audition for' she points out 'It's not as easy as "Oh you're a big star do this"'

Ireland on Sunday, 11 January 1998

Exercise 2.

1. Select a piece of writing of about 150–200 words from one of the following sources:
   - a book
   - a magazine
   - a newspaper
   - a textbook

2. Read it carefully, **circling** or **highlighting** every comma.

3. Write a **summary** of the passage in about one-third of its length (50–75 words), using commas correctly, but **sparingly**, i.e. **one** in a short sentence, and no more than **two** in a longer sentence – unless you are required to **list** items, of course!

Read the rules and examples again before attempting this exercise.

The Exam; Reading comprehension

Exercise 3.

The following is an extract from the Junior Cert. Higher level paper, Section 1, 2002, Reading. Read it carefully. **All the commas have been removed**. Can you replace them? You should have twenty-five.

THE JEANING OF AMERICA – AND THE WORLD

This is the story of a sturdy American symbol which has now spread throughout most of the world. The symbol is not the dollar. It is not even Coca-Cola. It is a simple pair of pants called blue jeans. They have been around for a long time and it seems they will outlive even the necktie.

This ubiquitous American symbol was the invention of a Bavarian-born Jew. His name was Levi Strauss. He was born in Bad Ocheim Germany in 1829 and during the European political turmoil of 1848 decided to take his chances in New York to which his two brothers had already emigrated. Upon arrival Levi soon found that his two brothers had exaggerated their tales of an easy life in the land of the main chance. They were landowners they had told him; instead he found them selling needles thread pots pans ribbon yarn scissors and buttons to housewives. For two years he was a lowly peddler hauling some 180 pounds of sundries door-to-door to eke out a marginal living. When a married sister in San Francisco offered to pay his way West in 1850 he jumped at the opportunity taking with him bolts of canvas he hoped to sell for tenting.

It was the wrong kind of canvas for that purpose but while talking with a miner he learnt that pants – sturdy pants that would stand up to the rigours of digging – were almost impossible to find. Opportunity beckoned. On the spot Strauss measured the man with a piece of string and for six dollars in gold dust had the canvas tailored into a pair of stiff but rugged pants. The miner was delighted with the result word got around about 'those pants of Levi's' and Strauss was in business. The company has been in business ever since.

Correct your work from your own set of exam papers.

And finally . . .

> *I was working on the proof of one of my poems all the morning, and took out*
> *a comma. In the afternoon I put it back again.*
>
> Oscar Wilde

How Do You Spell ...?

Learning to Spell: Some Strategies

'I'm no good at spelling.' Some students find spelling genuinely difficult. Others make spelling mistakes simply because they are careless or lazy. In this unit, we will look at ways in which you can become a better speller. But . . . be warned! There are no miracle cures. You will have to **work** at it!

Strategy 1 – Sound patterns in spelling

Sounding out words before you spell them heightens your awareness of **sound patterns**. Two or more letters can combine to make one sound.

> **Example** 'er' in talk**er**, walk**er**, jump**er**

Associating the sound with the letters will therefore help with the **spelling** of the word. Here are some more examples of common sound patterns:

'ing' in sing**ing**, danc**ing**, laugh**ing**

'tion' in sta**tion**, men**tion**, por**tion** (pronounced 'shun')

'ious' in env**ious**, grac**ious**, delic**ious** (pronounced 'y-us')

'ence' in pati**ence**, lic**ence**, sci**ence**

'ive' in effect**ive**, expens**ive**, detect**ive**

Exercise 1.

1. Read the example words out loud several times. In this way you will learn to link a particular **sound** to a particular **ending**.

2. Your teacher will now call out the words from the examples and ask you to write them down, **first** the ending, and then the complete word.

> **Example** a. Teacher calls out 'mention'.
> b. You **hear** the ending 'shun'.
> c. You **write** 'tion'.
> d. You write 'mention' – breaking it up into two parts if you wish.

Now you can see that certain words have a **sound pattern**, and that these patterns have the same spelling.

Exercise 2. Write five more words for **each** of these sound patterns. Consult your dictionary if you get stuck. Time limit: ten minutes.

1. 'ing'
2. 'tion'
3. 'ious'
4. 'ence'
5. 'ive'

Swop copies with your neighbour. Add his/her words to your own list, making sure the spelling is correct in each case.

Exercise 3. Write a short piece of **dialogue** *or* a **paragraph** in which all of your words from Exercise 2 are used once only.

N.B.! Be careful with the **spelling**!

Strategy 2 – 'Spell it well': words that rhyme

It is much easier to learn the spelling of words that **rhyme**.

Exercise 1. Write three more words which rhyme and end with the same spelling patterns as **highlighted** in the words listed below. It helps if you work through the alphabet.

> **Example**   baking, faking, making, raking, waking

1. diTCH _____ _____ _____
2. fiGHT _____ _____ _____
3. hoppING _____ _____ _____
4. aBLE _____ _____ _____
5. tASTE _____ _____ _____
6. hATCH _____ _____ _____
7. cANE _____ _____ _____
8. bOLD _____ _____ _____
9. tUMBLE _____ _____ _____
10. mAPPED _____ _____ _____

Exercise 2. For each of the following 'ie' words add **one** other word which rhymes with it, and ends with the same two letters:

> **Example**   relief: belief

1. die: _____
2. achieve: _____
3. pie: _____
4. niece: _____
5. belief: _____
6. field: _____
7. flies: _____

Add one other 'ei' word which rhymes with these (the first letter is your clue):

    8. receive: d _____   10. eight: w _____

    9. receipt: d _____   11. either: n _____

Exercise 3. Select **one or two** words from **each** of your sets and write a letter to a friend in which you use each word once only. Mind the spelling! (100–120 words)

Strategy 3 – 'Cloze' it!

A cloze-style exercise involves **filling in** a missing letter or letters in a word, in **stages**. The aim is to learn the spelling by **working through** it in stages, becoming **familiar** with each part or syllable of the word as you work.

> (**Example**) Let's use the word **hospital** as an example. It can be broken up into five stages. **Cover** up each stage as you complete it, before you attempt the next stage. By the time you get to stage 5, you should be thoroughly familiar with the word, and confident in your spelling of it.
>
> 1. ___pital (hos)
> 2. hos___al (pit)
> 3. hospi__   (tal)
> 4. _____tal (hospi)
> 5. **hospital**

Remember that you are concentrating on **one part** of the word only at each stage, and learning **that** part. Students often believe they are bad spellers because many words are marked as spelled wrongly in their copies. However, if you examine these words carefully and look them up in your dictionary, you will find that you have usually only misspelled one or two letters in each word. The rest of the spelling may be absolutely correct! So, become aware of how words break down into parts (syllables), and follow a certain **pattern**. Words can be broken up into more easily learned segments, for example **magazine**.

Exercise 1. Here are some more words for you to complete and learn. Remember to follow the guidelines for 'hospital'.

    1. microphone:

        a. ——crophone

        b. mic——phone

        c. micro——

        d. microph——

        e. ————

    2. symbolise

        a. ——bolise

        b. sym——ise

        c. symbol——

        d. ————ise

        e. ————

3. magazine
    a. ——azine
    b. mag——ine
    c. magaz——
    d. ——ine
    e. ————

4. disappointment
    a. ——appointment
    b. disapp——ment
    c. disappoint————
    d. ————————ment
    e. ————————

5. character
    a. ——racter
    b. char——ter
    c. charac——
    d. ——ter
    e. ————

6. development
    a. ——velopment
    b. de——opment
    c. devel————
    d. ————————ment
    e. ————————

Exercise 2.   Here are some more words that are commonly misspelled. Select **ten** of them and create your own **stages** 1–5, following the examples in Exercise 1.

1.	accommodation	8.	prejudice	15.	criticism
2.	beautiful	9.	appearance	16.	definite
3.	disappear	10.	humorous	17.	description
4.	literature	11.	advertisement	18.	immediately
5.	necessary	12.	athletics	19.	laboratory
6.	embarrass	13.	believable	20.	livelihood
7.	government	14.	calendar		

Exercise 3.   Write one sentence for each of the remaining **ten** words which clearly shows its use and meaning.

Strategy 4

1. Look
2. Cover
3. Write
4. Check

Do you remember this way of learning your spellings in primary school? It is still a very good method. Again you must follow stages 1–4 in learning a word.

Example Here is the word 'marriage', from a spelling list of ten words. It is often misspelled. Learn to spell this word in the following way:

1. **Look** at the word and try to learn the spelling; break it up into two parts: marr–iage.
2. **Cover** the word and **say** it to yourself a few times, trying to **visualise** it in your head.
3. **Write** the word as you remember it.
4. Uncover the word and **check** your spelling.
5. If **correct**, continue to the next word in the list.
6. If **incorrect**,
   a. **Look** at the word again.
   b. **Say** the word slowly, tracing it with your finger.
   c. **Cover** the word.
   d. **Write** the word.
   e. Uncover the word and **check** the spelling.

You will almost certainly get it right the second time round. Be patient! Good spelling needs **care** and **work**.

Exercise 1. Here is a list of ten words, beginning with 'marriage'. You will see that they all have the same ending – 'age'. So you don't have to learn this bit of the word – **patterns** again! Learn these spellings using Strategy 4.

1. marriage
2. average
3. language
4. postage
5. teenage

6. manage
7. courage
8. message
9. wreckage
10. advantage

Exercise 2. Write **five questions**, and **five answers** to those questions, using each of the words in Exercise 1 once only.

Exercise 3.

Test yourself

Here are some definitions of words that have been used so far in this unit. Write out each word, spelled **correctly** of course! Revise the spellings (using Strategy 4) **before** attempting the exercise.

1. Singers use one to make themselves heard at a large venue. _____
2. Every country has one of these. They are the ruling power. _____
3. The feeling we experience when we look forward to something and it doesn't happen. _____

4. We read a lot of this in school!   _____

5. Hotels and guesthouses provide this.   _____

6. What is left after a major car, plane or train crash.   _____

7. An adjective meaning funny.   _____

8. You have a favourite one which you will buy and read each week.   _____

9. A strongly held belief in favour of or against a particular idea,
   or race of people.   _____

10. The legal union of a man and woman.   _____

Swop copies with your neighbour and correct each other's spellings.

Strategy 5 – Words within words

Another useful way of learning spellings is to spot words **within** words. Look at the word 'assignment', for example. There is another word **within** this word: 'sign'.

Exercise 1. Here are some more examples. Can you find the word **within** the word? Underline or highlight it, when you do.

1. advance
2. important
3. banter
4. satisfactory
5. directory

6. continental
7. decode
8. microphone
9. orchestra
10. secondary

Exercise 2. Put the words in the list below into their correct spaces to make twenty more 'words within words'.

(Example)   disappointment

1. dis_____ment
2. __rel
3. pheas_____
4. sur_____
5. qu_____er
6. re_____
7. hair_____er
8. mis_____stood
9. re_____ment
10. _____ly

11. sp_____
12. trum_____
13. dis_____ion
14. th_____
15. pass_____
16. _____th
17. un_____ful
18. h_____ed
19. ex_____ive
20. _____able

connect, appoint, success, fresh, face, pet, port, live, ant, arrow, bar, aunt, row, art, ear, dress, pens, too, reason, under

Exercise 3.

1. Working in pairs, or in teams of three, construct twenty of your own 'words within words'. You may use a dictionary. Put them into an exercise like the one above. Time limit: twenty minutes.

2. At a signal from your teacher, exchange your exercise with another pair or team of students. You then have ten minutes to complete their exercise. The pair/team who finishes first wins!

Strategy 6 – DIY spelling

As its name suggests, this is the 'Do It Yourself' spelling strategy! If you **really** want to be a better speller, you have to take **control** of it. One very good way of doing this is to create your **own** spelling notebook or dictionary.

Suggestions for use:

1. An **address** or **index book** will make a good personal dictionary.

2. **Collect** words from your exercises and your textbooks once a week and file them **alphabetically** into your 'dictionary of spelling'.

3. Decide on a **number** of words per week that you can realistically learn. Ten would be a good start, for example. Too many will discourage you, and defeat the purpose.

4. In **choosing** words, be sure to include those words which you use most frequently, and those which you **misspell** frequently also.

5. Leave a space of a few lines at the end of each index page for **sentence practice** using the words on that page.

6. Consult your **exam papers**, and include words that regularly appear in questions. For example, in **English**, the following words are often used: **author, character, poet, scene, extract, text.**

7. Set some time aside once a month to **revise** your spellings, **re-learn** the words you've written in your notebook. There is no point in simply collecting words and never looking at them again!

Remember your aim – to be a better speller. Stick with it! It will work.

Also, in the following units you will be doing lots of spelling practice, which will give you confidence in this area.

Words at Work

Word Building

As you saw in Unit 1, it is possible to form new words from those you already know. In this way, we start **building** a vocabulary that is **more varied** and **less repetitive**. In this unit, we will be looking at words that relate to, or are associated with, a particular **keyword**, and also at how a **thesaurus** can help you to extend your vocabulary, thus increasing your word power.

Stage 1

Exercise 1. The keyword **beverage** may refer to any number of different drinks, for example **tea, coffee, water, juice, etc.**

Here are some more keywords. How many words can you think of that are associated with each of them?

1.	Food	6.	Television
2.	Travel	7.	Books
3.	Films	8.	Fashion
4.	Occupations	9.	Sport
5.	Art	10.	Music

Your teacher may choose a keyword and allow you to work in pairs on this exercise, with a time limit of ten to fifteen minutes, or you may do it as an individual challenge for homework.

Exercise 2.

1. Here are thirty nouns. They can be divided up into six groups of five words each. The keyword for each group is given to you. You must place each word under its appropriate heading.

   beach, oil, saucepans, microwave, cell, priest, luggage, reception, proposal, sink, exam, engagement, crime, computer, pupil, petrol, fridge, book, judge, hotel, fine, driver, service, tyre, dishwasher, ticket, honeymoon, study, sun, station

	Police	Garage	Kitchen	School	Holiday	Wedding
a.						
b.						
c.						
d.						
e.						

2. Now write a piece of **dialogue**, between **two** people, which features two of the word groups and connects them in some way, for example 'holiday' and 'wedding', or 'garage' and 'police'. Try to use each related word within a group once only. (150–200 words)

Exercise 3. Compare your lists of related words with others in your class. (ten minutes)

1. Add any you haven't thought of to your own. (five minutes)
2. Choose one keyword and write an article for the school magazine on that topic in which each **related** word is used once only. (100–120 words)

Stage 2

Exercise 1.

Find the missing link

Study the first pair of words below, and then complete the second pair, having worked out the 'link' between them.

> **Example**) Ireland, **island**. Asia, _____.
>   Ireland, island. Asia, **continent**.

1. Roy Keane, football. Ken Doherty, _____.
2. England, Prime Minister. Ireland, _____.
3. O'Casey, plays. Yeats, _____.
4. Cartoon, pictures. Dictionary, _____.
5. *Evita*, musical. *Swan Lake*, _____.
6. Apple, tree. Grape, _____.
7. *As You Like It*, comedy. *Romeo and Juliet*, _____.
8. Numbers, maths. Coins, _____.
9. Country, rural. City, _____.
10. January, month. Autumn, _____.

Exercise 2. Having completed Exercise 1, add as many **related** words as possible to each link word.

> **Example**) **snooker**: cue, ball, player, round, tournament, champion, cup, etc.

Suggestion: Your teacher may choose to make this a competitive exercise, as in a table quiz situation, in class.

●   In a class of thirty students, there could be six teams of five.
●   Each team confers on the list of related words.
●   The team which comes up with the most words for each link word wins!
●   Your teacher decides which starter word he/she will call out, and a time limit of three minutes per word is imposed. Your teacher chooses five words in all from Exercise 1.
●   Good luck!

Exercise 3. Read the poem 'Squaring Up' by Roger McGough, and answer the following questions:

1. Which 'key' word does the phrase 'Squaring Up' refer to?
2. Underline all the **nouns**, **verbs** and **adjectives** that relate to this topic; for example, boxing-gloves (noun); bob (verb); gloveless (adjective).
3. Write them all out in a **list** under these headings:

    Noun   Verb   Adjective
4. Write **a short article** for the school magazine in which you express your opinions on this topic, **referring to this poem** to support your points. Use as many of your list words from (3) as possible.

Squaring Up

When I was thirteen and crimping my first quiff
Dad bought me a pair of boxing-gloves
In the hope that I would aspire to the Noble Art.

But I knew my limitations from the start:
Myopia, cowardice and the will to come second.
But I feigned enthusiasm for his sake.

Straight after tea, every night for a week
We would go a few rounds in the yard.
Sleeves rolled up, collarless and gloveless.

He would bob and weave and leave me helpless.
Uppercuts would tap me on the chin
Left hooks muss my hair, haymakers tickle my ear.

Without glasses, only one thing was clear:
The fact that I was hopeless. He had a son
Who couldn't square up. So we came to blows.

Losing patience, he caught me on the nose.
I bled obligingly. A sop. A sacrifice.
Mum threw in the towel and I quit the ring.

But when the bell goes each birthday I still feel the sting
Not of pain, but of regret. You said sorry
And you were. I didn't. And I wasn't.

Roger McGough

Stage 3 ━━━━━━━━━━━━━━━━━━━━━━━━━━━━━━━━━━

Using a thesaurus

In 1805, a man called Peter Mark Roget began to compile a catalogue of words, classed together in sections. Under each topic, he placed many words that are associated with each other. Forty-seven years later (in 1852) the book was published and entitled **Thesaurus**, meaning a 'treasury of words'.

Here is a page from the *Webster Pocket Thesaurus*, with headwords ranging from 'go' to 'gossip'. Each headword has its own list of **context** words, e.g.

Go: Leave; Proceed; Function; Suit; Extend; Elapse; Die.

Unlike a dictionary, a thesaurus doesn't explain the meaning of a word, but rather gives you a number of **alternative** words for each headword. Using a thesaurus, therefore, allows you to find the **precise** word for the meaning you wish to convey. It also helps you to avoid **repeating** the same word, e.g. 'go' or 'good'.

---

go *v.* **LEAVE:** withdraw, depart, vacate, flee, fly, run, escape; **PROCEED:** advance, progress, move; **FUNCTION:** run, perform, operate; **SUIT:** conform, accord, harmonize, agree, fit; **EXTEND:** stretch, cover, reach; **ELAPSE:** transpire, pass; **DIE:** depart, succumb

goad *v.* prod, urge, prompt, spur, drive, press, push, impel, force, stimulate, provoke, encourage

goal *n.* aim, ambition, object, intent, end, purpose

go-between *n.* middleman, referee, mediator, agent

god *n.* deity, divinity, spirit

godly *adj.* righteous, devout, pious, holy

gone *adj.* moved, withdrawn, retired, departed, dissolved, decayed, extinct

good *adj.* **MORAL:** upright, honest, respectable, noble, ethical, fair, pure, decent, honourable; **KIND:** considerate, tolerant, generous; **RELIABLE:** trustworthy, dependable, loyal; **SOUND:** safe, solid, stable, reliable; **PLEASANT:** agreeable, satisfying, enjoyable; **HEALTHY:** sound, normal, vigorous; **OBEDIENT:** dutiful, tractable, well-behaved; **GENUINE:** valid, real, sound; **DELICIOUS:** tasty, flavourful, tasteful

good-for-nothing *n.* loafer, vagabond, bum, vagrant

good-looking *adj.* clean-cut, attractive, impressive, beautiful, handsome

good-natured *adj.* cordial, kindly, amiable, friendly

goodness *n.* decency, morality, honesty, virtue

goof *v.* err, flub, fail

> **gorge** *n.* chasm, abyss, crevasse, ravine
>
> **gorge** *v.* glut, surfeit, stuff, eat, fill
>
> **gorgeous** *adj.* beautiful, dazzling, superb, sumptuous, impressive, grand
>
> **gory** *adj.* blood-soaked, bloodstained, offensive
>
> **gossip** *n.* RUMOUR: scandal, meddling, hearsay, slander, defamation; TALEBEARER: snoop, meddler, tattler, scandalmonger, muckraker, backbiter

Exercise 1. Examine all of the headwords on your Thesaurus page from **go** to **gossip**. Now fill in the blanks in the following sentences with a word chosen from one of the **context** words given with each headword.

> (**Example**) Headword: **go**; Context words: leave, proceed, function, etc.
>
> You must **vacate** the building immediately. The basement is on fire.

The obvious choice here is 'vacate', from the context word 'leave'. Your intelligence will tell you this, of course, once you have examined all the context words and eliminated those which do not apply.

N.B.! The headword is in brackets at the end of each sentence.

1. I'm not sure this climate ____ with you, Mark. (Go)
2. Rita is a very dependable person and extremely ____ to her friends. (Good)
3. Barry is not just a harmless gossip. He is a ____ in other people's affairs. (Gossip)
4. Before I ____ this world, I really must change that wallpaper. (Go)
5. Her ____ is to be an astronaut. (Goal)
6. I wouldn't give it away. It's very ____. (Gorgeous)
7. Con is making real ____ in his relationship with Rachel. (Go)
8. That Mexican dish was very ____. (Good)
9. Bill has a nasty tongue. He's a notorious ____. (Gossip)
10. I'm not sure if the rope will ____ that far, Jan. (Go)

Exercise 2. Here are some more entries from the *Webster Pocket Thesaurus*. The words **great** and **nice**, for example, are much overused.

> **funny** *adj.* COMIC: laughable, comical, whimsical, amusing, entertaining, diverting, humorous, witty, jocular, droll; SUSPICIOUS: curious, unusual, odd
>
> **futile** *adj.* useless, vain, fruitless, hopeless, impractical, unsuccessful, purposeless, ineffective, ineffectual, unproductive, empty, hollow
>
> **glum** *adj.* sullen, moody, morose, sad
>
> **gnaw** *v.* tear, crunch, champ, masticate, bite, chew

> **great** *adj.* **LARGE**: numerous, big, commanding, vast; **EXCELLENT**: exceptional, surpassing, transcendent; **EMINENT**: grand, majestic, exalted, famous, renowned, celebrated, distinguished, noted
>
> **nervous** *adj.* **EXCITABLE**: impatient, restless, uneasy, unstable; **EXCITED**: fidgety, jittery, agitated, bothered
>
> **nice** *adj.* likable, pleasant, agreeable, amiable
>
> **noise** *n.* sound, clamour, racket, fracas, din, uproar

Read the following description of a school tour. The words in bold are all taken from the above thesaurus entries, but they do not fit the **context** in which they are used. Can you find more **suitable** words from the entries above and insert these instead, in order to make more sense of the story? You will need to read the **headwords** and their **context** words very carefully.

Arriving at Disneyland, Paris in the pouring rain made us all **morose**. Tommo was making his usual **fracas**, shouting out 'I'm singin' in the rain . . . I'm singin' in the rain!!'

He thought he was being **whimsical**, but not Mr. Barrett who thought it was far from **comical**.

'It is **fruitless** talking to you, Tommo Hayes, truly **vain**. Here we are in this **celebrated** theme park, and all you can do is make a **din**!'

Meanwhile Shirley Lambert was **champing** a **vast** toffee bar she'd bought at the airport.

'You're like a dog with a bone, the way you're **tearing** at that bar, Shirl,' said Tommo.

'Very **diverting**, Tommo Hayes. Get lost,' said Shirley. 'You're not a bit **agreeable**, so you're not.'

'Now, now. That's enough, you two,' said Mr. Barrett, who knew it was **purposeless** trying to talk sense to these two. He checked them all through the gate and everyone was really **agitated**. Whacker Ryan had an **exceptional** camera, and was very **restless**, waiting for the parade to start.

'You should get a **vast** view of the parade from Main Street, Whack . . . em . . . Williams,' Mr. Barrett said.

'Yeh, Sir,' said Tommo, 'specially of Mickey Mouse. Whacker and him can compare their **majestic** ears, can't they, Sir?!'

'Tommo Hayes! Behave yourself. That's not a very **likeable** attitude. Really, it's not **humorous** to make fun of a classmate like that. Not **amusing** at all.'

'Sorry, sir,' Tommo grinned. 'I promise I'll be really **pleasant** for the rest of the trip. Honest, sir.'

'That's what worries me, Tommo,' Mr. Barrett said, looking **moody**. 'You and the word "pleasant" don't exactly go together! Now, get off, the lot of you, and have a **transcendent** time. I'll see you back here at five o'clock. No doubt I'll be **gnawing** my hair out by then,' he muttered to himself, as class 3B all charged off down the Main Street, making a dreadful **clamour**.

The Exam; Functional writing

Exercise 3.

1. The school tour
2. The debating final
3. My favourite film
4. Gossip hurts

Choose one of the above topics and write an **article** for the school magazine. (150–200 words approximately) Try to use as many related words as possible from the thesaurus entries in this section. Avoid **repeating** overused words like 'good' and 'great'!

Unit 3

Grappling with Grammar

Adjectives

 Question   What is an adjective?

Answer   An adjective is a word that describes a noun. It tells us more about people, places, things, animals and feelings.

Adjectives make our writing lively, interesting and colourful. Charles Dickens, for example, uses adjectives to wonderful effect in his books: *'Mrs. Gradgrind, a little, thin, white, pink-eyed bundle of shawls.'*

(Hard Times).

Now compare these two sentences:
- The street ran down to the factory.
- The **dusty**, **bustling** street ran down to a **black**, **foul-smelling** factory.

The adjectives 'dusty' and 'bustling' give life to the street, and 'black' and 'foul-smelling' appeal to our senses. We can visualise the scene because of the adjectives. They 'paint' pictures for us.

Stage 1

Exercise 1.

In pairs

The list below contains fifteen adjectives and fifteen nouns, all jumbled up together. Can you pair them off, as in the following example?

Example		**Adjective**	**Noun**
	a	busy	office

Your teacher will time you (five minutes), and the first pair of students to complete the task wins!

> beautiful, sky, interesting, castle, strong, programme, fresh, lovely, car,
> view, fast, glue, chest, golden, worm, girl, loaf, golden, black, duckling,
> tooth, hairy, rotten, rude, hole, wound, comedian, deep, wriggly, ugly

Exercise 2. In pairs, or as individuals, think of a good and interesting adjective of your own for each of the nouns below.

Example		Adjective		Noun
	an	amusing		visitor

1.	_____	boy	6.	_____	driver
2.	_____	film	7.	_____	friend
3.	_____	day	8.	_____	drug
4.	_____	dinner	9.	_____	experience
5.	_____	teacher	10.	_____	game

Exercise 3.

1. Write one interesting adjective for each letter of the alphabet. Think hard and only consult your dictionary when you are really stuck – as in adjectives beginning with 'x', 'y' or 'z'! Give yourself a time limit of fifteen minutes for this exercise.

2. **Combine** your list of **adjectives** with twenty-six **nouns** beginning with the same letter.

> (Example) an adventurous ant
> a beautiful bowl
> a cheerful chap

Try to create some funny or unusual combinations, if you can. Time limit: twenty minutes.

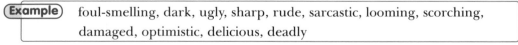

Stage 2

Types of adjectives

1. **Descriptive.** This type of adjective includes a broad range of words including those that appeal to the **senses.**

> (Example) foul-smelling, dark, ugly, sharp, rude, sarcastic, looming, scorching, damaged, optimistic, delicious, deadly

2. **Possessive.** These adjectives show **ownership** or **possession.**

> (Example) **my** car, **your** book, **his** problem, **her** friend, **our** school, **your** teacher, **their** pitch

3. **Demonstrative.** These adjectives **point out** or **refer to a specific** object or person.

> (Example) **this** page, **that** man, **these** flowers, **those** students

4. **Proper.** These adjectives come from **proper nouns** and are always written with a **capital letter.**

> **Example**   the **Celtic** tiger, our **Irish** heritage, the **French** language,
> the **Atlantic** Ocean

Exercise 1.

1. **Locate** and **underline** each of the adjectives in the following sentences.

2. Indicate which **type** of adjective it is by writing the letter 'D' over a **descriptive** adjective, 'P' over a **possessive** adjective, 'DM' over a **demonstrative** adjective and 'PR' over a **proper** adjective.

    a. You can get a really tasty curry in the local Indian restaurant.

    b. This pink ticket has some interesting but illegible writing on it.

    c. Did you see those amazing pictures that Tom took of that French vineyard?

    d. Scorching weather, long cold drinks, intelligent attractive company. What more could you want on a Mediterranean holiday?

    e. The African continent is beautiful, but there are fierce and angry conflicts between its various countries.

    f. An industrious, good-humoured student is optimistic about the future and confident in terms of the exam.

    g. 'What an appetising smell! Your lasagne is as delicious as you are beautiful, my darling,' the oily charmer said.

    h. This room is freezing! I have never been so cold. My hands and feet are numb.

    i. John is very intelligent and studious, but he panics before an exam and is terrified he will fail.

    j. In the soft light of morning, the worn gravestones looked less sinister, less frightening than the night before.

Exercise 2.

1. Write the corresponding adjective for each of the following nouns.

> **Example**   Noun   Adjective
>   monster   monstrous

	Noun	Adjective		Noun	Adjective
a.	beauty	_____	k.	energy	_____
b.	courage	_____	l.	nation	_____
c.	poet	_____	m.	power	_____
d.	sincerity	_____	n.	truth	_____
e.	patience	_____	o.	clarity	_____
f.	thought	_____	p.	artist	_____
g.	risk	_____	q.	suspicion	_____
h.	innocence	_____	r.	mystery	_____

	Noun	Adjective		Noun	Adjective
i.	silence	_____	s.	effect	_____
j.	strength	_____	t.	doubt	_____

2. Now choose ten adjectives from the list and write a sentence for each one, remembering that adjectives describe **nouns**. Make them as interesting as possible, and vary the type of sentence, i.e. question, negative, exclamation, statement.

> **(Example)**
>
> | | adjective | noun |
> |---|---|---|
> | Jane's a very | thoughtful | person. |

The Exam; Personal writing

Exercise 3.

Here are two lists of adjectives that describe **feelings** and qualities, both good and bad. There are forty in all.

Good		Bad	
amazed	amused	afraid	angry
calm	confident	anxious	awful
cool	delighted	bored	depressed
enthusiastic	excited	disappointed	frightened
fascinated	friendly	frustrated	guilty

Good		Bad	
happy	interested	helpless	hurt
loving	optimistic	impatient	jealous
pleasant	proud	lonely	mean
quiet	sensitive	sad	uncomfortable
surprised	warm	upset	worried

Using words from these lists, write a **prose composition** on one of the following titles:

1. Write a story which at some point includes the sentence: 'I was only messing – honestly!'. (Junior Cert. Ordinary level, 2003)

2. The time I was sick **OR** lucky **OR** embarrassed **OR** sad. (Junior Cert. Ordinary level, 2002)

3. It's a weird and wonderful world. (Junior Cert. Higher level, 2003)

Stage 3

Comparative and superlative of adjectives

Rules:

1. Most adjectives simply add '**er**' for the comparative and '**est**' for the superlative.

(**Example**) tall, tall**er**, tall**est**

2. If the adjective **ends in 'y'**, the 'y' **changes to** 'i' before adding 'er' or 'est'.

(**Example**) happy, happ**ier**, happ**iest**

3. If an adjective ends in a **consonant** and the **letter before** the last one is a **vowel**, then the **consonant letter** is **doubled** before adding 'er' or 'est'.

(**Example**) big, big**ger**, big**gest**

4. Adjectives of **two or more syllables** usually add '**more**' for the comparative and '**most**' for the superlative.

(**Example**) useful, **more** useful, **most** useful

5. Finally! There are some **irregular adjectives** which change **completely** in the comparative and superlative. You just have to learn these.

(**Example**)

good	better	best
little	less	least
many	more	most
bad	worse	worst

N.B.! 'Worser' is **not** good English!

Exercise 1. Write the comparative and superlative forms of the following adjectives:

Adjective	Comparative	Superlative
1. smooth	_____	_____
2. wise	_____	_____
3. sunny	_____	_____
4. fat	_____	_____
5. foolish	_____	_____
6. dangerous	_____	_____
7. bad	_____	_____
8. noisy	_____	_____
9. truthful	_____	_____
10. beautiful	_____	_____
11. safe	_____	_____

	Adjective	Comparative	Superlative
12.	long	_____	_____
13.	strong	_____	_____
14.	many	_____	_____
15.	soft	_____	_____
16.	slim	_____	_____
17.	delicious	_____	_____
18.	efficient	_____	_____
19.	good	_____	_____
20.	cool	_____	_____

Exercise 2. Look at the following sentence in which the **comparative** form of the adjective is used.

> **(Example)** The **more** I run, the **fitter** I feel.   more \ run \ fit \ feel

Using the above sentence as an example, write ten more sentences according to this pattern, from the following words and phrases. Begin each sentence with 'The'.

1. warm \ weather \ happy \ are
2. more \ earn \ more \ spend
3. long \ wait \ impatient \ become
4. more \ see her \ less \ like her
5. big \ car \ more petrol \ use
6. more \ eat \ fat \ get
7. soon \ leave \ better
8. more \ merry
9. more \ work \ more \ builds up
10. less \ say \ better

Exercise 3. Look at this sentence which uses the **superlative** form of the adjective:

> **(Example)** The **happiest** day of my life was when our team won the Leinster Cup.

Write **one complete** sentence in answer to each of the following questions. Then choose one of them and write a little more about the experience in the form of a **paragraph** (100–120 words), a **poem** or a **piece of dialogue**. Use as many interesting adjectives from this unit as you can.

1. What was the **happiest** day of your life?
2. What was the **worst** day?
3. What was the **most embarrassing** experience you've ever had?
4. What was the **most shocking** experience?
5. What was the **most exciting** moment?

The Exam; Poetry

Exercise 4.

(Junior Cert. Higher level, 2003, Poetry)

Here is the unseen poem from the Junior Cert. Higher level paper, 2003. Read it carefully, then answer the questions which follow. They will focus your attention on the poet's use of **adjectives** in particular.

Space Shot

Out of the furnace
The great fish rose
Its silver tail on fire
But the slowness
Like something sorry
To be rid of earth.
The boiling mountains
Of snow white cloud
Searched for a space to go into
And the ground thundered
With a roar
That set teacups
Rattling in a kitchen
Twenty miles away.

Across the blue it arched
Milk bottle white
But shimmering in the haze.
And the watchers by the fence
Held tinted glass against their eyes
And wondered at what man could do
To make so large a thing
To fly so far and free.
While the unknown Universe waited;
For waiting
Was what it had always been good at.

1. Highlight those adjectives in the poem that best describe the rocket at the very moment of its launch from the shuttle pad.
2. The '**boiling** mountains . . .'. What does the adjective 'boiling' suggest to you?
3. What were the 'watchers by the fence' holding against their eyes? And Why?
4. Which **adjectives** do the watchers use to describe the rocket in flight?
5. You are one of the 'watchers by the fence', looking at this spectacle. Describe what **you** see. Use as many adjectives from the poem as you can.

Punctuation Please!

Semi-colons and Colons ; :

Stage 1

Semi-colons ;

Question When do we use semi-colons?

Answer 1. When we want to mark a longer or more important break in a sentence than is served by a comma.

Example *Love is like the measles; we all have to go through it.*

Jerome K. Jerome

In this sentence a comma wouldn't have been sufficient. A full stop, however, would have been too much! So, the **semi-colon** was just right. Its job lies **between** a comma and a full stop. It also serves to unite two elements of the sentence that are closely connected.

Example **To lose one parent**, Mr. Worthing, may be regarded as a misfortune; **to lose both** looks like carelessness.

Oscar Wilde

2. When we want to separate complicated things in a list of connected items.

Example Mum loaded up the trolley with delicious food for the party: barbecued chickens coated in crisp golden breadcrumbs; a whole ham glazed with pineapple and honey; fresh bread rolls swimming in garlic butter; chocolate chip and toffee crunch ice-cream.

3. When we want to separate statements that are connected, in a comparative sense.

Example All the guys are posing; all the girls are bored.
All the male tigers are spotted; all the females striped.

4. When two ideas are connected by one of the following words: **however**, **therefore**, **indeed**, **besides**, **nevertheless**, **consequently**.

Example I waited for over an hour; **however**, she never arrived.

Exercise 1.

Class exercise, oral, in pairs

Your teacher will call out the following:

'The members of the committee are: Peter Ryan, teacher; Sheila Fox, dentist; . . .'

The teacher will then ask each pair of students to add a person and his/her profession to the list. Your teacher will allow you **thirty seconds** to come up with both. You must also say the word '**semi-colon**' after his/her job description.

> **Example**   'Tom Murphy, builder; – **semi-colon**.'

Exercise 2.   Complete the following sentences with a statement **connected** to the first part by the word in bold in each case.

> **Example**   The guest speaker never arrived; **therefore**, we all went home.

1. Tim's father approved of his plans; **indeed**, _____.
2. Shauna didn't really believe in ghosts; **nevertheless**, _____.
3. He practised hard for his driving test; **however**, _____.
4. You can't leave at this hour of the night; **besides**, _____.
5. The pitch was waterlogged; **therefore**, _____.

Exercise 3.   Complete the following sentences. There should be some **comparative connection** between the first and second half of the sentence.

> **Example**   The rain fell in sheets; it _____.
>   The rain fell in sheets; it soaked me through to the bone.

1. Tom turned on the football; Joan _____.
2. Everyone ate Sarah's curry; it _____.
3. Some students travel by bus; some _____.
4. Joe's teacher approved of his plans; Joe's Dad _____.
5. I love the summer holidays; they _____.

Exercise 4.   Here is an extract from *Oliver Twist* by Charles Dickens. Read it, carefully noting the use he makes of the **semi-colon** in his description of the children, the man and the old woman.

There was no fire in the room; but a man was crouching, mechanically, over the empty stove. An old woman, too, had drawn a low stool to the cold hearth, and was sitting beside him.

There were some ragged children in another corner; and in a small recess, opposite the door, there lay upon the ground something covered with an old blanket. Oliver shuddered as he cast his eye towards the place, and crept involuntarily close to his master; for though it was covered up, the boy felt that it was a corpse.

The man's face was thin and very pale; his hair and beard were grizzly; and his eyes were bloodshot. The old woman's face was wrinkled; her two remaining teeth protruded over her under lip; and her eyes were bright and piercing. Oliver was afraid to look at either her or the man. They seemed so like the rats he had seen outside.

Here is another extract from *Oliver Twist*, from which I have removed eight semi-colons. Write it out into your copybook, replacing the semi-colons where you feel they are appropriate. (Look at No. 2 in the list of uses of the semi-colon at the start of this Unit, and read the above extract again before you begin.) Note how the **comma** is also skilfully used in this extract.

'Stop thief! Stop thief!' There is magic in the sound. The tradesman leaves his counter and the carman his waggon the butcher throws down his tray the baker his basket the milkman his pail the errand-boy his parcels the schoolboy his marbles the child his toys. Away they run, pell-mell, helter-skelter, slap-dash tearing, yelling and screaming knocking down passengers as they turn round corners, and rousing up the dogs. The streets and squares re-echo with the sound.

Exercise 5. Now choose a **character** from a short story, novel or play you have read, and write a brief description of that character (70–100 words) using **semi-colons** to balance your sentences, in the way that Dickens does in the extracts above.

Stage 2

Colons :

Question When do we use colons?

Answer When we want to make a **stronger** punctuation mark than a semi-colon. It is very useful for:

1. introducing a **list** or a note, and after expressions like 'for example': and 'the following':

Example Students going on the Paris trip should bring the following: their passport, comfortable shoes, one bag or suitcase and an umbrella.

2. introducing a **title** or **quotation**.

Example The first line of the poem is: 'I wandered lonely as a cloud.'

3. introducing **direct speech**.

Example Dad looked up from his paper and said:
'Are you going somewhere, Susan?'

4. separating different parts of a sentence where the idea or thought is connected. In this situation a colon is used in the same way as a dash.

Example No excuses this time: your work must improve.
I like work: it fascinates me. I can sit and look at it for hours.

In these examples the **colon** pulls us up sharp, forcing us to make a significant pause before continuing.

5. introducing the main **theme** or **subject matter** of a piece.

Example Drug abuse: the menace of the age
Ireland: the best address on Earth

6. moving a thought from its **premise** (introduction) to its **conclusion** (summary of the point).

Example Punctuation is important (premise): it helps the reader to make sense of what you write (conclusion).

Two points to note:
- Don't add a dash after a colon when introducing a list.
- Don't put a capital letter after a colon in the same sentence.

Watch Your Language!

Exercise 1.

Oral, teacher directed

Your teacher will call out a **situation** which requires a **list** of items, and will then select students at random to supply one item each.

> **Example**
>
> | Teacher: | Give me a list of items you would need if you were planning a trip to a **jungle** in Central America. |
> |---|---|
> | Student A: | I would need: a rucksack |
> | Student B: | insect repellent |
> | Student C: | sunscreen . . . |
> | Student D: | . . . |

The teacher continues on round the class until there are **ten** items. At the same time as the items are being called out, **each student must try to write them all down.** The one who lists the **most** items wins!

Remember! Each list must be **introduced** by a **colon**, and **commas** must be put after each item, **except** between the last two – where you will write 'and'. Swop lists with your neighbour, and check for his/her correct use of semi-colons.

Exercise 2.   Write out these sentences, inserting a colon where necessary in each case:

> **Example**   Sugar: a sweet source of tooth decay.

1. Smoking a serious hazard to your health.
2. School can be OK it's here we make friends for life.
3. Homework a necessary evil.
4. To make a sickeningly delicious dessert, you'll need five tins of golden syrup, two pounds of butter, two pounds of brown sugar. *Et voilà*! Toffee fudge sauce for the whole class!
5. The weather continued as it had for several days hot and humid with storms at night.
6. The dogs began to bark they must have sensed an intruder.
7. There was a wonderful surprise waiting at home my new car had been delivered.
8. I don't watch soaps they're too predictable.
9. I was very late for work there was a pile-up on the M50.
10. Punctuation a vital component in good writing.

Exercise 3.   Place a colon after each of the following **titles**, and write a short statement about each of them:

> **Example**   *Coronation Street*: the longest-running 'soap' in television history.
>
> | 1. *Eastenders* | 4. *The Full Monty* |
> |---|---|
> | 2. *Titanic* | 5. *Romeo and Juliet* |
> | 3. *Match of the Day* | |

Exercise 4. Now choose ten titles of your own. They may be the names of books, films, TV programmes, CDs, magazines or comics. Write a statement about each one, as you did for Exercise 3. Remember to **begin** with the title followed by a colon.

Stage 3

Exercise 1.

Colons, semi-colons and commas combined

Write out the following sentences, inserting colons, semi-colons and commas in each one, as required:

1. The line-out is John O'Leary back Tom Murphy wing forward Sean Duignan scrum half Barry O'Neill hooker. Everyone else as was.

2. The film crew consists of Stan Carey camera operator Mary Slevin assistant to the producer Paul Thornton best boy Brian Nutley clapper loader Laura Ryan scenic artist Tom Shanahan carpenter.

3. Miss Lopez requests the following for her concert tour John Lyle piano tuner Stacey Grant masseuse Stanley Moorehead stress counsellor Michael Sullivan stage manager Irene Coates choreographer.

4. When in Paris, please contact the following people Michel Dumont chef 'Café de Paris' Odette Brumard couturier Marcus Ryan restaurateur Yves Montand movie star Jeanne Auban cabaret artiste.

5. The cast is as follows Joe Ryan caretaker Teresa Tancred landlady Tom Shaw salesman Denise Schneider German visitor Sean Lyons barrister.

The Exam; Media studies

Exercise 2.

Go colon hunting! Search through a **newspaper** or **magazine** and cut out the sentences you can find that use a colon. **Headlines** are a good place to start.

Stick these sentences into a single page of your copybook. Think of a suitable **title**, which includes a colon, for your page; for example, **Colossal Colon Hunt: The Search Starts Here**!

Exercise 3.

Litter: the scandal of our age

Write a **short article** on this subject for your school magazine (100–150 words). You might use this anti-litter poster from the Junior Cert. Ordinary level paper, 2003, as your inspiration.

How Do You Spell . . .?

Decisions! Decisions! Spelling Traps

- 'ie' or 'ei'?   - 'able' or 'ible'?   - 'ful' or 'full'?
- 'e' or no 'e'?   - 'ce' or 'se'?

Decisions, decisions! Which do we use? It's often difficult to decide in spelling, but there are some rules that govern the above 'traps'. Let's look at some examples, and then exercise them.

Trap 1 'ie' or 'ei'?

Rules: 1.   Usually the 'i' comes **before** the 'e'.

> (**Example**)   priest, believe, niece, grief

2.   But 'e' comes before 'i' after 'c'.

> (**Example**) ceiling, receipt, deceive

3. Exceptions (weird ones!). These must be learned, as the rule simply doesn't apply.

> (**Example**) weird, seize, foreign, either, neither, protein, leisure, neighbour, weight, Sheila, Keith, Neil

Exercise 1. Fill in the blanks in the following sentences with suitable words from the box below.

1. My _____ is always baking cakes. Her _____ is constantly in use!
2. There were only _____ of them left on the _____, battling it out for the cup.
3. Our _____, Sheila, _____ all day at her son's wedding.
4. No matter how hard he _____, he simply couldn't find the _____ for his suit.
5. The _____ was covered in scenes from the _____ of Pope Gregory.

> **eight, niece, field, sieve, reign, receipt, cried, neighbour, tried, ceiling**

Exercise 2. Write a paragraph (70–100 words) in the form of **a story** which uses each of the **exceptions** listed under Rule 3 **once** only. You might, for instance, begin with this sentence: 'Keith didn't look foreign, but Neil did.' You may, of course, compose your own opening sentence.

Trap 2 'ful' or 'full'?

Rule: When you want to add 'full' to another word, drop the final 'l'.

> (**Example**) **joy** plus **full** becomes **joyful**
> **use** plus **full** becomes **useful**

So, the rule is very simple. A word **cannot** end in 'full' – it must end in 'ful'.

Exercise 1. Fill in the blanks in the following sentences with suitable words from the box below.

1. He was my _____ friend for many years, kind and _____.
2. Granny was _____. Even when times were hard she was always _____.
3. Tom is _____ never to make mistakes in his spelling, because he hopes to become a _____ journalist.
4. Karen's love life is _____ at the moment. She's just too _____ around boys.
5. 'How could Brian be so _____? I think he's _____!', Sarah muttered.

> **bashful, deceitful, uneventful, thoughtful, successful, wonderful, awful, cheerful, careful, faithful**

Exercise 2. Write a short descriptive paragraph or piece of dialogue (70–100 words) which **connects** each of these five **adjectives** in some way:

1. painful
2. beautiful
3. doubtful
4. disgraceful
5. spiteful

Trap 3 'ce' or 'se'?

Rules: 1. The word with 'c' is a **noun** (the/a practice).

> (**Example**) Selling alcohol to underage teenagers is a widespread **practice**.

2. The word with 's' is a **verb** (to practise).

> (**Example**) Barry **practises** the guitar for three hours every day.

Exercise 1. In the following sentences, decide which one of the two words in brackets is **correct**, in terms of the context in which it is being used, i.e. as a **verb** or a **noun**.

1. 'That's good ——— (advice/advise),' the man said. 'I'll speak to my solicitor tomorrow.'
2. A publican is ———d (licence/license) to sell alcohol.
3. Inventors ——— (device/devise) new ways of doing things.
4. ——— (practice/practise) makes perfect.
5. 'I ——— (advice/advise) you to watch out for pickpockets in this street,' said the guide.
6. 'If you ——— (practice/practise) hard, you really will succeed,' her piano teacher said.
7. The man lost his ——— (licence/license) when he was found drunk at the wheel of his car for the third time.
8. What is it? It's a ——— (device/devise) for extracting salt from water.

Exercise 2. Practise the above words in sixteen sentences of your own – using each of the words as both **noun** and **verb**, for practice. Vary your sentences i.e., four statements, four questions, four negative statements, four dramatic sentences ending with an exclamation mark (!).

Trap 4 'able' or 'ible'?

Rule: Although it's difficult to remember whether a word ends in 'able' or 'ible', the fact is that **most** words end in 'able'. Here are ten commonly used 'able' words.

1. acceptable
2. reasonable
3. accountable
4. biddable
5. capable
6. considerable
7. comfortable
8. fashionable
9. miserable
10. reliable

Exercise 1.   In the following piece of dialogue, fill in the blanks with a suitable '**able**' adjective from the list above. (One word has been used twice.)

Dad: Really, Tina, it is not _____ to your mother and me that you come home at this hour!

Tina: Chill out, Dad. I'm quite _____ of taking care of myself. I am fourteen, you know.

Dad: Yes, but not very _____, it seems! You promised to be home by eleven.

Tina: But it's only ten past twelve. Everyone in Sarah's house was still up. We were just getting _____ in fact, when I had to leave.

Dad: Oh were you now?! Listen to me, young lady, this is the second time you've been late this week. What's wrong with you? You used to be so _____, so trustworthy.

Tina: That's not fair, Dad! I am trustworthy. If you and Mum were just a little bit more _____, you'd know that it's just not _____ for teenagers to behave exactly as you 'oldies' want us to any more. This is 2004, Dad, not 1904!

Dad: _____ __ or not, young lady, we're not talking about clothes here, we're talking about behaviour! Your mother and I have gone to _____ trouble to bring you up properly.

Tina: And to make my life _____, you mean! It's not fair. You're always on my back.

Dad: No, Tina. That is not true. We just want you to be _____ for your actions, that's all.

Exercise 2.

Note: The 'ible' ending **sounds** like a suffix to the word: sens**ible**, terr**ible**. Saying the word **aloud** may help. Now fill in the blanks in the following sentences with 'ible' words from the box below.

1. 'Who's _____ for the mess in here?' roared the Head.
2. What an _____ story! Did you make that up?
3. 'Is that cheese _____?' she asked, wondering about the grey fuzzy bits on one side.
4. 'Correcting your homework would be a lot easier if your handwriting were _____, John,' sighed Miss Cronin.
5. Sarah's very _____. She always does the right thing.
6. 'I can be a little _____ about your hours of work, if that helps,' the Manager said.
7. That's _____ news. I'm really sorry.
8. You're so _____, Peter! You believe everything she tells you.
9. He's the most _____ bachelor in Kerry.
10. What a _____ day! It hasn't stopped raining since 7 a.m.

   **flexible, responsible, horrible, legible, gullible, sensible, incredible,
   terrible, edible, eligible**

Trap 5 'e' or no 'e'?

Words ending in 'e' can cause problems, when we wish to add a new ending (suffix). What do we do? Keep the 'e' or drop it? Here are the rules.

Rules:
1. When the suffix begins with a **vowel**, or a 'y' is added, we **drop** the 'e'.

(Example)
dive	div**ing**	div**ed**
bone	bon**y**	

2. When the suffix begins with a **consonant**, we **keep** the 'e'.

(Example)
bare	bare**ly**
face	face**less**
refine	refine**ment**

3. There are some exceptions. Learn these, as they are often spelled incorrectly:

argue	arg**um**ent
true	tru**ly**
due	du**ly**
whole	who**lly**
humble	humb**ly**
courage	courag**eous**
notice	notic**eable**
like	lik**eable** or lik**able**

Exercise 1. Add 'ing' and 'ed' to these words, **dropping the 'e'** according to Rule 1. The first one is done for you.

1. hate   hating   hated
2. cycle   _____   _____
3. starve   _____   _____
4. save   _____   _____
5. rave   _____   _____
6. bake   _____   _____
7. declare   _____   _____
8. hope   _____   _____
9. love   _____   _____
10. live   _____   _____

Exercise 2. Add 'ly', 'less' or 'ment' to the following words, **keeping the 'e'**, as in Rule 2. But you must decide which suffix you can add to the word given! The first one is done for you.

	ly	**less**	**ment**
1. advance	_____	_____	**advancement**
2. care	_____	_____	_____
3. refine	_____	_____	_____
4. late	_____	_____	_____
5. nice	_____	_____	_____
6. face	_____	_____	_____
7. definite	_____	_____	_____
8. hope	_____	_____	_____
9. require	_____	_____	_____
10. precise	_____	_____	_____

Exercise 3.   Write out the following paragraph with the correct spelling of the words **in brackets**, according to the rules you have studied, and to their use and meaning within the passage.

Margaret was (hope) for a miracle. She couldn't believe that Kevin actually (hate) her. Claire was (rave) surely? After all, Margaret (love) him and they were (save) for a house, weren't they? He was (definite) in line for (advance) at work, and her mother had already (bake) the wedding cake, for heaven's sake! She had even sold her car in order to save money and was now (cycle) to work every day. (Late), however, she had noticed that Kevin was getting (care) about time, and wasn't quite as (love) as he'd been. Perhaps Claire was right. Kevin hadn't actually (declare) his intention to marry her, but he had said he'd always wanted to marry a woman of (refine) and taste – like her.

'To hell with him!' she thought. 'I have (starve) myself for that man! How dare he hate me?'

'(Precise)!' a little voice inside her said. 'You're better off without him, Margaret. Off you go and find some nice, (name), (face) bureaucrat with lots of money instead.'

'Too true!' said Margaret to the teddy on her desk. 'That'll do me (nice)! I'll be (live) it up this weekend, Kevin Ryan, but without you. Hasta la vista, baby! – as Arnold would say.'

Words at Work

Opposites Attract . . . Synonyms and Antonyms

Question What is a synonym?

Answer A synonym is a word or phrase which means **exactly** the same as another word or is **very close** in meaning to it.

Example **Student** is a synonym of **pupil**.

When you use synonyms you avoid needless repetition and your writing becomes more interesting as a result. A **thesaurus** is a book with an alphabetical list of words and their synonyms. It is a very useful tool in your writing (see Unit 2 pages 49–51).

Question What is an antonym?

Answer An antonym is a word which is **opposite in meaning** to another word.

Example **Happy** is an antonym of **sad**.

Exam questions often ask you to **compare** and **contrast** things, for example images, characters, plots and styles of writing. Having a variety of **synonyms** for **comparison**, and **antonyms** for **contrast**, will help you to write better answers to these kinds of questions.

Let's practise.

Stage 1

Exercise 1. Sort these words into ten pairs of synonyms:

Example large – big

small, expensive, neat, shut, reply, difficult, tidy, closed, right, large, dear, ill, answer, despise, tiny, correct, big, hate, hard, sick

Exercise 2. Replace each of the words in bold in the following sentences with a synonym from the list below.

1. Golf takes up almost all of my **spare** time. _____
2. You can get a lot of **fun** out of solving puzzles. _____
3. Tom is an enthusiastic member of his local drama **club**. _____
4. I find Maths **difficult**. _____
5. Miss Hurley is very nice but she can be a bit **cutting** at times. _____
6. That film was really **dull**! _____
7. It's **icy** out there. _____

8. Sarah actually **likes** housework. _____
9. Richard Branson is extremely **wealthy**. _____
10. Dad discovered an **old** sword in the attic. _____

pleasure, leisure, affluent, antique, society, tedious, glacial, enjoys, scathing, arduous

Exercise 3. Sort these words into ten pairs of antonyms:

> **Example**) appear – vanish

relaxed, intolerant, fresh, understanding, strict, majority, pessimistic, friendly, vanish, wrong, minority, nervous, optimistic, appear, tense, easygoing, hostile, right, calm, stale

Exercise 4. Write the antonyms of these words. The first letter is given to you as a clue.

		Antonym				Antonym
1.	absence	p_____		11.	war	p_____
2.	cheap	e_____		12.	sense	n_____
3.	failure	s_____		13.	difficult	e_____
4.	innocent	g_____		14.	honest	d_____
5.	kind	u_____		15.	pleasant	u_____
6.	careful	c_____		16.	selfish	u_____
7.	obey	d_____		17.	capable	i_____
8.	trust	d_____		18.	approval	d_____
9.	true	f_____		19.	mature	i_____
10.	vague	d_____		20.	encourage	d_____

Stage 2

More about synonyms

Because some synonyms are very close in meaning to another word, but not always exactly the same, we must be careful which synonym of a word we use in a particular **context**. For example, if your Mum made you a cup of tea, and you appreciated it, you might say: 'Thanks, Mum. That was a **great** cup of tea.' But you would hardly say: 'That was a **momentous** or **magnificent** cup of tea.' These two words are indeed synonyms of 'great', but they would be inappropriate in this context. (Incidentally, *The Wordsworth Thesaurus for Home, Office and Study* has over 125 synonyms for 'great'!)

Exercise 1. Fill in the blanks in the sentences below with the most **suitable** (appropriate) synonym from the four options given.

1. If you don't lift that saucepan carefully, you may _____ yourself.
   - **a.** blister   **b.** sear   **c.** scald   **d.** singe
2. Mr. Murphy has been asked to _____ the next meeting of the Parents' Committee.
   - **a.** present   **b.** preside   **c.** lead   **d.** chair
3. Miss Simpson was _____ of stealing money from the till.
   - **a.** accused   **b.** alleged   **c.** charged   **d.** denounced
4. The deer in the Phoenix Park are quite _____.
   - **a.** biddable   **b.** tame   **c.** broken in   **d.** domesticated
5. Margaret never bought anything for her friend's birthday. She was too _____.
   - **a.** close   **b.** tight   **c.** mean   **d.** miserly
6. The President's personal _____ never left her side during the State Visit.
   - **a.** defender   **b.** lifeguard   **c.** protector   **d.** bodyguard
7. She couldn't believe that he had bought her a _____ diamond ring.
   - **a.** imitation   **b.** fake   **c.** artificial   **d.** false
8. There have been many changes in the _____ for Junior Certificate.
   - **a.** plan   **b.** syllabus   **c.** agenda   **d.** programme
9. The sea was so _____ that many of the passengers were seasick.
   - **a.** uneven   **b.** choppy   **c.** wavy   **d.** billowy
10. Mary buys most of the _____ she sees advertised on TV.
    - **a.** goods   **b.** products   **c.** commodities   **d.** merchandise

Exercise 2. Below are five sets of words, each of which comprises a headword and three synonyms for it, taken from the *Wordsworth Thesaurus*. Write one sentence for each synonym in the set. Your sentences should **clearly** show the difference in **usage** of each word, depending on the **context** in which it is used. Try to keep your sentences short and clear.

(Example)	bother	1. annoy:	That man annoys me!
		2. disturb:	I don't want to disturb you.
		3. upset:	I hope this won't upset you.

	Word	Synonyms
Set 1.	bother (verb)	annoy, disturb, upset
Set 2.	courtesy (noun)	consideration, kindness, politeness
Set 3.	deep (adjective)	bottomless, grave, mysterious
Set 4.	enterprise (noun)	activity, business, project
Set 5.	foreign (adjective)	alien, distant, strange

N.B.! Think of these exercises as a means of increasing your **word power**. This will make your writing much more interesting and varied.

More about antonyms

You can also form antonyms by:

1. adding a prefix to a word.

(Example)		
	happy	**un**happy
	correct	**in**correct
	obey	**dis**obey
	perfect	**im**perfect

2. changing the prefix.

(Example)		
	ascend	**de**scend
	internal	**ex**ternal

3. changing the suffix:

(Example)		
	careful	care**less**
	useful	use**less**

Exercise 1. Using prefixes and suffixes, make antonyms from the following words:

		Antonym				Antonym
1.	just	unjust	7.	selfish	_____	
2.	convenient	_____	8.	sane	_____	
3.	advantage	_____	9.	like	_____	
4.	patient	_____	10.	possible	_____	
5.	increase	_____	11.	encourage	_____	
6.	hopeful	_____	12.	merciful	_____	

Some other less common prefixes can also be used to make antonyms:

(Example)						
	ab	+	normal	=	**ab**normal	
	il	+	legal	=	**il**legal	
	non	+	sense	=	**non**sense	
	ig	+	noble	=	**ig**noble	

You will find a lot more examples and exercises on prefixes and suffixes in Unit 6 – How Do You Spell . . .?

Exercise 2. Write a paragraph or a piece of dialogue in the form of a **story** which uses each of the antonyms from Exercise 1 once only. Here is a starter sentence: 'George felt that it was very **unjust** to dismiss Shane, but the rest of the team felt it was **impossible** to work with him.' You may compose your own, of course!

Stage 3

The Exam; Personal writing

Exercise 1.

'Write the conversation (in dialogue form) that might occur between a parent and a teenager after the parent comes home from a parent/teacher meeting.' (Junior Cert. Higher level, 1997)

Imagine that the following is the **first draft** of the above personal writing exercise. You will notice that certain words are in bold, because they are **repeated**. Can you write a **second draft** using **synonyms of your own** for those words in bold? Use a thesaurus if you get stuck!

Dad: Well, Pat, that was a terrific parent/teacher meeting, really . . .

Pat: **Terrific**? That's great Dad, really **great**!

Dad: Will you let me finish?! I was about to say that I was **really** . . .

Pat: I know, I know, Dad, but there's no need to say it, like. I'm a **great** son, and that's all there is to it.

Dad: No! That is not all there is to it! I have never been so embarrassed in my entire life. Did you hear me? **Embarrassed**, dreadfully **embarrassed** for you, Pat. I . . .

Pat: Yeh. Yeh. I heard. You've never been so embarrassed in your **entire** life, etc., etc. So what's the problem? It's only the Mocks, right?

Dad: Only the Mocks?! Oh, well, that's all right then, Pat, isn't it? It's only three months to your exam. You'll have no **problem** there at all, will you? Not my brainy son, oh no!

Pat: Yeh, well, I am **brainy**. You just don't see it, that's all. You don't understand, do you? I'm under a lot of pressure, you know, a lot of **pressure**. You parents never **understand** that – **never**.

Dad: Oh, so I don't understand now. I know nothing about **pressure**, I suppose. I'm only your **parent**, right?!

Pat: Got it in one, Dad! It's not your fault entirely, of course. You are getting on a bit and the old grey matter doesn't work too well. Hey! No sweat. It happens.

Dad: Getting **on a bit**, am I? Listen, sunshine, I may be ancient in your eyes, but I still have all my **grey matter** intact, I can assure you! What's more, I'm still your Dad! Up those stairs this minute and get studying, or this **old** man, whose brain doesn't work too well, will ground you for a month!!

The drama continues

Exercise 2.

Now, **continue the dialogue** and complete the personal writing exercise, using **synonyms** and **antonyms** from this unit as far as possible. (200–250 words)

And finally . . . A joke!

Teacher: Who can explain what a synonym is?
Peggy: I can, Miss! It's a word you use instead of the one you can't spell.

Unit 4

Grappling with Grammar

Adverbs

> **Question** What is an adverb?
> **Answer** An adverb is a word that tells us more about a **verb**.

Adverbs:

1. give us more **information** about verbs, about **how** something is done.

> **Example** The dinner was   planned **precisely**,
>   cooked **carefully**,
>   and   eaten **quickly**.

2. can also tell us **when** something is done.

> **Example** She wrote home **immediately**.

3. can tell us **where** something happens.

> **Example** The match was played **away**.

There are levels of **comparison** for adverbs, as there are for adjectives.

> **Example** carefully   **more** carefully   **most** carefully

Lots of adverbs are **formed** very easily from **adjectives**. In most cases, you simply add '**ly**'.

> **Example** clever (adjective) → cleverly (adverb)

Be careful, though, because some **adjectives** also end in 'ly'.

> **Example** friendly, lively, elderly, lonely, silly, lovely

In some cases, there will be a slight change in the **spelling** when forming adverbs from adjectives.

> **Example** 1. When an adjective ends in 'y', in order to make the adverb, we
> drop the 'y' and put in 'i' before adding 'ly'.
> angry → angrily

> 2. When an adjective ends in 'e' and has **two** consonant letters before the 'e', we **drop** the 'e' before adding the 'ly'.
> gentle → gently.
>
> 3. However, if an adjective ends in 'e' but has just **one** consonant letter immediately before the 'e' then we **keep** the 'e' before adding 'ly'.
> sincere → sincerely
> wise → wisely
> delicate → delicately

So you can see that dealing with adverbs needs a careful eye!

Stage 1

Exercise 1.   Fill in the blanks in each of these sentences with a suitable adverb from the list below.

1.   She ate _____, taking tiny bites.
2.   'I don't frighten _____ ,' said Tom.
3.   Mr. Riordan drives very _____, at a steady forty miles per hour.
4.   'You may speak _____, Simon,' the Principal said. I'm listening.'
5.   The mother gazed _____ at her new baby.
6.   Drinking _____ makes good sense.
7.   'To _____ go where no one has gone before.' (*Star Trek*).
8.   _____, it won't be long before we can go home.
9.   Rose has been behaving very _____ lately, don't you think?
10.   They've been _____ married for over forty years.

boldly, carefully, moderately, happily, slowly, lovingly, easily, strangely, openly, hopefully

Exercise 2.

1.   Write the **adverb** for each of the adjectives below. (Remember to check the spelling rules given in the introduction).

Adjective	Adverb		Adjective	Adverb
a. annual	_____	f. passionate	_____
b. beautiful	_____	g. quick	_____
c. definite	_____	h. reluctant	_____
d. gradual	_____	i. skilful	_____
e. menacing	_____	j. superb	_____

2. Now write one sentence for each adjective and adverb.

> **Example** annual (adjective). He pays an **annual** visit to his Aunt Sarah
> in Cardiff.
>
> annually (adverb). His subscription to the *National Geographic* is paid
> **annually**.

N.B.! Highlight the **noun** to which each **adjective** refers, and the **verb** to which each **adverb** refers, in your sentences.

Test yourself!

Exercise 3.

1. In pairs, decide who's A and who's B. Your teacher will **spell** out **twenty adjectives** from this section. You must form **adverbs** from them.
2. You must decide how the adverb will be spelled from the explanations given in the introduction (points 1–6).
3. There will be a time limit of **thirty seconds** per example. A and B may consult on the spelling of the adverb. B must write **both** adjective and adverb into his/her copy.
4. At the end, the teacher will ask you to **exchange** copies with another pair of students, and you will correct each other's work. Consult your dictionaries if in doubt about any of the spellings. The **pair** with the most correctly spelled adjectives **and** adverbs wins! (Time limit: ten minutes)

Stage 2

Types of adverbs

HOW?   WHERE?   WHEN?   HOW OFTEN?

1. **Adverbs of manner** answer the question **How?**

> **Example** **How** did the old lady dress? She dressed **elegantly**.

2. **Adverbs of place** answer the question **Where?**

> **Example** **Where** did he leave his coat? He left it **here**.

3. **Adverbs of time** answer the question **When?**

> **Example** **When** did you last see Stephen? I saw him **yesterday**.

4. **Adverbs of frequency** answer the question **How often?**

> **Example** **How often** do they eat out? They eat out at weekends, **usually**.

Exercise 1. Place each of the twenty-four adverbs from the list below under its correct heading in the following table:

	Manner	Place	Time	Frequency
1.	_____	_____	_____	_____
2.	_____	_____	_____	_____
3.	_____	_____	_____	_____
4.	_____	_____	_____	_____
5.	_____	_____	_____	_____
6.	_____	_____	_____	_____

> never, eagerly, yesterday, seldom, now, outside, stubbornly, soon, kindly,
> early, usually, seriously, loudly, here, somewhere, sometimes, everywhere,
> tomorrow, always, there, today, painfully, often, anywhere

Exercise 2. Now choose the most **suitable** adverb from Exercise 1 to complete the following sentences:

1. When May was ill, Tom treated her _____.
2. Brendan lives _____ else now.
3. 'Will I see you _____?' Karen asked.
4. 'How _____ do you see Paul?'
5. The children waited _____ for their Dad to bring home the new car.
6. Barry has concluded (however _____) that Susan doesn't fancy him.
7. You can see posters for *Lord of the Rings* _____ these days.
8. 'I can't believe you're actually _____ for once!'
9. He's _____ very punctual.
10. Eminem is _____ rich!

The Exam; Writing dialogue

Exercise 3.

Using at least **three** of each type of adverb exercised so far (manner, place, time, frequency), write a 3–5 minute **scene** for a TV soap involving just **three** characters, entitled: *Never Too Late.* Keep it credible, and use as many adverbs from this unit as possible.

Stage 3

Combinations

Although we mainly use adverbs to describe **verbs**, there are times when we combine:

1. adverbs and adjectives

(**Example**) reasonably cheap

2. adverbs and adverbs!

(**Example**) incredibly quickly

3. adverbs and past participles

(**Example**) badly organised

Exercise 1. Choose **two** words, one from each box, to complete the sentences below.

Adverbs	Adjectives / past participles
absolutely, incredibly, badly, completely, seriously, fully, really, unusually, slightly, barely	easy, huge, organised, changed, ill, quiet, damaged, insured, ready, sorry

(**Example**) adverb: reasonably   adjective: cheap
Liam thought the restaurant was expensive, but I thought it was **reasonably cheap.**

1. Sean's mother is _____ _____ in hospital.
2. The fire destroyed our house, but fortunately we were _____ _____.
3. What a big ship! It's _____ _____.
4. It wasn't a serious accident. The car was only _____ _____.
5. Lots of things went wrong because the trip was _____ _____.
6. The kids are usually very boisterous but they're _____ _____today.
7. When Brian returned home after forty years in the States, everything had _____ _____.
8. I'm _____ _____ about losing your book. I'll buy you another one.
9. Denis was _____ _____ when the taxi arrived.
10. I'm pleased to say this exercise has been _____ _____.

Exercise 2.   Complete these sentences with a **second** adverb. Remember! It need not necessarily end in 'ly'. Look back at all the different types exercised so far.

1.   The police were on the scene incredibly _____.
2.   For such skilled technicians, they worked terribly _____.
3.   We got home reasonably _____ from the match.
4.   '4.30 a.m. is extremely _____, in my opinion, Gráinne!'
5.   Everything went perfectly _____ on the day.
6.   Bridget has behaved fairly _____ under the circumstances.
7.   'Do you come here _____?'
8.   The garden is a mess! There are weeds absolutely _____.
9.   'How does she usually play?' 'Very _____!'
10. 'How will we approach the subject of the wedding?' 'Extremely _____!'

The Exam; Personal writing

Exercise 3.

Adverbs of **manner** are used more frequently than any other type of adverb.

> (**Example**)   sleep **soundly**, eat **greedily**

1.   Match each of the following **verbs** to an adverb of **manner** from the list below.
   a.   feel _____   f.   speak_____
   b.   argue _____   g.   behave _____
   c.   whisper_____   h.   remember _____
   d.   investigate _____   i.   listen _____
   e.   react _____   j.   fall _____

   softly, frequently, angrily, clearly, deeply, attentively, thoroughly, stupidly, convincingly, continuously

2.   Now write a **short story** (110–120 words) in which you make an **imaginative connection** between the above verbs and adverbs. The situation might be one of conflict perhaps, **or** of reconciliation. Try not to **repeat** any of your verb/adverb combinations. Here is a possible starter for you: 'Although Donnacha tried to **listen** (verb) very **attentively** (adverb) to what she was saying, his mind was really on the match.'

What does B.C. stand for? Before Calculators.

What is a forum? Two-um plus two-um.

Your son has the ability to go places – I wish he would!

Punctuation Please!

Question Marks and Exclamation Marks ? !

1. Question marks

Question | When do we use question marks?
Answer | Simple. We use them every time we ask a question.

Example | What's all this about then?
But do **not** put a **full stop** or a **comma** after a question mark.

Example | Who won the match?. Wrong!
Who won the match? Right!
N.B. Do not use a question mark after an indirect question.

Example | **I asked him** who had won the match.

2. Exclamation marks

Question | When do we use exclamation marks?
Answer | **Not** so simple! We use them:

1. when giving an **urgent message** or **order**.

Example | Ambulance, please!
Stop doing that! Sit down!

2. when expressing **surprise or disbelief**.

Example | A million pounds! I can't believe it!

3. in **newspaper headlines**. It suggests to the reader that what has been written is funny, exciting, dramatic or extraordinary in some way.

Example | Amazing triumph for home town team!
It's snow joke! Blizzards in Bailieboro!

4. after **exclamatory expressions** (interjections).

(Example) Wow! Well really! No way! Ow!

Oh! Help! Stop! As if! Go away!

5. to emphasise **a strongly felt emotion**, perhaps anger or joy.

(Example) 'I hate you!' Jill screamed.

'I'm so happy!' Hannah sighed.

Stage 1

Exercise 1.

In pairs, oral and written

1. Decide who's A and who's B.

2. Both A and B take **five minutes** to write out **five questions** on one or more of the topics from the list below. Do not let the other person see your questions!

3. When the time is up, A asks B each of his/her five questions. B must answer with an **exclamation**-style sentence, which A must write down, with an exclamation mark, under his/her own question.

(Example) A. Do you like Blue?

B. Yeh! They're brilliant!

4. Swop roles and repeat the exercise. This time, B must write down all the answers – with exclamation marks – to his/her own questions.

5. Compare each other's work for correct use of exclamation marks **and** question marks. (Time limit: ten minutes)

    TV, groups, teams, holidays, food, subjects in school, films, friends, weekends, clothes

Exercise 2. Here are some answers to a quiz. Can you supply possible **questions**? Write them out. Remember those question marks! Time limit: ten minutes.

1. Dublin	6. Coldplay
2. France	7. Seamus Heaney
3. Stratford-upon-Avon	8. *Friends*
4. *Romeo and Juliet* (film)	9. Mount Everest
5. Wimbledon 2003	10. Mary McAleese

Exercise 3.   Write out the following sentences with **either** a question mark or a full stop at the end, depending on whether you understand the sentence to be a **direct** or an **indirect** question.

1. Can you tell me when the next train leaves
2. He asked me when the next train left
3. Why don't you ring her
4. Is that all you've written
5. She asked me if I could help her
6. Are you ever happy, Paula
7. That time is it
8. They asked for directions to the school
9. Do you know what you're saying
10. Hannah wanted to know if Jill was coming out to play

Stage 2

Writing dialogue

When writing **dialogue**, we put question marks and exclamation marks **inside** the quotation marks.

> **Example**   'Do you really hate me?' asked Paul.
> 'No, of course not!' snapped Diane.

Exercise 1.   Punctuate the following piece of dialogue with **question marks** and **exclamation marks** where appropriate. Write it out into your copybook, with a new line for each character, as you see here.

Stephen: Are you coming home
Tina: What
Stephen: Home. Are you coming home
Tina: No. Not yet.
Stephen: Why
Tina: Why what
Stephen: For God's sake, Tina Don't do this to me
Tina: Don't shout at me
Stephen: I'm not shouting. Sorry. I just want to know if you're coming home
Tina: Yeh, Yeh OK. I know Just don't keep going on about it
Stephen: But why aren't you coming home
Tina: I told you I don't know Now, leave it, will you You're doing my head in
Stephen: OK. OK. I'm sorry. I was only asking.

Tina: Yeh, well, don't

Stephen: Right I won't

Tina: Good.

Stephen: I'll see ye then. Next week. OK

Tina: Yeh. Yeh. Whatever

Stephen: Bye .

Tina: Yeh. Bye.

Exercise 2.   Politely **contradict** these questions or statements using **do/does/did** and an exclamation mark.

> (Example)   'Why didn't you finish it?'
> 'But I **did** finish it!'

1.   I'm sorry you don't want to go out with me.
2.   I am surprised that your mother doesn't drive.
3.   Why don't you practise?
4.   It's a pity Sarah doesn't like Maths.
5.   Why didn't you tell me it was your birthday?
6.   I know you don't really love me.
7.   It's a shame your brother doesn't like pizza.
8.   I suppose they've cut off your phone because you didn't pay the bill.
9.   You would play much better if you practised.
10. You would have passed if you'd studied harder.

Exercise 3.

Look at this statement, followed by a question:

> (Example)   'You can sing, **can't you?**'

Complete the following statements with a **question**. Don't forget the question mark!

1.   You can dance, _____
2.   He knows what he's doing, _____
3.   They are coming with us, _____
4.   You've got the tickets, _____
5.   You haven't been fighting, _____
6.   She's mad about me, _____
7.   He's not totally daft, _____
8.   We won't get in trouble, _____
9.   It's over, _____
10. He can go as well, _____

Stage 3

The Exam; Media studies

Newspapers and magazines frequently use **exclamation marks** to:

1. **Promote a competition or offer.**

WHAT A GOOD IDEA!

Ideas that are so good, we wonder why they weren't thought of before …

Win Bon Jovi!

Win Justin Timberlake!

2. **Advertise a product or service.**

3. **Highlight or emphasise a particular article.**

Sugar scoop!

PAT IN HUNGRY LION HORROR!

Eastenders' Pat Evans, a.k.a. Pam St. Clement, narrowly escaped a wild animal recently – and we don't mean Grant Mitchell! On safari in Africa, Pam was checking out some lion tracks when their owner emerged from the bushes to scoff her up! She made it to the jeep in the nick of time and word from the jungle is that her huge multi-coloured earrings frightened him off. Eek!

Question marks are also used in the same way.

Was she trying to tell me something?

Who'll look after them if you die? The Sun Life MoneyBack Plan will!

Exercise 1.

1. Look for some more examples of the use of question marks and exclamation marks in **magazines** and **newspapers**. Cut them out and paste them into a copybook/notebook under two headings 'Question Marks' and 'Exclamation Marks'.

2. Choose **two** of each and write a brief comment on how effective the punctuation marks are in each case, in terms of persuading you to read the article or advertisement.

3. Are there occasions where the **exclamation mark** seems overly dramatic or unnecessary? Comment on one example from a magazine or newspaper you've read.

Exercise 2.   In the following article, from *Bliss* magazine, three soap stars describe their most embarrassing moment. Note how the **exclamation mark** is used in each case. Now write a paragraph of similar length (60–90 words) in which you describe your own most embarrassing moment! Try not to use more than **three** exclamation marks.

Philip Olivier, *Brookside's Tinhead*

'I was filming the famous parade explosion scene and they had artificial rain on the set. I had to run off after saying my line, which was "I'm going to see Mum and Ben". But as I turned round, I ran straight into the camera! When they re-shot the scene, I said: "I'm going to see Burns and Men". I was talking gibberish!'

A. J. McLean,

Backstreet Boys

'We were in a hotel in Texas and we went into the balcony to wave to our fans. I was munching on a hot doughnut when I noticed this cute girl in the crowd smiling at me. Just then I bit into the jammy bit and scalded my mouth. I spat out a mouthful and ... it landed on her head! I was too ashamed to go back out and say sorry'.

Michelle Williams,

Dawson's Creek's Jen

'We were on set and the director wanted to shoot us sliding down the hall, so they put baby powder on the floor and greased our shoes so we'd slip along nicely. On the first take I did a run-up, started gliding ... then fell over and nearly knocked myself out. Everyone cracked up – I'm such a klutz!'

Exercise 3.

1. Using either question marks **or** exclamation marks, write **a caption** for each of the pictures numbered 1 to 6.
2. What do you imagine Chandler (*Friends*) in Picture 2 is saying/thinking?
3. What do you imagine Joey (*Friends*) in Picture 5 is saying?

1.
2.
3.
4.
5.
6.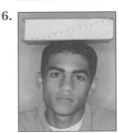

How Do You Spell . . .?

Doubling Up: Double-letter Words 1

One of the most common errors made in spelling double-letter words is to leave out one of the two letters.

Example	hoby	wrong!	hobby	right!
	rubish	wrong!	rubbish	right!

There are no hard and fast rules here. You just need to **learn** the correct spelling through **practice** and by **being careful**. In this unit, you will be exercising double-letter words from double 'b' to double 'l'. So let's begin!

1. Double 'b' words

Here are some of the most common ones:

abbreviate	robber
flabby	rubbish
gobble	scribble
hobby	stubborn
lobby	wobble

Exercise 1.

1. Study the ten words above for five minutes in class. Remember it will be easier to learn these spellings because each word contains a **double 'b'** and they are written in **alphabetical** order.

2. When the five minutes are up, your teacher will call out each word in the order in which you have learned them. Write them out, one underneath the other, in a list, being very careful with those **double 'b's**!

3. Exchange your copy with the person next to you. You will now correct his/hers, and he/she will do likewise with yours. Please refer to the **original spelling list** when correcting each word.

4. Give **one** mark for each word spelled correctly, and a total mark out of ten.

5. If a word has been spelled **incorrectly**, cross it out and write the **correct** spelling of the word beside it, again checking from the original list.

6. Take back your own copy and write out any words you have spelled incorrectly, **five** times each.

Exercise 2.

Now look again at the ten double 'b' words listed above, this time for **meaning**. Then fill in the gaps in the following sentences with the most suitable word from the list.

1. Sometimes it's very handy to _____ a word, especially when writing notes.

2. 'Simon! Please don't _____ your food!'

3. Everyone should have a _____.

4. I know I write _____ at times, but I just can't help it!

5. Mum is always talking about her _____ thighs. Dad just ignores his.

6. The bank _____ got away with fifty thousand pounds and a box of the manager's cigars.

7. The _____ of the hotel in New York was huge!

8. 'I can't understand a word you've written, Paul! It's such a _____.'

9. Jelly _____s.

10. 'Why are you so _____?!'

The Exam; Personal writing

Exercise 3.

Using your imagination, write a series of **questions** and **answers**, in dialogue form, using all ten double 'b' words from the list, once only.

> **Example** 'Do you think I have **flabby** thighs?'
> 'No. But they do **wobble** a bit!'

2. Double 'c' words

accent	account
accept	occasion
accident	occupation
accommodation	occur
according	succeed

Six of the list words begin with '**acc**', three with '**occ**' and one with '**succ**'. This should make them easier to learn and remember.

Do you remember those spelling strategies from Unit 2? Look for **sound** patterns in the double 'c' list.

> **Example** accommoda**tion**, occupa**tion**

You **hear** the ending 'shun'. You spell it '**tion**'. (See Unit 2, Spelling Strategy 1, Exercise 1.)

Exercise 1.

As for double 'b' words.

Exercise 2.

1. Underline the **ending** of each of the double 'c' words.

> **Example** accen**t**, acce**pt**

Say the words **out loud**, making the connection between the **sound** and the **spelling**. These same sounds will occur in other words, remember. Therefore, the same spelling will apply.

2. Play **What's the Word**? with the student next to you.* It's a bit like charades, but you use words instead of gestures. This is how it works:
    a. Decide who's A and who's B.
    b. A selects **five** words from the list, but does not tell B what they are.
    c. A gives a **definition** of each word to B, and/or an explanation of its use, where one might find it, who might need it, etc. For example, 'This word means a place to stay or rent' . . . (accommodation).

d. B has to try to guess what each word is, but **quickly, and then spell it**. There is a time limit of three minutes for all five words. The aim is for B to **guess and spell** all five words within the time, or he/she loses the game!

e. Change roles, with B testing A this time with the five remaining words – which must be guessed **in the order** in which they are presented to A.

Have fun!

*The **teacher** may also direct the game, choosing students at random. Everyone must **write down** the words guessed.

Exercise 3. Write ten sentences of your own, each one using one double 'c' word from the list above. Write the following types of sentences:

- **Three question**-style sentences
- **Three negative-statement**-style sentences
- One exclamation-style sentence
- **Two statement**-style sentences
- **One** type of your **own choice**.

3. Double 'd' words

add	odd
address	puddle
fiddle	riddle
giddy	shudder
middle	suddenly

Notice the pattern in the **four** words that end in '**le**'. Also notice that '**suddenly**', which is often misspelled, does not contain a '**t**'.

Exercise 1.

As for double 'b' words.

Exercise 2. Go back and read Spelling Strategy 3 in Unit 2.

Here is another **cloze-style** exercise; but **without** the word being given to you at the top of the staged exercise. You must supply the complete word, once you have studied the stages and filled in the gaps in each one.

(Example)
1. _____ly
2. su_____
3. __dd__
4. ____en__
5. _____ (completed word: **suddenly**)

Remember! This is an exercise designed to help you to **spell** better. Therefore, it doesn't matter if you guess the whole word straight away. The point is to make you aware of how letters **combine** to form a complete word, and to learn to spell it **correctly**. Two-syllable words may be completed in only three or four stages.

1. a. ___ress
    b. add___
    c. _____

2. a. _____er
    b. ___dd__
    c. shu__er
    d. _____

3. a. ____le
    b. ri__le
    c. ridd__
    d. _____

4. a. ____le
    b. mi__le
    c. midd__
    d. _____

5. a. ____le
    b. pu__le
    c. pudd__
    d. _____

Exercise 3.   Consult your dictionary and see if you can find one double 'd' word for every letter of the alphabet.

> **Example**   'a' for adder
> 'b' for bidder
> and so on.

You may have a problem with some letters, but the **search** is the important thing. (What about 'Yiddish' for 'y'?)

4. Double 'f' words

affair	efficient
affection	effort
afford	sufficient
coffee	toffee
daffodil	traffic

Did you notice how the double 'f' in all these words is followed by a **vowel**? This is also the norm with double 'c' words, for example accept, accident.

Exercise 1.

As for double 'b' words.

Exercise 2.   Can you **unjumble** these words from your double 'f' list?

1. LODAFDIF _____
2. FOIATNFEC _____
3. TEFCINFEI _____
4. INSFUCFETI _____
5. CFTFAIR _____

Exercise 3. Write **a nonsense poem**, entitled 'Daffodil Traffic' or 'The Toffee Affair'. Use each double 'f' word from the list, repeating a particular word for effect perhaps, as in a chorus of a song. Be as imaginative and crazy as you want. After all, Edward Lear got away with it, didn't he? (Read 'The Dong with the Luminous Nose'.)

5. Double 'l' words

cellar	excellent
challenge	illustration
collar	intelligent
collect	million
collision	villain

Again, notice how double 'l' is followed by a **vowel**. Notice too how some words have two **syllables** while others have three. If you break the words up into **syllables**, it will be easier to learn the spelling.

> (**Example**) ill-us-tra-tion, ex-cell-ent

Exercise 1.
As for double 'b' words.

Exercise 2. In pairs, play **What's the Word?**, following the instructions given in double 'c' words, Exercise 2.

Exercise 3. Now look again at the ten double 'l' words listed above, this time for **meaning**. Then fill in the gaps in the following sentences with a suitable word from the list.

1. 'What a wonderful _____!' she thought, admiring his drawing.
2. Uncle Colm has an impressive wine _____.
3. 'I _____ you to a duel, Sir!' the angry lover declared.
4. His car was in _____ with a lorry at the junction of Seahaven Road and Northbrook Avenue.
5. Everyone dreams of winning a _____ on the Lotto.
6. We're hoping for _____ results, as Marianne is a very _____ and hardworking student.
7. After the rugby match, Tom's _____ was not exactly white.
8. Sheila will _____ the pizza on her way home.
9. He will never be any good. He's an out and out _____.

Words at Work

Similes and Metaphors

Question What is a simile?

Answer A simile is a **comparison** between two things or people **using** the words 'like' or 'as'.

Example
1. He is **as** strong **as** an ox.
2. She sings **like** an angel.

Question What is a metaphor?

Answer A metaphor is a **comparison** between two things or people **without using** the words 'like' or 'as'. The comparison is imaginative, but stronger than a simile.

Example
1. He **is** an ox.
2. She **is** an angel.

In sentence 2, for example, the girl is so wonderful that the one who admires her believes she is **actually** an angel.

Poets are especially fond of similes and metaphors.

Example
simile
    Like flames across the sky,
    With wings all bristling,
    Came the angel striding by.
                  from 'Tom's Angel' by *Walter de la Mare*

metaphor
    The moon was a ghostly galleon tossed upon
    cloudy seas.
               from 'The Highwayman' by *Sir Henry Newbolt*

Stage 1

Similes

Exercise 1. Your teacher will call out the first part of ten well-known similes, with 'as', and you must supply the ending.

> **Example** Question: He was as brave as _____?
> Answer: a lion.

Write your answers into your copybook. Your teacher will impose a time limit of **twenty seconds** per example. When all of the similes have been called out, you will be asked to swop your copy with another student. Your teacher will then call out the endings and you will correct them. The student with the highest number of correctly completed similes wins!

Exercise 2. Complete the following well-known similes, in under three minutes:

1. as cold as _____
2. as mad as a _____
3. as light as a _____
4. as fresh as a _____
5. as sober as a _____
6. as bold as _____
7. as regular as _____
8. as weak as a _____
9. as blind as a _____
10. as busy as a _____

Exercise 3. Now write each of the above similes in a sentence of your own. Then extend the image into a **second** sentence which **explains** or **develops** the simile.

> **Example** Aunt Jane was **as mad as a hatter**. She wore purple socks all year
> round and swore Elvis lived in her attic.

Stage 2

Metaphors

Look at these examples of metaphors in use:

1. He **was** a **scarecrow** of a man.
2. The desert **was** a vast sea of sand.

Remember a metaphor is different from a simile, in that a simile says one thing is **like** another, whereas a metaphor says that one thing **is** another.

Exercise 1. Rewrite the following sentences, using a **metaphor** instead of the simile in each:

(Example)	Simile	His mind is **like** a vast library of facts.
	Metaphor	His mind **is** a vast library of facts.

Simile   The grass felt like a carpet underneath her feet.

Metaphor   _____

Simile   His tongue is as sharp as a blade.

Metaphor   _____

Simile   She is as immovable as a rock.

Metaphor   _____

Simile   A picture is like a poem without words.

Metaphor   _____

Simile   The pitch was like a battlefield.

Metaphor   _____

Simile   She is as busy as a bee.

Metaphor   _____

Simile   He is like a live wire.

Metaphor   _____

Simile   The frozen lake was like a sheet of glass.

Metaphor   _____

Simile   He is like a giant in her eyes.

Metaphor   _____

Simile   Having no direction in his life, he is like a ship without a compass.

Metaphor   _____

Exercise 2. There is only **one metaphor** in each of the following sets of three sentences. Identify it by underlining it in each case. Explain your choice.

1. He was like a devil.
   He was the devil incarnate.
   He was evil.

2. Her life was hell.
   She led a miserable life.
   She felt like she was living in hell.

3. All the world's a stage.
   The world is full of actors.
   The world is like a stage.

4. He was a great leader.
   He was a very tall man.
   He was a giant among men.

5. She was a rock of sense.
   She was very sensible.
   She was like a rock.

Exercise 3. Choose ten metaphors from Exercises 1 and 2 and write ten sentences **of your own** with them. Extend the metaphor in each case into a **second** sentence which **explains** or **develops** the metaphor.

> **Example** David Beckham **is a giant** in their eyes. When he walks onto the pitch, every youngster wants to be him, **to be a star.**

Stage 3

The Exam; Poetry

Exercise 1. Do you remember the example of a metaphor from Sir Henry Newbolt's poem, 'The Highwayman'? Here is the verse from which it was taken:

> *The wind was a torrent of darkness among the gusty trees,*
> *The moon was a ghostly galleon tossed upon cloudy seas,*
> *The road was a ribbon of moonlight over the purple moor,*
> *And the highwayman came riding up to the old inn door.*

1. Identify three metaphors used in this verse.
2. Write a sentence for each one in which you **comment** on the comparison being made. For example, how good a metaphor is it? What **picture** is the poet painting for us?

Exercise 2.

1. Identify the metaphors in the following extracts from two poems – one by Norman MacCaig, one by Michael Hartnett.

> *She was buckets*
> *and water flouncing into them.*
> *She was winds pouring wetly round house-ends.*
> *She was brown eggs, black skirts and a keeper of threepenny bits in a teapot.*
>
> Norman MacCaig
>
> *She was a summer dance at the crossroads.*
> *She was a cardgame where a rose was broken.*
> *She was a song that nobody sings.*
> *She was a house ransacked by soldiers.*
> *She was a language seldom spoken.*
> *She was a child's purse, full of useless things.*
>
> Michael Hartnett

2. Select three metaphors from the above poems and write a sentence or two on each one, in which you comment on the **comparisons** being made between the **woman** and the **object** in each case. What image of the woman is conveyed in each metaphor?

The Exam; Poetry

Exercise 3.

(Junior Cert. Higher level, 2003)

Poem for Lara, 10

An ashtree on fire,
the hair of your head
coaxing larks
with your sweet voice
in the green grass,
a crowd of daisies
playing with you,
a crowd of rabbits
dancing with you,
the blackbird
with its gold bill
is a jewel for you,
the goldfinch
with its sweetness
is your music.
You are perfume,
you are honey,
a wild strawberry:
even the bees think you
a flower in the field.
Little queen of the land of books,
may you be always thus,
may you ever be free
from sorrow-chains.

Here's my blessing for you, girl,
it is no petty grace –
may you have your mother's soul
and the beauty of her face.

Michael Hartnett

1. 'An ashtree on fire'. To what does this metaphor refer?
2. 'You are perfume, you are honey, a wild strawberry:' What impression of Lara do you gain from these metaphors/images?
3. 'may you be ever free from sorrow-chains'. What might the 'sorrow-chains' refer to, do you think? Support your answer by reference to the poem.
4. Can you find other examples of **similes** and **metaphors** in the literature you are studying for Junior Cert.? Try to find at least **five examples of each**, and write them out into your copy. Try making up your own similes and metaphors. Your writing will appear more imaginative and interesting as a result.

Unit 5

Grappling with Grammar

Verbs

Question What is a verb?

Answer 1. A verb is a word that tells us what someone or something **does**. Every sentence must have one.

Example Birds **sing**. (**Sing** is the verb. It tells us what birds do.)
Tom **works** in an office. (**Works** is the verb. It tells us what Tom does.)
My computer **stores** information. (**Stores** is the verb. It tells us what my computer does.)

2. A verb can also tell us what someone or something **is**.

Example Birds **are** beautiful.
Tom **is** an accountant.
My computer **is** the latest model.

3. Verbs are also used in **commands** or **orders**.

Example **Eat** your vegetables!   **Do** your homework!
Shut that door!   **Phone** your gran!

Stage 1

Alphaverb challenge

Exercise 1.

Oral and written

1. Your teacher will ask you to form **teams of three**.

2. You will be given a number: Team 1, Team 2, Team 3, etc. (In a class of thirty, therefore, there will be ten teams.)

3. Your teacher will choose a team at random, and ask them to call out **three verbs** beginning with **A, B** and **C.** The team may confer – but must call out their three verbs in under thirty seconds.

4. One member from **each** of the ten teams writes down **all the verbs** that are called out by the other teams.

5. Your teacher then continues to call out other teams at random, who must also think of three verbs, working their way through the alphabet. So, the second team chosen at random will call out three verbs beginning with **D, E, F**; the next team **G, H, I**; the next team **J, K, L**; and so on, to the letter 'W'.

6. Teams 9 and 10 may be asked to supply verbs for any three letters of the alphabet, chosen by the teacher. The team who has answered the fastest, and has a clearly written list of all the verbs called out, in **alphabetical order**, wins!

Exercise 2.

Written, in pairs

1. Your teacher will call out the following instructions: 'I want **five** verbs associated with each of the following **situations**. You will have **thirty seconds** to write down your **five verbs**, in each case. Are you ready? Here we go.'

   a. Five things you do at home every evening.

   b. Five things you do at the weekend.

   c. Five things you do at Christmas.

   d. Five things you do in the summer holidays.

   You should now have twenty verbs.

2. Compare your list of verbs with those of other pairs of students in the class. Add **five** more verbs to your own list, for each of the situations called out. You should now have **ten** verbs per situation, and forty overall!

3. **Individual exercise** for homework or class.

   Choose one of the four situations above, and write the **opening paragraph** of an essay inspired by that situation. Use as many of the verbs you have written for Exercise 2 as possible. Try not to repeat a verb. Write your paragraph in the **present tense** and stay with this one tense throughout. (75–100 words)

Watch Your Language!

Exercise 3.

Crossverb

1. There are **thirty-seven** verbs hidden in this Crossverb.
2. In order to find them, write the **letter** in the space that is **the same as the number** in the box.
3. You have been given seven of the letters.
4. You must work out the other nineteen letters for yourself.
5. The verbs are all in the **present tense**.
6. The verbs can go **across** or **down** only.
7. Fill in the letters in the box also as you find them.
8. In some cases one letter doubles as the last letter of one word **and** the first letter of another word.

Main grid:

T₃	R₁₅	22	A₆	T₃	S₁	9	6	15	13	23	24	7
6		20		8		15						8
7	8	3		15	1	11	2	23				19
		22		20		20			9	8	19	19
1		15	11	1	11	20	2	23				26
3			20	20		15	22	6	12	23	22	
15	24	18	1	1		24		1		24		
6			11	7		6			7	11	12	13
5			1	11		20	22	22	16	1	6	
1	23	8	3			15					3	
	6					22	14	8	11	7	12	
	21					17					23	
9	22	6	10			22	10		4	11	3	10
24						12	24			11		11
18	24	15	13		3	24	18	1	6	21	22	25

Key box:

S₁	2	T₃
4	5	A₆
7	8	9
10	11	12
13	14	R₁₅
16	17	18
19	N₂₀	21
22	23	24
25	L₂₆	

Stage 2

Exercise 1. Listed below are five everyday words. What can we **do** with each one? Write out as many **verbs** (actions) as you can for each word.

(Example)	Cake: We can	bite it	bake it
		cut it	sell it
		eat it	buy it
		share it	long for it

Use your imagination. Extend the action a little, as with some of the following examples for 'cake':

(Example)	Cake: We can	fight for it	have it with tea
		give it to a friend	put it away for Sunday

Now you do it! Choose two of these words, and write as many verbs as you can for each one. Then **extend** the action into three to four sentences.

    1. Football   **2.** DVDs   **3.** Friends   **4.** Money   **5.** Books

Exercise 2.

Finding verbs

1. Find the verbs in these sentences and **underline** them. Each sentence has **two** verbs.

    a. Dad fried the eggs and burnt the chips.

    b. You have to score the goal before you boast about it.

    c. Claudia Schiffer is beautiful and has lots of money.

    d. Mary sang, and cleared the hall in minutes.

    e. The fire crackled and roared up the chimney.

    f. Tina sulked all through class because she got detention.

    g. Mrs. O'Neill fainted when she won the Lotto.

    h. Mrs. O'Neill invited us all to swim in her pool in the Bahamas.

    i. Tom Cryan buys six sports magazines every week and reads them all from cover to cover.

    j. The class had good fun doing these exercises on verbs!

2. Now write **ten sentences of your own** with **two** verbs in each sentence chosen from those in the list below:

      played, is, ate, were, worked, ran, broke, jumped, was, seemed, lost,

      learned, rang, waiting, told, kicked, disappeared, cooked, left, travel

Exercise 3. Using the **right** verb for the context is important. In the following sentences, you must choose the verb which **best** completes the sentence in each case. Only **one** verb is correct. **Circle** the verb you choose, and **write it** into the space provided.

1. I lay on the beach and happily _____ in the heat of the sun.
   a. searched   b. burnt   c. basked   d. bathed

2. A stone hit the windscreen and it instantly _____ into thousands of tiny pieces.
   a. shattered   b. splattered   c. cracked   d. burst

3. The cost of buying a house has _____ considerably in the last few years.
   a. soared   b. zoomed   c. taken off   d. risen

4. If you don't lift that saucepan carefully, it will spill and you may _____ yourself.
   a. skim   b. peel   c. scald   d. singe

5. Sean is always _____ about how well he plays football.
   a. puffing   b. boasting   c. flaunting   d. parading

6. The intruder was badly _____ by the guard dog at the factory.
   a. mauled   b. damaged   c. eaten   d. torn

7. The thief _____ the flat in an attempt to find cash.
   a. looted   b. ransacked   c. pilfered   d. invaded

8. Mrs. Ryan has just _____ the couch in her living-room.
   a. sewn   b. dressed   c. upholstered   d. recovered

9. When it saw the dog by the water, the swan _____ its wings and rose into the air.
   a. flipped   b. flicked   c. flapped   d. folded

10. Sitting by the river, we could hear the _____ of the sheep in the field behind us.
    a. bawling   b. braying   c. barking   d. bleating

Stage 3

Verbs as nouns

Exercise 1. Verbs ending in 'ing' (participles) can also be used as **nouns**.

> **Example**   The old lady was **walking** (verb) slowly, but she enjoyed **walking** (noun).

Complete the second sentence in each of the following with a noun made from the verb in bold in the first sentence:

1. Jane is **knitting** a jumper. She enjoys _____.
2. Tom **paints** every day. _____ is his hobby.
3. 'Don't **shout** at me! _____ is rude!'
4. Why don't you **smile** a bit more? _____ is good for your facial muscles.
5. Liz **shines** every object in the house. _____ things is her passion.
6. They **fight** all the time. _____ is second nature to them.

7. We all need to **cry**. Sometimes _____ really helps.
8. 'Please don't **whisper**! _____ in the library is forbidden.'
9. Aileen always **listens** to my problems. _____ is one of her best qualities.
10. Sheila **jogs** to work. She says _____ is excellent exercise.

Nouns as verbs

Exercise 2.

Here are ten sentences. The word in bold in each one is a **noun** that can **also** be used as a **verb**. Write ten sentences of your own, in the spaces provided, in which you use the word in bold as a **verb**. You may change the spelling of the word, for example 'fall' to 'fell', and the meaning and situation may change also.

> **Example**   *The Hobbit* is a good **book**. (noun)
>   Did the guard **book** you for speeding? (verb)

1. Sean had a nasty **cut** over his eye.

   _____

2. The enemy **attack** was fierce and merciless.

   _____

3. There was a **fall** in the price of oil last month.

   _____

4. 'There is a **charge** for that service, Madam,' the bank official said.

   _____

5. The Phoenix Park in Dublin is the largest inner-city **park** in Europe.

   _____

6. Matching up **paint and paper** takes time.

   _____

7. It's a long **walk** to the station from here.

   _____

8. Barbara won €500 in the **draw**.

   _____

9. Emma put on an **act**, but it didn't fool her mother.

   _____

10. The **departure** time is 9.30, for the train to London.

    _____

Verbs and adjectives

Exercise 3.

Some words can be used as an **adjective** or a **verb**.

> (**Example**) dry: It was a **dry** day. (adjective)
> **Dry** those clothes properly now! (verb)

The following words can be used as an adjective **or** a verb:

1.	light	**6.**	tidy
2.	clean	**7.**	idle
3.	clear	**8.**	paint
4.	free	**9.**	stolen
5.	empty	**10.**	broken

Can you write two sentences for each word, one in which the word is used as an **adjective**, and one in which the word is used as a **verb** – without changing the **spelling** of the verb?

> (**Example**) light: adjective: Margaret wore a light suit for the Christening in June.
> verb: You can't light a fire without matches.

The Exam; Personal writing

Exercise 4.

Below is an extract from the Fiction section of the Junior Cert. Ordinary level paper, 2002.

1. Read it carefully, and underline all the **verbs**. You should find thirty (**excluding** auxiliary or helping verbs, like 'could', 'was' and 'had').

2. Write out the thirty verbs as a **list**.

3. Write a **short story** based on **one** of the following titles:
   a. In the dark, something moved . . .
   b. A terrifying night
   c. Waiting
   d. The first thing he noticed was the smell . . .

   Try to use as many of the **verbs** from the exam extract as possible and also from the other exercises in the unit. Try not to **repeat** a verb.

   He collapsed at the door, gasping for breath. And the first thing he noticed was the smell. For a second he drew back, uncertain. Then he squirmed quickly inside. The hut was small and dark. It had no window or chimney, and the door was a couple of sods. From the inside, Eric blocked out the wind with the sods. The sound of the storm faded, and the last glimmer of light was snuffed out. The smell – foul and strong – rose sharply out of the dark. On the far side of the hut, something moved.

Eric peered into the darkness, suddenly afraid. Twin balls of red glowed in the dark. And Eric shrank back, terrified. Something was in the hut. Some wild and terrible animal – a great bear, maybe, with claws that could rip your guts out in a single slash? Eric spun round. He tore at the sods in the doorway. Then he remembered the storm.

He stood very still, teeth clenched, eyes screwed tight. Waiting. But the wild and terrible animal did not spring at him. Everything was very quiet – everything except his pounding heart. He peered into the blackness. At first he could see only the red of the eyes. But gradually as he became accustomed to the dark he could make out more: a shadowy mass, coiled and menacing.

Punctuation Please!

Apostrophes ′

Question	When do we use an apostrophe?
Answer	We use an apostrophe:
	1. to show **possession**.
Example	Laura's dog Matthew's car
	2. to **shorten** two words to one
Example	I have → I've Colette is very nice → Colette's very nice He is → he's Freddy is a good golfer → Freddy's a good golfer
	This is also called contraction.

N.B.!

1. Do not use **apostrophes** when writing the **plural of a noun**.

Example	Shop's	Book's	Friend's	**Wrong!**
	Shops,	Books,	Friends	**Right!**

2. Sometimes shopkeepers, stallholders and restaurants get them wrong in their signs.

Example	Hot Dog's for sale	**Wrong!**
	Hot Dogs for sale	**Right!**
	Tomato's, Carrot's and Potato's sold here.	**Wrong!**
	Tomatoes, Carrots, and Potatoes sold here.	**Right!**

3. 'Its' often creates a problem. Students put in an apostrophe when it is grammatically incorrect to do so.

> **Example**   a.   The toy train is in it's original box.   **Wrong!**
>   b.   The toy train is in its original box.   **Right!**

Why? Because in **b.**, 'its' is a **possessive adjective** describing the noun '**box**' (its box). 'Its' may only have an apostrophe when we want to shorten '**it is**' or '**it has**' to '**it's**'. If in doubt, say the expression or sentence out loud. Can you say 'The toy train is in **it is** original box'? No. So you don't need an apostrophe.

4. The **possessive pronouns** (ours, yours, theirs, hers) **never** take an apostrophe.

> **Example**   our car   **ours**
>   your car   **yours**
>   their car   **theirs**
>   her car   **hers**

Now that you know the rules, let's exercise them!

Stage 1

Exercise 1.

1. Study the following contractions for five minutes:

I have	→ **I've**	I am	→ **I'm**	cannot	→ **can't**
you have	→ **you've**	you are	→ **you're**	could not	→ **couldn't**
he has/is	→ **he's**	we are	→ **we're**	will not	→ **won't**
she has/is	→ **she's**	they are	→ **they're**	would not	→ **wouldn't**
we have	→ **we've**			should not	→ **shouldn't**
they have	→ **they've**	I will	→ **I'll**	is not	→ **isn't**
		you will	→ **you'll**	was not	→ **wasn't**
		we will	→ **we'll**	were not	→ **weren't**
		they will	→ **they'll**	does not	→ **doesn't**

Note that with **negatives**, the apostrophe replaces the 'o' in 'not'.

2. Your teacher will select students at random, and call out an example from your list, for instance 'she has'. The student selected must:

   a.   **call out** the contraction, e.g. 'she's'

   b.   **spell** it out loud.

   All within ten seconds! Any student who fails to complete the task within this time is out!

3. play the game with each other, but this time the contracted verb must be extended into a **sentence**.

> **Example**
>
> | Student A | | calls out 'we are'. |
> | Student B | **a.** | says 'we're' |
> | | **b.** | spells it out loud |
> | | **c.** | writes it, **plus** another few words, to make a complete sentence. For example 'We're playing a game with apostrophes.' |

Time limit **thirty seconds** per example this time, to allow for writing the sentence. Swop roles between each example.

Exercise 2. Imagine you are the teacher and correct the following piece of writing from a student who clearly isn't too familiar with the correct use of the apostrophe! Write out the corrected version as you go.

My little brothers always getting into scrape's. If its not cutting the knee's off himself on the garden wall, its climbing the neighbours tree's or teasing his dog's. He has three and each has it's own kennel. They're very expensive pedigree dog's and Donnacha doesnt' understand that he's not supposed to go near them. Youll appreciate that its not easy being his sister when he brings all his friends around to look over the wall at Mr. Behans dogs'. They dont just look, you see. Theyre always whistling and shouting at them and then Mr. Behan gets' mad and threatens them with my Dad.

Im thinking of emigrating. They're must be countrie's with no little brothers' **somewhere** on the planet!

Note: Sometimes we have to decide whether to put an apostrophe **before** an 's' or **after** it. This is how it works:

> **Example**   The teacher praised the **girl's** work.

Here the apostrophe **before** the 's' indicates that the teacher praised just one girl. However, look at this sentence.

> **Example**   The teacher praised the girls' work.

Here, the apostrophe after the 's' indicates that the teacher praised two or more girls.

So, placing the apostrophe before or after the 's' can convey very different meanings. Here is another example.

> **Example**   My friend's parties are great! (**one** friend). But . . .
>
> My friends' parties are great! (more than one friend – perhaps **all** your friends).

Exercise 3. Now invent five examples of your own, like the above, practising inserting the apostrophe in the correct place, i.e. before or after the 's' depending on the meaning you wish to convey.

Stage 2

Exercise 1. Rewrite the following shortened sentences **in full**.

> **Example**
> He hasn't fed the dog yet.
> He **has not** fed the dog yet.

1. They don't like Maths. *do not*
2. We can't see the telly. *can not*
3. She's always late. *she is*
4. We're never going to understand this. *we are*
5. It's really easy once you try. *It is*

6. They'll have a great time in Paris. *They will*
7. I couldn't contact him by phone. *could n*
8. They're late, as usual. *They are*
9. He doesn't listen to anyone. *does not*
10. You shouldn't have any difficulty *should* with apostrophes – if you're careful! *you have*

Exercise 2. N.B.! Students often confuse **possessive adjectives** (its, your, their, whose) with **contractions** (it's, you're, they're, who's). Remember that contractions take apostrophes because the apostrophe is **replacing** a letter or letters in a word.

> **Example** it's = it is
> they're = they are

Now choose the correct form of the words in each of the following sentences and write them in the spaces provided.

1. (It's, Its) *It's* a tragedy that the horse broke (its, it's) *its* leg during the big race.
2. (Your, You're) *You're* not serious about (their, they're) *their* offer, are you?
3. (Whose, Who's) *Whose* car is it, anyway?
4. (Their, They're) *Their* holiday was spoiled during (its, it's) *its* first week, by rain.
5. (Your, You're) *Your* handwriting needs work.
6. (Whose, Who's) *Who's* the idiot who took my keys?
7. (Their, They're) *They're* leaving the baby with (their, they're) *their* sister.

Exercise 3. You can use apostrophes with **time words** (today, tomorrow, etc.).

> **Example** **Today's** meeting has been cancelled.
> Have you got **tomorrow's** schedule?

Read the following sentences and write a new sentence for each, using 's for the words in bold. Begin each sentence with the time word or words.

> **Example** The match **today** has been cancelled.
> **Today's** match has been cancelled.

1. The earthquake **last year** caused a lot of damage.

    _____

2. The figures for **last month** were poor.

    _____

3. *The Irish Times* next **Saturday** will carry the results of the referendum.

    _____

4. Have you got the timetable for **tomorrow**?

    _____

5. They will show the Premiership match on TV3 **this evening**.

    _____

Stage 3 ──

The Exam; Other drama

Exercise 1. The following is an extract from the Junior Cert. Higher level paper, 2003 (Other Drama). I have removed all the **apostrophes** from the dialogue. Can you **replace** them? (There are **thirty-four** in all.)

N.B.! Be **very careful** where you **place** the apostrophe in a word. Read back over the rules and examples in this unit.

Background to the extract:
●   Lelum is the son of Mary and Michael.
●   They live in Ireland in the 1940s.
●   As this extract begins Michael has gone to the river to collect more gravel for the wall he is building.

Lelum: If he doesnt come back soon this stuff will be gone hard. Where did he go anyway?

Mary: To the river for more gravel.

Lelum: What a wall this is going to be.

Mary: Come here Lelum and hold this yank of wool for me.

(He sits on the seat and extends his hands. She entwines the wool round them and starts to make a ball of thread)

Lelum: I think he is using the wall to avoid reality.

Mary: I suppose in a way youre right but were all the same arent we? We all need something to hide behind at times. You and he dont seem to be hitting it off lately. I think youre under the impression hes failed you.

Lelum: Well hasnt he?

Mary: You mean because he didnt send you to university?

Lelum: Among other things.

Mary: If you were an only son Lelum or if there were only two or even three of you the university would be no problem but there are four of you and then there are the girls. You dont know how lucky you are to have received a secondary education. When I was a girl only one in a hundred was so lucky.

Lelum: If he didnt drink so much.

Mary: Hes never refused me anything. We dont know what hunger is. We have a fine home.

Lelum: I dont know what to do. Ive no job.

Mary: You have your job in the fields.

Lelum: We both know theres no future there. Anyway theres only another month of it.

Mary: Youll get a job and whats more youll get a good job. You have brains Lelum and youre a good worker. Youre young and strong and youre good looking. Its only a matter of time.

Lelum: I know what Id really like to do but Im almost afraid to say it.

Mary: You can say it to me. Thats as far as twill go. Come on Lelum. You and I are too fond of each other to have secrets.

Lelum: Well . . . Id like to become a professional actor . . . arent you going to laugh?

Mary: Why would I laugh?

Lelum: Nobody from this town ever became a professional actor.

Mary: I should think that would be a reflection on the town.

Lelum: You mean youd approve?

Mary: If its what you really want Lelum I approve. Ill do all in my power to help you. Have you done anything about it?

Lelum: I spoke to Mr. McMaster the last time he was here and he promised me an audition this time round. Theyll be in town next week.

from *The Crazy Wall* by J. B. Keane

The drama continues

Exercise 2.

Write the scene which you imagine took place between Lelum and his father when Lelum told him of his wish to be an actor.

Be careful in your use of **apostrophes** and other punctuation marks, e.g. **question marks and full stops.**

How Do You Spell ...?
That Dumb Thumb! Silent-letter Words 1

Silent-letter words can be difficult to spell correctly, simply because we don't **pronounce** the 'silent' letters.

Example dumb thumb

If you say these words out loud you will notice that the **sound** stops at the 'm'. So what we **hear** is 'dum' and 'thum'. When we come to **write** this type of word, therefore, we often misspell it.

In this unit we will be exercising silent-letter words from silent '**b**' to silent '**gh**'. So let's begin.

1. Silent 'b' words

bomb	doubt
climb	dumb
comb	numb
crumb	plumbing
debt	thumb

Did you notice that **seven** of the list words **end** in 'mb', and that in 'debt' and 'doubt' the silent 'b' is the **second last** letter in the word? Plumbing is the only two-syllable word in the list. Before you learn the spellings, it would be a good idea to underline or highlight the silent 'b' in each word. This will help you to **remember** to include it.

Exercise 1.

1. Study the ten words above for five minutes in class. Remember it will be easier to learn these spellings because each word contains a silent 'b' and they are written in **alphabetical** order.

2. When the ten minutes are up, your teacher will call out each word in the order in which you have learned them. Write them out, one underneath the other, in a list, being very careful with those **silent 'b's**!

3. Exchange your copy with the person next to you. You will now correct his/hers, and he/she will do likewise with yours. Please refer to the **original spelling list** when correcting each word.

4. Give **one** mark for each word spelled correctly, and a total mark out of ten.

5. If a word has been spelled **incorrectly**, cross it out and write the **correct** spelling of the word beside it, again checking from the original list.

6. Take back your own copy and write out any words **you** have spelled incorrectly, **five times** each.

Exercise 2.

1. Which **five** words from the list are hidden in boxes 1 and 2? Complete box 2 with the correct part from box 1.

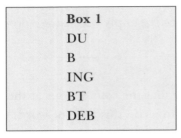
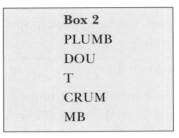

Box 1	Box 2
DU	PLUMB
B	DOU
ING	T
BT	CRUM
DEB	MB

2. Make your own boxes for the remaining five words from the list. Swop copies with your neighbour, and give yourself a time limit of **two** minutes to figure out his/her words and **write them out**. The one who finishes first and whose words are **spelled correctly** wins!

Exercise 3.

Use your imagination and compose **five** questions, and **five** answers to those questions, using each of the silent 'b' words from the list once only.

> **Example**   Q: Is that my **comb** you're using?
> A: I **doubt** it.

2. Silent 'c' words

scenario	sceptre
scene	scheme
scenery	school
scenic	science
scent	scissors

In many 'sc' words, the 'c' is silent, as in the above list. Read them out loud and you will not hear the 'c', so it is very easy to forget it. Circle the 'c' in each word. It will remind you to **keep it in** when you are spelling the word. The list words are also in **alphabetical order** as found in the dictionary. Notice how the first six words begin with 'sce', the next two with 'sch' and the last two with 'sci'.

Exercise 1.

As for silent 'b' words.

Exercise 2.

1. Unjumble the following words from the list of silent 'c' words:
   a. E N S C E I C
   b. T S R C P E E
   c. O N S A C E I R
   d. E N S C E
   e. S I R S C O S S

2. Jumble up the remaining five words yourself. Swop with the person next to you. You must each unjumble the words in under two minutes. The one who completes the task first – **with correct spelling** – wins. Remember to **check** the spellings with your **original** list.

The Exam; Personal writing

Exercise 3.

Write the **opening paragraph** (70–90 words) of a composition entitled '**School scene**'. Use each of the list words once only. You will need to think a little about how you can include the word 'sceptre', but it will be a good exercise for your imagination!

3. Silent 'e' words

awake	frame
brake	gate
complete	hate
disgrace	invite
explode	judge

Notice that the above silent 'e' words are in alphabetical order, one for each letter from A to J. **Underline** the silent 'e's before you learn them.

Exercise 1.

As for silent 'b' words.

Exercise 2.

1. Go to your dictionary and find ten more silent 'e' words from the letters **K** to **T**. Write them out in a list, and highlight the silent 'e' in each word.

2. Play **What's the Word?** with the student next to you. It's a bit like charades, but you use words instead of gestures. This is how it works:
   a. Decide who's A and who's B.
   b. A selects five words from his/her list, but does not tell B what they are.
   c. B must try to guess what each word is from A's description of its use or meaning.
   d. Have a time limit of **two minutes** for B to guess all five words and **write** them out, **spelling** them correctly!

e. Swop roles. B now presents five words from his/her list for A to guess.

f. The one who guesses and correctly spells the most words, within the time limit, wins!

Exercise 3. Using your **own** list of silent 'e' words from K to T, and the original list from A to J, write a complete sentence for each word, **underlining** the silent 'e' every time.

> (Example) That boy's hair is a disgrace!

4. Silent 'g' words

consignment	gnash
design	gnaw
designer	neigh
foreigner	resign
gnarled	sign

Notice that silent 'g's are usually followed by 'n' and the 'n' is **sounded**.

> (Example) design, sign

It is useful to remember this when learning to spell the words. Circling the letter 'g' in each word will also help.

Exercise 1.

As for silent 'b' words.

Exercise 2. Now look again at the silent 'g' words listed above, this time for **meaning**. Then fill in the gaps in the following sentences with the most suitable word from the list.

1. The President must _____ at once, before the scandal breaks.
2. We are expecting a _____ of Maxi Stor shelving this afternoon.
3. The branches of the ancient oak tree were _____ and twisted with age.
4. 'Don't _____ anything until you've read the small print, Pauline!'
5. I love to hear my horse _____ in greeting when I approach her.
6. Susan would prefer to _____ her own wedding dress.
7. They are kind to him because he is a _____, and away from home.
8. 'There shall be weeping and _____ing of teeth.'
9. _____ clothes are expensive.
10. The puppy will _____ away at that bandage until it comes loose.

Exercise 3.

Silent 'g' words quiz

This exercise is for fun – but will also enlarge your vocabulary. You will need your dictionary, preferably the *Concise Oxford Dictionary*, but any good-sized one should do. It may be done in class, with your teacher imposing a time limit of **20 minutes**, or as an exercise for homework. (Clue: **all** the words **begin** with a silent 'g'.)

1. What is a small two-winged biting fly called? _____
2. What is an aboriginal waterhole called? _____
3. What is an Italian dish of small dumplings called? _____
4. This is a dwarfish legendary creature supposed to guard the earth's treasures underground (or your garden!). _____
5. What is the rod or pin on a sundial called? _____
6. This is a coarse-grained metamorphic rock foliated by mineral layers, principally of feldspar, quartz and ferromagnesian mineral. _____
7. This is a type of antelope, native to South Africa, also called a wildebeest. _____
8. What is the knowledge of spiritual mysteries called? _____
9. This is the adjective of Number 8, relating to knowledge, especially mystical knowledge. _____
10. This is an adjective: of or relating to the jaws. _____

5. Silent 'gh' words

although	eight
bought	fight
caught	high
cough	light
daughter	might

There are lots of silent 'gh' words! Did you notice how different the **sounds** are?

> **Example**   although (-oh)
>   bought (-aw-)
>   cough (-off)

The 'gh' is silent though, and therefore often misspelled. So watch those spellings!

Exercise 1.

As for silent 'b' words.

Exercise 2.

1. Which is the **correct** spelling of the following words from the list? **Underline** your choice, and write it into your copy.

a.	Fite	Figte	Fight
b.	Douhter	Daughter	Dauhter
c.	Bought	Bouht	Bote
d.	Cawte	Caught	Cauht
e.	Alltough	Altdough	Although

2. a. What rhymes with 'high' and means a long sad breath? _____

    b. What rhymes with 'light' and is the opposite of 'wrong'? _____

    c. What rhymes with 'bought' and is the past tense of 'catch'? _____

    d. What rhymes with 'cough' and is a watering place for animals? _____

    e. What rhymes with 'fight' and is the opposite of 'loose'? _____

Exercise 3.   Here are some more silent 'gh' words. Write five sentences with two of the words below in each sentence.

1.	enough	6.	nightmare
2.	lighthouse	7.	rough
3.	naughty	8.	sleigh
4.	neighbour	9.	through
5.	night	10.	weigh

> **Example**   I think I weigh enough now.

Be as silly as you like!

Remember. The spelling's the thing!

Words at Work

Colour Your Words: Idioms

> **Question**   What is an **idiom**?
>
> **Answer**   An idiom is a group of words, in the form of a phrase or expression, that is in everyday use. An idiom is also known as a **colloquialism**. The interesting thing is that an idiom often means something quite different from the meaning of the **individual** words within it.

(Example) 1. **A piece of cake**. This describes something which is easy to do, but has nothing whatsoever to do with cake!
2. Similarly, we say: **in hot water**, meaning in trouble or disgrace.
3. Or **to let the cat out of the bag**, meaning to tell or reveal a secret – usually without meaning to!

All languages have their own idioms, and English is no exception. These phrases, when used wisely and imaginatively, will add colour and interest to your writing. In this unit, we will exercise a variety of idioms, under certain headings; for example, those that have to do with:

- families and/or friends (chip off the old block, thick as thieves)
- attitudes (to pay lip service to)
- parts of the body (to pull someone's leg).

So, let's begin.

Stage 1

Exercise 1. The following idioms can all be used when writing about **families** or **friends**. Match each idiom in Column A to its **meaning** in Column B. If you are not sure, check in your dictionary.

A	B
1. generation gap	1. family ties are stronger than friendship
2. chip off the old block	2. not a bit like one another
3. thick as thieves	3. difference in ideas and attitudes between old and young people
4. blood is thicker than water	4. person who looks or behaves like one of his/her parents
5. flesh and blood	5. extremely friendly with one another
6. different as chalk and cheese	6. member of the same family

Exercise 2. Write some fictional notes about a family called 'The Gogarty Gang', in which you use each of the six idioms from Exercise 1 at least once. In addition, use the following idioms (which are also similes) to make comparisons about the **appearance** of people in the family:

1. as bald as a coot	4. as fit as a fiddle
2. as pretty as a picture	5. as deaf as a post
3. as blind as a bat	

This exercise lends itself to humour, so have fun!

Stage 2

Exercise 1. Here are some idioms using **parts of the body**.

1. to pull someone's **leg**
2. to keep an **eye** on something
3. to be a pain in the **neck**
4. to talk behind someone's **back**
5. to fall on one's **feet**

Write a sentence for each of these, which **clearly** shows the meaning and usage of the idiom.

> **Example**   to be a pain in the neck
>
> He's in such bad form these days, interfering all the time and being such a bore! He's a **real pain in the neck**.

Exercise 2. Some idioms are used to describe people's **attitudes** to life or the way they react to situations. Here are some examples:

	Idiom	Meaning
1.	to live and let live	to be tolerant of others
2.	it's no use crying over spilt milk	no point in regretting something that went wrong
3.	to have your cake and eat it	to desire more than you can have
4.	to have several irons in the fire	to have many plans and projects at one time
5.	to keep up with the Joneses	to always do what your neighbours do
6.	to go by the book	to do everything strictly according to the rules
7.	to pay lip service to	to pretend to agree with an idea or belief
8.	to stand out like a sore thumb	to be different, but in a bad way
9.	to take the law into one's own hands	to act independently of the law; to do something illegal
10.	to be like a fish out of water	not to feel at home or to be uncomfortable in a certain situation

A. **Replace** the words in bold in the following sentences with an **idiom** from the list above:

1. When I was Treasurer of the drama group, I only **pretended to agree with** their ideas, for a quiet life.

2. Siobhan is not very adventurous. She always **does everything according to the rules.**

3. **Let people live as they want to**, that's what I say.

122

4. With that bright pink hair and blackened teeth, Terry certainly **looks different**!

5. There's no point in **regretting the past**. What's done is done.

B. Write sentences of your own for the remaining five idioms.

Exercise 3. Fill in the missing words in the following passage with an idiom **not** previously given to you. The word in bold in each sentence is the clue to the idiom you require. Check with your **dictionary** (or your teacher) if you get really stuck.

> My Dad didn't ___ __ **eyelid** when I told him I wanted to travel to the Himalayas after school. In fact, instead of _____ ___ **roof** as I expected, and _____ ___ ___ **handle**, he was quite good about it. He even offered to pay my air fare. I couldn't _____ __ **ears**! He usually takes everything I suggest ____ _ _____ __ **salt**. This time, however, he said that he'd ____ ____ _ ___ **leaf** in his attitude towards me, and that it was time for me to _____ __ _ ___ ___ **feet**. Of course, I wouldn't ___ __ **past** ___ to change his mind. I've always had to ___ ___ **line** up to now, haven't I?

Stage 3

Adjective idioms

Exercise 1. Here are ten adjective idioms:

bone idle	bolt upright
pitch black	soaking wet
stark naked	stark raving mad
dog tired	piping hot
dead straight	stone cold sober

Choose a suitable idiom from the list above to complete the following sentences:

1. Can you switch on the light? It's ___ ___ in here.

2. I can't believe it. He was ___ ___ ___ coming home from the pub last night.

3. Sheila is ___ ___. She's too lazy even to put her own sugar in her tea.

4. I love the smell of pizza when it comes _____ ___ from the oven.

5. By the time we got to school, the rain was bucketing down and we were _____ ___.

6. Give you €500 for a motorbike?! Are you _____ _____ ___?!

7. The crowd whistled and cheered when Eugene ran _____ _____ on to the football pitch.

8. When we visited Gran in hospital, she was sitting ____ _____ in the bed, not a bother on her.

9. I won't wait up for the late film. I'm ___ _____.

10. In Technical Graphics, Gerry draws _____ _____ lines.

Exercise 2. Now write a paragraph in which all ten idioms are used just once. (80–100 words). Here's a 'starter' suggestion for you – but of course, feel free to choose your own.

> Sean wondered how the hell he'd ended up standing **stark naked**, outside his own hall door!

Exercise 3.

Idiom 'families'

Some words can be written in the form of:

- a **noun** idiom   you old **dog**!
- an **adjective** idiom   **dog** tired
- a **verb** idiom   to **dog** someone's footsteps

From each of the following families of idioms, see if you can make **one noun** idiom, **one adjective** idiom and **one verb** idiom – if possible! Use your dictionary if you get stuck.

(Example)	Animals	a dark **horse** (noun idiom)
		a **catty** person (adjective idiom)
		to **fish** for compliments (verb idiom)

1. Animals   (Clues: dog, cat, pig, horse, fish)
2. Body   (Clues: hand, leg, neck, finger, head, feet, stomach, heart, elbow)
3. Clothes   (Clues: hat, sock, boot, cuff, sleeve, trousers)
4. Food   (Clues: jam, pop, soup, goose, salt)
5. Colour   (Clues: white, blue, black, green, red)
6. Numbers   (Clues: one, two, three, nine)
7. Weather   (Clues: weather, cold, wet, wind)
8. Water   (Clues: swim, deep end, tide, canoe)
9. Sport   (Clues: line, game, cricket, belt)
10. Time   (Clues: clock, dot, wound up, chime)

The Exam; Media studies

Exercise 4.

1. Study these three **advertisements**, marked A, B and C. They each contain **an idiom**. Identify it, and write it out into your copy.

2. Now look at how the idioms are **used** in the three advertisements.

   a. What is the **meaning** of the idiom in each case in relation to the **product** being advertised?

   b. Do the idioms **work**, in terms of selling the products being advertised? Why? Give a reason for each one.

   c. Which idiom is the most humorous? Give a reason for your choice.

1.

2.

3.

Unit 6

Grappling with Grammar

The Past Tense 1

The past simple

When you change from the **present** tense to the **past** in your writing, the verb must change too.

> **Example** I walk (present tense) → I walked (past simple)

Rules:

1. Usually, you add '**ed**' to the verb, to make it past, as in the example above.
2. However, some verbs do not change at all from present to past.

> **Example** I **read** textbooks every day. I **read** several yesterday, too.

3. Verbs ending in '**y**' in the present tense change the '**y**' to '**ied**' in the past.

> **Example** I **fry** everything. I **fried** everything last week, too.

4. Some verbs **double** their last letter before adding '**ed**'.

> **Example** Prices drop all the time. Prices dro**pped** dramatically last year.

5. A large number of verbs are **irregular** and change quite a lot in the past.

> **Example** Jane **runs** everywhere. She **ran** to school yesterday.

These are the ones you are most likely to speak and write incorrectly. So **watch** them!

Stage 1

Exercise 1.

Oral

Your teacher will select individual students at random from the class roll, and call out a sentence in the **present tense**. The student must change it to the **past simple** tense and add a **time** word.

> **Example** Teacher: Paul **visits** Canada every summer.
> Student: Paul visit**ed** Canada **last** summer, too.

Other time words are: **ago, yesterday, last week/month/year, 2003**, etc.

Exercise 2. Here are some more verbs in the present tense. Write a **short** sentence for each in the past simple tense, and add a **time** word as in Exercise 1.

> (**Example**)   The dog attacked the postman **yesterday**.

attack, beg, come, direct, express, find, grow, hear, know, loan

The past simple and the present perfect simple

Look at these two sentences:

> (**Example**)   1. Paul **wrote** to Linda **last week**. (past simple)
> 2. Paul **has written** to Linda three times already **this week**. (present perfect simple)

In Sentence 1, the action is **finished**, and took place at a **specific time** in the past. In Sentence 2, the action is still in the past ('has written') but with the strong possibility of it being **repeated** in the future.

Time words associated with the present perfect simple are: **already, yet, just, now, up to now, so far, for ages/weeks/years.**

Exercise 3. Now write the correct form of the verb in brackets (past simple or present perfect simple) in the following sentences, according to the **time** references at the end of each sentence:

1. Sally _____ (do) her Junior Cert. two months **ago**.
2. They _____ (drive) to France three times **already this year**.
3. Donna _____ (eat) six doughnuts **yesterday afternoon**.
4. The thief _____ (steal) five thousand pounds from the old lady's house **last Christmas**.
5. I haven't _____ (be) to that film **yet**.
6. Have you _____ (finish) it **already**?
7. John _____ (become) very angry and threatened to leave **last night**.
8. Sheila _____ (work) there **for ages**.
9. They _____ (emigrate) to America a long time **ago**.
10. Ireland _____ (host) the Special Olympics World Games in **2003**.

Exercise 4. In pairs, or on your own, can you complete the following **table** in under ten minutes? Consult your dictionary if you get stuck.

Present	Past simple	Present perfect simple
1. I begin	I_____	I have_____
2. I bring	I_____	I_____
3. I buy	I_____	I_____
4. I catch	I_____	I_____

Present	Past simple	Present perfect simple
5. I do	I_____	I_____
6. I drink	I_____	I_____
7. I fall	I_____	I_____
8. I fly	I_____	I_____
9. I get	I_____	I_____
10. I give	I_____	I_____
11. I go	I_____	I_____
12. I keep	I_____	I_____
13. I know	I_____	I_____
14. I mean	I_____	I_____
15. I ride	I_____	I_____
16. I ring	I_____	I_____
17. I see	I_____	I_____
18. I shake	I_____	I_____
19. I sing	I_____	I_____
20. I sleep	I_____	I_____
21. I speak	I_____	I_____
22. I stand	I_____	I_____
23. I swear	I_____	I_____
24. I take	I_____	I_____
25. I teach	I_____	I_____
26. I think	I_____	I_____
27. I throw	I_____	I_____
28. I understand	I_____	I_____
29. I wake	I_____	I_____
30. I wear	I_____	I_____

Exercise 5. **Correct** the verbs in bold in the following sentences. Watch out for the **time** reference, to help you decide which **form** of the past to use, i.e. the past simple or present perfect simple.

1. I **throwed** the book away last week.
2. Tracy **run** to school yesterday.
3. Mr. Butler **rung** the bell late last Friday.
4. Donna has just **ate** six doughnuts!
5. My pigeon has **flew** over Mr. Ryan's wall twice this week.
6. The bank **rised** the interest rates last month.
7. The baby **begun** to bawl the minute Mam walked in.
8. Ralph has **blew** that trumpet until 2.00 a.m. every night this week.

9. I **seen** him kiss her at the disco last Saturday.
10. I already **done** lots of exercises in this unit!

Stage 2

The past continuous and the past simple

Look at this sentence:

(**Example**) I **was doing** my homework when the phone **rang**.

'Was doing' is an example of the **past continuous** tense. As you can see, it is often combined with the **past simple** ('rang'). Writers frequently use the past continuous tense.

(**Example**) Mr. Gilmer **was standing** at the window talking to Mr. Underwood.
Bert, the court reporter, was **chain-smoking**.

Harper Lee, *To Kill a Mockingbird*

Uses

1. The past continuous is formed with '**was/were**' plus '**ing**'. This tense refers to an action **in progress** in the past, but not **completed**. The action was **continuous**, going on for some time.

2. We use the past continuous for **two** actions in the past, happening **at the same time**.

(**Example**) I **was minding** my brother while Mum **was making** the dinner.

The word 'while' is often used with this tense.

3. The past continuous is also used to describe the **typical or habitual** behaviour of people in the **past**.

(**Example**) Gordon **was always moaning** about work.
Karen **was smoking** for three years before she gave up.

Exercise 1. In the following passage, write the verbs in brackets in **either** the past **continuous or** the past **simple** tense. You must decide, from the **context**, which one is correct.

Last Thursday, Donna and her pal, Susan, _____ (walk) through the park on the way home from school when two lads from Fifth Year _____ (stop) them. They _____ (look) for money and they _____ (ask) the girls for some. 'No way!' _____ (say) Donna. 'Get lost!' The two lads _____ (think) of bullying the girls into giving them the money, when Mr. Macken, their Maths teacher, suddenly _____ (appear).

'What's happening here?' he _____ (ask). 'I thought you two lads _____ (do) detention this week. You _____ (smoke) in the changing room, weren't you? Get back to school this minute, do you hear?!'

Donna and Susan _____ (laugh) when Mr. Macken_____ (make) the two lads turn round and they _____ (head) back in the direction of school. 'Thanks, Sir,' _____ (say) Susan. 'You were brilliant!'

'Now, now. No need for that,' Mr. Macken _____ (say). 'Off home with you now. See you tomorrow.'

'Did you notice he _____ (wear) the good suit?' _____ (say) Donna when he _____ (leave).

'Yeh! Must have a heavy date, wha!' _____ (grin) Susan. 'Still, he's OK old Mac.'

Stage 3

The present perfect simple and the present perfect continuous

So far in this unit, you have exercised:
1. the past simple (I ate)
2. the present perfect simple (I have eaten)
3. the past continuous (I was eating).

Now, look at this sentence:

> **(Example)** Donna **has been eating** doughnuts all day.

This sentence is written in the **present perfect continuous** tense. It is formed with '**have/has been**' plus '**ing**'. We use this tense when we are talking about an action that **began** in the past, but has **not** yet finished. Donna is **still** eating doughnuts and is likely to eat even more before the day is out! There is always a strong suggestion or possibility of the action **continuing** for some time into the future, with this tense.

Exercise 1. Let's exercise the **present perfect continuous** tense. Write ten complete sentences beginning with '**I have been** (verb) + **ing**' in answer to each of the following questions:
1. What have you been doing since nine o'clock this morning?
2. What have you been learning about in this unit so far?
3. How long have you been living in your area?
4. How many hours' study per night have you been doing this term?
5. How long have you been day dreaming about the holidays?

(Use your **imagination** on the next five.)
6. Where have you been hiding all this time?
7. What have you been saying to him/her?
8. Why have you been reading my diary?

9. How have you been without any money?
10. Why have you been following me?

N.B.! Students often leave out the **have/has** of the present tense in their speech. So, when it comes to **writing**, the following type of error is common:

> (**Example**) I **seen** Tom twice this week. (Ouch!)
>
> I **have** (or **I've**) seen Tom twice this week. (Right!)

Since **writing** is a much more formal exercise, you must be careful to avoid this mistake.

Exercise 2. Using the skeleton notes below, write out the complete sentence in each case, in **either** the **present perfect simple** or **present perfect continuous**, depending on the **context**. The time words will help you to decide.

> (**Example**) 1. I/just/finish/homework
>
> I **have** just finished my homework.
>
> 2. I/play/golf/Forrest Little/**for years**
>
> I **have been** playing golf in Forrest Little for years.

1. Sheila/not/sing/competition/**yet**.
2. Peter/forget/my birthday/ **every year since**/child.
3. Have you/wait/long?
4. I/not/understand/a word **so far**!
5. Mary/bring me/magazines/**for years now**.
6. We/go/same resort/**for ten years now**.
7. Has she/speak/Tracy/**yet**?
8. I/not/sleep/well/**for ages**.
9. Donna/eat/doughnuts/**all day**!
10. I/just/complete/this exercise.

Exercise 3. Read the following text carefully, correcting the verbs in bold as you go. Use **either** the **past simple**, **past continuous**, **present perfect simple** or **present perfect continuous** tense. Read the previous explanations and examples before you start!

Paul just **done** a really bad thing. He **is dating** Donna for six months now, but last Friday, while **he's going** to town on the bus, he **seen** Tracy, her pal, and **begun** to chat her up. They were **haven** a great time, until Paul looking out the window at the next stop **seen** Donna who **got** on the bus.

'**I just remembered** something, Tracy,' he said hurriedly. 'I have to get off here. See ya!' While Tracy **thinks** about this sudden change in Paul's behaviour, Donna is **paying** her fare. She **spots** Paul and **says**: 'How ya babe! **I just done** me homework. I **comin'** to see ya!' 'Yeh? Great!' Paul is **sweaten** bricks. 'I . . . eh . . . I **been thinking** about you, all day. I **didn't done** me Maths yet, and I **been** kind of hoping you might give us a hand – like.' 'I wish I could!' **laughs** Donna, 'but I **never been** much good at Maths. I **been studying** Calculus for three months now, and I still don't get it! Hey! There's Tracy! Hiya Tracy! Now, she **done** really well in Maths in the Mocks. Why don't you ask her to help you?'

Paul **smiles** weakly at Donna and at Tracy. Things were **got** complicated. 'Right. I will. But . . . eh . . . not now. OK? I'd much rather be with you. Let's get off here, and go for a burger, eh? I **been dying** to see you all week! What **was** you doin' anyway?' With that, the smarmy Paul whisks Donna off the bus, **winks** back at Tracy at the same time, and **steers** her off down the road to McDonald's at the rate of knots!

I tell ye, so far, that fella **had** the luck of the gods. Fair play to him!

The Exam; The drama continues

Exercise 4.

Write **a scene** with the three characters from Exercise 3 in it, **perhaps** set in a **disco** the following week or in **school**. There should be some **confrontation** between them. Use **all of** the tenses you've been practising throughout this unit. (200–300 words)

Punctuation Please!

Quotation Marks ' '

Question	When do we use quotation marks (also called inverted commas)?
Answer	When we want to indicate:
	1. **direct speech**
Example	'I love you,' he said. 'Do you?' she yawned.
	2. **quotations**
Example	'She ran the whole gamut of emotions, from A to B.' (Dorothy Parker speaking about the actress Katherine Hepburn)

Uses

1. It's a matter of personal choice whether you use single or double quotation marks. Writers tend to prefer single marks, and magazines and newspapers double. However, if you are writing a quote **within** a quote, it might be wise to do it as follows:

Example	Tim said, 'Honestly, I can't believe that man! I have just spent two years completing this design and all he could ask was, "Does it come in yellow?" What a stupid question!'

2. All **other** punctuation marks **except** for colons and semi-colons are placed **inside** the quotation marks:

(Example) Exception: (semi-colon) Laura said, 'Of course not'; and she meant it.

3. Sometimes quotation marks surround **a single word** that is **unusual**, or even **invented**:

(Example) 'When he asked me to go "**surfing**" with him, I was thrilled, until I discovered he meant the Internet!'
'I've been "**teddy-sitting**" with my niece's collection of bears.'

4. Always write the **first** word of **direct speech** with a capital letter, even if the speech starts **within** the sentence:

(Example) The woman shouted hysterically, 'It's my son. They've killed him!'

However, if the direct speech **continues** on after the speaker has been named, do **not** use a capital letter:

(Example) 'In that case,' Colm said, 'wouldn't it be better to hire a car?'

5. If a **new** sentence starts after the speaker has been named, use a capital letter:

(Example) 'We had a puncture,' Colm explained. 'We didn't get home until 2 a.m.'

6. Notice the **commas** in the following sentence **interrupted** by the unspoken words 'he said':

(Example) 'Mole,' he said, 'you're the best of fellows!' (*The Wind in the Willows*)

7. Quotation marks are used for **titles** of poems, songs, episodes of TV and radio series, book series and idiomatic phrases:

(Example) *Star Trek*'s 'The Borg' episodes
Point Horror's 'Babysitter 11' series
'Spirit in the Sky'
'Digging' by Seamus Heaney
Helen had a cosy 'tête-à-tête' with Terry.
Ben was thoroughly 'cheesed-off' with his job.

Watch Your Language!

Stage 1

Exercise 1.
Classroom activity, in pairs

1. Decide who's A and who's B. Within a time limit of **two minutes** student A asks student B **five questions** about himself/herself, which B must answer, in **short** statements.

2. After two minutes, the teacher says 'Stop!'. B must now write out the **questions** he/she has heard, from memory, and A must write out the **answers**, also from memory! Time limit of **two minutes** again. N.B.! **Quotation marks** must be used in both cases!

3. Now compare each other's work. You may dispute the **content** of the written questions or answers at this stage! (How well have you **listened** to each other, for example?) Watch those **quotation marks**!

Exercise 2. Write out the following sentences, inserting **quotation marks** where necessary:

1. I live in Galway, said Mary.
2. Did you have a good holiday? asked Jim.
3. I'm starving, said Donnacha. I hope there's something good for dinner.
4. I hope you realise, Dad said, that money doesn't grow on trees.
5. They missed the last bus, Sheila explained. That's why they're late.
6. Get out of my flower beds! Mr. Ryan roared.
7. Playing a battlement, no doubt. (Dorothy Parker, speaking about an elderly actress in Camelot.)
8. On hearing that President Calvin Coolidge had died, Dorothy Parker remarked: How could they tell?
9. Teacher: Who wrote To a Mouse?
   Gerry: I don't know, Miss, but I bet they didn't get an answer!
10. Teacher: How long can someone live without a brain?
    Gerry: How old are you, Sir?

Stage 2

Writing dialogue

Students like writing dialogue, but sometimes it's handled pretty badly, and the page can end up looking as if it's been sprayed with quotation marks!

 'I think someone, or something, is moving about in there,' Susan whispered. 'And I don't like it.' 'Should we not just go in and have a look?' 'Well, I'm certainly not putting a foot inside there! It's spooky.' 'Oh don't be such a wimp!' 'I just don't want to get my head blown off.' 'Don't be stupid. This is not Exterminator 2 remember.' 'It could be, though, couldn't it?' 'You go in if you're so brave, but I'm staying right here.'

As you can see, the dialogue is lively, and starts off well in terms of punctuation. However, as it progresses, it becomes **unclear** who is saying what at any one time and the quotation marks, inserted back to back, are very confusing.

Exercise 1. Rewrite the above piece of dialogue, using **separate** lines for each character, as they speak. Give the name 'Peter' to the other person in the conversation.

The drama continues

Exercise 2.

Now continue the dialogue for a further ten to twelve lines only remembering to give each character a **new** line, each time they speak, even if it's only a short **interruption**.

 'Susan?' Peter whispered.
'Yes, what?'
'Can you still see him?'
'Yes. I . . .'

Once you separate out the characters in this way, there is no need to keep repeating their names. The reader can figure out for himself/herself who is speaking at any one time. You will have noticed that this is how dialogue is written in novels, short stories and plays.

Exercise 3.

1. Read the following extract from 'Louise', a short story by Somerset Maugham. You will see that I have removed all the quotation marks. Can you replace them?
   Well, I hear that Iris isn't going to be married, I said after a while.

   I don't know about that. She's not going to be married quite as soon as I could have wished. I've begged her on my bended knees not to consider me, but she absolutely refuses to leave me.

Don't you think it's rather hard on her?

Dreadfully. Of course it can only be for a few months, but I hate the thought of anyone sacrificing themselves for me.

My dear Louise, you've buried two husbands. I can't see the least reason why you shouldn't bury at least two more.

Do you think that's funny? she asked me in a tone that she made as offensive as she could.

I suppose it's never struck you as strange that you're always strong enough to do anything you want to and that your weak heart only prevents you from doing things that bore you?

Oh, I know, I know what you've always thought of me. You've never believed that I had anything the matter with me, have you?

I looked at her full and square.

Never. I think you've carried out for twenty-five years a stupendous bluff. I think you're the most selfish and monstrous woman I have ever known. You ruined the lives of those two wretched men you married and now you're going to ruin the life of your daughter.

I should not have been surprised if Louise had had a heart attack then. I fully expected her to fly into a passion. She merely gave me a gentle smile.

My poor friend, one of these days you'll be so dreadfully sorry you said this to me.

Somerset Maugham, 'Louise'

2. Now imagine the dialogue that took place **earlier** between Louise and her daughter, Iris. Write about twenty lines of an imaginary dialogue between Louise and her daughter on that occasion. Watch those quotation marks!

Stage 3

The Exam; Media studies

Magazine and newspaper articles are written in short paragraphs. Each paragraph is set in a little from the left of the column, and quotations also. Read this article from the *Irish Examiner* (20 March 2003), and answer the questions which follow.

N.B.! You must use **quotation marks** in your answers.

Schoolgirls whisper their way into the Guinness Book of Records

By Mícheál Lehane

Hundreds of Dublin schoolgirls whispered their way into the history books yesterday to help raise money for charity.

Some 557 Chinese whispers put Mayfield College on Glandore Road, Drumcondra, Dublin, into the Guinness Book of Records.

The school's staff and students took 22 minutes to demolish the previous record of 270 whispers which was set by a British company last year. In true Chinese whisper style the last word differed dramatically from the original quote.

The first whisper spoken by school principal Gerard Wrigley was: "They inherited the earth. Then the army came and scorched it."

At the end of a long chain that stretched throughout the grounds and corridors of the school, the final whisper ended with the words: "Mayfield College." Second year student Aoife Matthews had the last word. The novel record-breaker raised over €1,000 for Amnesty International's Irish branch.

Organiser and biology teacher Tommy Murtagh said the school doesn't expect to hold the world record for long.

"We were happy just as long as the whisper was clean when it finished," he said.

'It changed a bit, but we're delighted to have made it into the Guinness Book of Records," Mr Murtagh said. The students could have beaten the record spectacularly if all 630 pupils were at school.

However, two camogie teams were playing matches yesterday and couldn't participate.

Teachers at Mayfield College believe this was the perfect time to raise money for Amnesty.

"Hopefully it will increase awareness of world issues among the students," Mr Murtagh said.

Exercise 1.

1. What was the first whisper spoken by the school principal, Gerard Wrigley?
2. The final whisper ended with which words?
3. What did the organiser and biology teacher, Tommy Murtagh, have to say about the 'novel record-breaker'? (two points)
4. How did the other teachers at Mayfield College feel about the event?
5. What was Mr. Murtagh's final comment?

Exercise 2.   Read this newspaper article about David Beckham and answer the questions which follow. Again, you must use **quotation marks** in your answers.

Going, Going, Gone: Beckham joins Real Madrid for €35 million

Manchester United's David Beckham will join Real Madrid after the two clubs yesterday agreed a fee of around €35 million for the England captain. Beckham is expected to earn around €6 million a year plus bonuses at the nine-times European champions.

He will undergo a medical in Madrid on July 1st.

The midfielder, travelling to Japan today as part of a promotional tour of Asia for his sponsors, issued a statement through his agents SFX saying he was delighted to move to Spain.

"I recognise that this is an amazing opportunity for me as this stage in my career and a unique and exciting experience for my family," he said.

"I know that I will always regret it later in life if I had turned down the chance to play at another great club like Real Madrid.

"I will always hold precious memories of my time at Manchester United and Old Trafford as well as the players, who I regard as part of my family, and the brilliant fans."

Madrid sporting director Jorge Valdano said: "We are delighted with the arrival of David Beckham. It is a signing that will help us become more competitive."

Italian clubs Inter and AC Milan showed an initial interest in Beckham, but a week ago United announced it had agreed a conditional deal to sell him to Barcelona. Beckham's agents issued a statement saying he was "surprised and disappointed" at United's announcement and within days Barcelona's greatest rivals, Real, emerged as favourites for his signature.

(The Irish Times, 14 June 2003)

1.   According to the article, how does David Beckham view the move to Spain at this point in his career?

2.   How does he feel about playing at Real Madrid?

3.   How does he feel about leaving Manchester United?

4.   What did the Real Madrid sporting director, Jorge Valdano, say about Beckham's signing to the club?

5.   According to Beckham's agents, what was the football star's first reaction to Manchester United's announcement that they were selling him to Barcelona?

How Do You Spell ...?

Prefixes and Suffixes

Students often make mistakes in spelling when adding a prefix or a suffix to a word.

> **Example**
> injoyable   instead of **en**joyable
> Listen**d**   instead of listen**ed**

Quite often this is due to carelessness, but also to a lack of understanding of how words are constructed and what the prefix or suffix actually means. In this unit, you will find a broad range of prefixes and suffixes. Your task is to learn to spell and use them correctly.

1. **Prefixes**: A prefix is a letter or group of letters placed at the **beginning** of a word in order to:
    a. change its meaning, or
    b. form a new word.

> **Example**
> a. un   +   fair   =   unfair
> b. im   +   prove   =   improve

2. **Suffixes**: A suffix is a letter or group of letters placed at the **end** of a word to:
    a. change its meaning,
    b. form a new word, or
    c. form a plural, past tense, comparative, superlative, etc.

> **Example**
> a. heart   +   less   =   heartless
> b. enjoy   +   able   =   enjoyable
>   faint   +   ed   =   fainted (past tense)
>   box   +   es   =   boxes (plural)
>   soft   +   er   =   softer (comparative)
>   soft   +   est   =   softest (superlative)

Prefixes

Rules:

1. There is usually **no change** in the spelling when you add a prefix to a word.

> **Example**   un   +   safe   =   unsafe

But – be careful when adding the prefixes '**un**', '**dis**' and '**mis**' to words which begin with 'n' or 's'. You must **keep** the double letter when you are spelling the new word.

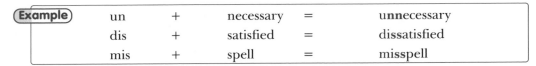

Example	un	+	necessary	=	unnecessary
	dis	+	satisfied	=	dissatisfied
	mis	+	spell	=	misspell

2. Each prefix has it own meaning. The most common prefixes are:

re	meaning	**a.** again	e.g.	**re**appear
		b. back	e.g.	**re**turn
pre	meaning	before	e.g.	**pre**paid
post	meaning	after	e.g.	**post**graduate study
ex	meaning	**a.** out of	e.g.	**ex**port
		b. former	e.g.	**ex**-president
over	meaning	excessive	e.g.	**over**rated
out	meaning	surpass	e.g.	**out**do
un			e.g.	**un**happy
dis	} opposite in meaning		e.g.	**dis**satisfied
mis			e.g.	**mis**understanding
in			e.g.	**in**ability

3. Many prefixes **change** the meaning of a word:

   a. from the positive to the **negative**:

Example	happy	**un**happy
	possible	**im**possible

   b. to its opposite:

Example	**en**courage	**dis**courage
	exterior	**in**terior

4. Some prefixes are **whole words** in themselves:

a.	out	e.g.	outline	**c.**	under	e.g.	underground
b.	over	e.g.	overtake	**d.**	up	e.g.	uproot

5. Lots of prefixes have to do with numbers:

mono	meaning	one	e.g.	monosyllable
bi	meaning	two	e.g.	bifocals
tri	meaning	three	e.g.	tripod

Let's exercise them.

Exercise 1.

1. Match the prefixes in the box on the left to the words in the box on the right, in under one minute:

dis, re, in, over, bi, un, under	paid, sensitive, lingual, rated, appear, agree, decisive

2. Now cover over your new words and see if you can write them from memory – **spelled correctly**, of course!

Exercise 2.

1. Put an appropriate prefix from the list below before the following words. The same prefix may be used for more than one word. Time limit: three minutes.

un, im, in, dis, mis, ir

___active	___appropriate	___spell
___usual	___understand	___tasteful
___approve	___responsible	___patient
___detected	___regular	___movable

2. Check your dictionary to see if your **spellings** are correct.
3. Write **one sentence** for each word. Vary the type of sentence, i.e. three questions, three negative statements, two exclamation-style sentences, two humorous sentences and two serious sentences. Watch the spelling!

Exercise 3.   Here are some definitions of words beginning with:

out, over, under, up

Can you supply the words? Write them in the spaces provided:

1. a sudden explosion of anger: _____
2. to ask too high a price for something: _____
3. to draw a line under, to stress: _____
4. loud and noisy shouting from a crowd: _____
5. the edge of a town or village: _____
6. deceitful and sly; secretive: _____
7. liquid spilling over: _____
8. sophisticated and expensive: _____

Watch Your Language!

And finally . . .

Here is a list of sixteen words with prefixes that come from Latin and Greek (like the number ones in Rule 5). These prefixes are common to many words, and once you have learned to spell them, you will have learned the hardest part of lots of related words. You will also have an important clue as to their meaning!

Prefix	Meaning of prefix	Word
ante	before	antenatal
anti	against	antisocial
auto	self	autobiography
bi	two	bicentennial
chrono	time	chronological
de	from	depart
fore	before	forewarn
inter	between	international
micro	small	microscope
mono	one, single	monorail
post	after	postscript
semi	half	semi-circle
tele	far	telephone
trans	across	transatlantic
uni	one, single	unilateral
vice	acting for	vice-principal

Exercise 4.

1. With the aid of your **dictionary**, find **one** other word for each of the prefixes in the above list.

2. Write the words and their **meanings** into your copy.

(Example) Prefix	Meaning of prefix	Word	Meaning of word
ante	before	antenatal	before birth

3. Write one sentence for each new word.

Suffixes

Suffixes are extremely useful. If you understand them and how they are used, you can increase your word power and improve your spelling at the same time!

Rules:

1. Adding a suffix to a word is usually quite simple:

(Example)	enjoy	+	able	=	enjoyable
	suburb	+	an	=	suburban
	sing	+	ing	=	singing

But when the root word ends in a silent 'e', you **drop** the 'e' before adding the suffix:

(Example)	tune	+	ing	=	tuning
	hate	+	ed	=	hated

There are two important **exceptions** to this rule:

  a. Words ending in 'ce' or 'ge' **keep the** 'e' before the suffixes '**able**' and '**ous**':

(Example)	courage	+	ous	=	courageous
	notice	+	able	=	noticeable

  b. When adding a suffix beginning with a **consonant**, you also keep the 'e' of the root word:

(Example)	care	+	full	=	careful
	amaze	+	ment	=	amazement

2. When the root word ends in 'y', change it to 'i' before adding the suffix:

(Example)	happy	+	ly/ness	=	happily, happiness

3. Words ending in 'l', 'm', 'n', 'p' and 't' usually **double** their last letter before adding the suffixes 'ed', 'er', 'in', 'est' and 'ing':

(Example)	patrol	+	ing/ed	=	patrolling, patrolled
	begin	+	ing/er	=	beginning, beginner

4. Words ending in 'ic' add 'k' before a suffix:

(Example)	panic	+	ing/ed	=	panicking, panicked

5. By adding a suffix, you can make:

  a. **nouns from adjectives:**

(Example)	good (adj.)	+	ness (suffix)	=	goodness (noun)

  b. **adjectives from nouns:**

(Example)	mind (noun)	+	less (suffix)	=	mindless (adj.)

Watch Your Language!

c. **verbs from adjectives and nouns:**

| (Example) | damp (adj.) | + en (suffix) | = dampen (verb) |
| | terror (noun) | + ise (suffix) | = terrorise (verb) |

Exercise 1.

1. Match the suffixes in the box on the left to the words in the box on the right, in **two minutes**. Make any necessary **small spelling** changes.

able, ful, less, ship, ly, en, ing, ness, ous, ment	resent, rare, recognise, mind, harm, glory, strength, begin, good, friend

2. Now check that your spellings are **correct**, by consulting your dictionary.

Exercise 2.

In pairs

1. Write down as many words as you can that **end with the suffixes from the box in Exercise 1**. Time limit: ten minutes.

2. Exchange copies with **another pair of students** who will check the **spellings** of your words in a dictionary, giving **one mark** for each correctly spelled word. If a spelling is incorrect, they should write the correct version in the space beside it. Time limit: fifteen minutes.

3. The pair of students with the **most** words spelled correctly wins!

Exercise 3.

1. Make **adjectives** from these nouns using the suffixes in the list below. Watch the **spelling**!

y, ly, ish, like, ful

a. child_____
b. truth_____
c. fool_____
d. prince _____
e. coward_____
f. hunger_____
g. life _____
h. snob _____
i. father_____
j. youth _____
k. plenty_____
l. skill_____
m. noise_____
n. leisure _____
o. fun _____

2. Write a short piece of dialogue between two people using each word once only. (75–100 words)

Begin with:

Ann: Lisa is really snobbish, don't you think?

Tracy:

Exercise 4.

1. Form **nouns** from these adjectives and verbs using the suffixes in the list below. Watch the **spelling**! Check the rules.

ness, ment, er, ism

a. swim_____   **f.** write_____

b. govern _____   **g.** improve_____

c. kind _____   **h.** cool_____

d. real_____   **i.** win _____

e. agree _____   **j.** autistic _____

2. Write one sentence for each new word, in the **question form**.

(**Example**) Is he a good swimmer?

Prefixes and suffixes combined

Exercise 1. Make adjectives from these verbs using the **suffix 'able'**. Mind the spelling!

1. value _____   8. obtain_____

2. work_____   9. recognise_____

3. advise_____   10. rely_____

4. forget_____   11. avoid _____

5. transfer _____   12. vary _____

6. predict_____   13. repeat _____

7. believe _____   14. profit _____

Exercise 2. Form the **negative** of the new adjectives by adding the **prefix** 'un' or 'in' to each of them. Be careful! Which is the correct spelling: 'un' or 'in'? Check your dictionary if you're not sure.

And finally . . .

Exercise 3.

1. Make **two lists** headed **Prefixes** and **Suffixes** from all the words that you have learned and exercised in this section.

2. Include also those new words that you yourself have created.

3. Write them out into your copy or folder in **alphabetical** order, as in a dictionary.

4. Set aside a little time each week to learn the spellings of **ten** words from your lists.

5. Refer to them when you are doing a homework assignment. **Use them**. Make them part of your speech and writing.

Words at Work

Action Words

> (Question) So what's an action word, then?
>
> (Answer) It's a word that **leaps**, **soars**, **struts**, **flicks**, **screams**, **whispers**, **sighs**, **sprints** or **pounces**! It has life, movement and feeling in it. Every sentence must have a verb, but many students never move beyond the same dull, overused ones: see, show, say, tell, etc. Let's exercise with more exciting ones!

Stage 1

'Walk this way!': verbs of movement

The verb 'to walk' is in common use, but there are many different ways of walking. Here are just some of them:

amble	hobble	plod	strut
crawl	limp	shuffle	tiptoe
creep	march	stagger	trek
dash	meander	stride	trudge
dawdle	pace	stroll	wander

Exercise 1.

Oral, class activity

1. Your teacher will begin a story in this way with the verb 'amble':
   'Pat was happy. He'd worked hard all week and now he'd decided to **amble** down to his favourite local for a pint and a game of snooker . . .'

2. There are twenty verbs in alphabetical order in the above list. Your teacher will select nineteen students **at random** to **continue** the story, each one contributing one sentence which must contain the next verb on the list. Begin with '**crawl**'. If an individual can't continue the story within thirty seconds, his/her turn goes to the next student selected. The game ends when your teacher gets to the verb '**wander**'. You should aim to conclude the story with this verb. Your teacher will impose a time limit of ten minutes for this exercise. Have fun!

Exercise 2.
Choose the **best** 'movement' verb from those in brackets in order to complete each of the following sentences:

1. When I struggled out of the ditch, I _____ (walked, slipped, staggered) up the hill to the nearest house.

2. Sheila fell off the wall and had to _____ (walk, plod, hobble) home in great pain.

3. Rita _____ (dashed, dawdled, strolled) all the way to school.

4. The injured hurler _____ (ambled, marched, limped) off the pitch.

5. Mrs. Molloy _____ (walked, strode, trudged) wearily home, the heavy bags biting into her hands.

Exercise 3. Now select any **ten** movement verbs from your list, and create a character for each one. Think about what kind of person might walk in a particular way, at what pace and in which situation.

> (**Example**) Paul **struts** around the school yard like a peacock.
>
> 'For heaven's sake, Tina Roche, will you stop **shuffling** those feet and get a move on!' said Mrs. Ryan.

Stage 2

'Sounds interesting!': sound verbs

Exercise 1. Write out the twenty 'sound' verbs from the list below into two lists of quiet and loud verbs, ten in each list.

	Quiet	Loud		Quiet	Loud
1.	_____	_____	6.	_____	_____
2.	_____	_____	7.	_____	_____
3.	_____	_____	8.	_____	_____
4.	_____	_____	9.	_____	_____
5.	_____	_____	10.	_____	_____

bang	gurgle	rustle	swish
blare	howl	sigh	thud
boom	hum	slam	tinkle
clatter	patter	sob	whimper
crash	purr	squeak	yelp

Have you noticed how some 'sound' verbs can be either loud or quiet depending on the **situation** in which they are used? For example, a child could **sob** quietly **or** loudly, depending on whether it wished to be heard or not!

> (**Example**) Amy wanted everyone to hear her, so she sobbed as loudly as she could.

Exercise 2. Choose an appropriate sound verb from your lists to complete the following sentences:

1. The baby _____ contentedly in its pram.
2. The wind _____ round the corner of the house.
3. The puppy _____ in pain when the boy kicked him.
4. The champagne glasses _____ as the old ladies smiled and _____ the old melodies of their youth.
5. The rain _____ on the roof of the car.
6. The head chef _____ the door on his way out while the youngest trainee _____ quietly in a corner of the kitchen.
7. He remembered how her gown had _____ as she danced across the floor.

Exercise 3. Choose five 'quiet' verbs and five 'loud' ones and write a continuous piece of prose, **or** a short poem (8–10 lines), in which each verb is used once only. Be imaginative. Consider the context in which the sound might be made, the kind of person, animal or object **associated** with that sound. Try to create an **atmosphere** appropriate to the situation.

Stage 3

'It's all talk!': talking verbs

Believe it or not, there are more ways of speaking than simply 'say' or 'tell'. Here are twenty really vibrant 'talking' verbs:

babble	jeer	bark
scream	moan	shout
chat	murmur	snap
mutter	drone	stammer
pray	gossip	preach
grunt	rant	whisper
rave	yell	

Exercise 1. Fill in the blanks in the following sentences with a suitable 'talking' verb from the above list. N.B.! More than one verb may be correct in some sentences, and you'll need to make some changes in the spelling.

1. I couldn't understand why she was _____ for rain!
2. He _____ something about losing his wallet, but it wasn't very clear.
3. 'Help!' she _____. 'He's going to kill me!'
4. Sarah never stopped _____ all through the film. It was really irritating.
5. I wish Harry practised what he _____.
6. The Principal _____ on and on about discipline for at least twenty minutes.

7. Maurice doesn't actually speak. He merely _____ whenever he wants something.
8. Barbara is forever _____ about her boyfriend not appreciating her.
9. They _____ him all the time about his clothes. It is very cruel.
10. 'I love you, too,' he _____ in her ear.

Exercise 2.   Read carefully the following extract from George Orwell's *1984*, and answer the questions which follow.

'Thirty to Forty group!' yapped a piercing female voice. 'Thirty to Forty group! Take your places please!'

Winston sprang to attention in front of the telescreen, upon which the image of a youngish woman, scrawny but muscular, had already appeared, dressed in a tunic and gym-shoes.

'Arms bending and stretching!' she rapped out. 'Take your time from me. One, two, three, four! One, two, three, four! One, two, three, four!'

As Winston mechanically shot his arms backwards and forwards, he wore the look of grim enjoyment on his face, which was considered proper during the Physical Jerks.

'Stand easy!' barked the instructress, a little more genially.

Winston sank his arms to his sides and slowly refilled his lungs with air, but the instructress had already called them to attention. 'And now let's see which of us can touch our toes!' she said enthusiastically. 'Right over from the hips please. One, two! One, two!'

He loathed this exercise, which sent shooting pains all the way from his heels to his buttocks and often ended by bringing on another coughing fit.

'Smith!' screamed the shrewish voice from the telescreen. '6079, Smith W.! Yes, you! Bend lower please! You can do better than that! You're not trying. Lower, please! That's better, much better. Now stand at ease, the whole squad, and watch me!'

1. Can you find six 'talking' verbs in the above extract which relate to the instructress? Underline each one.
2. What impression do they give us of the instructress? Why does she speak the way she does, do you think?

The Exam; Personal writing

3. Write a short piece of **dialogue** or **narrative** (150–200 words), in which you use as many of the talking verbs from this section as possible. Try not to repeat a verb. Here is a 'starter' sentence (but you are free to create your own, of course):

'You're not afraid of me, are you?' she **murmured**, as she passed his chair . . .

Stage 4

'Action please!': dramatic verbs

Verbs can also be **dramatic**, conveying a sense of tension, mystery or violence. These **action** words give life and energy to a text, creating an immediate excitement for the reader.

Exercise 1. Read the following passage from *Cider with Rosie* by Laurie Lee. It describes Miss B., the Head Teacher, whom I think you'll agree was absolutely terrifying! Answer the questions which follow.

> Miss B., the Head Teacher, to whom I was now delivered, was about as physically soothing as a rake. She was a bunched up and punitive little body and the school christened her Crabby; she had a sour yellow look, lank hair twisted round her ears, and the skin and voice of a turkey. We used to be afraid of the gobbling Miss B.; she spied, she pried, she crouched, she crept, she pounced – she was a terror.
>
> Each morning was war without declaration; no one knew who would catch her attention next. We used to stand to attention, half-crippled in our desks, till Miss B. walked in. She had a habit of whacking the walls with her ruler, and then fixed us with her squinting eye. We would sometimes say a prayer; but scarcely had we bellowed the last Amen than Crabby coiled, uncoiled and sprang, and knocked some poor boy sideways.

1. Underline those **verbs** the writer uses to describe Miss B, at the end of the first paragraph.
2. What did she do with her ruler?
3. How did the class say the last Amen of the prayers?
4. '. . . than Crabby **coiled**, **uncoiled** and **sprang**, and knocked some poor boy sideways.' What do you think 'coiled' and 'uncoiled' refer to, in terms of Miss B.? Is 'sprang' **dramatic**, and why? (30–50 words)

Exercise 2. Here is another short passage, describing the **violence** of an attack upon a house, during a burglary.

> In a burglary in Meadow Drive last night, considerable damage was done to interior fittings and decorations. Doors were ripped off their hinges, soft furnishings were slashed, mirrors and pictures were broken, and paint daubed over walls and carpets. The intruders made off with a small collection of valuable paintings. Items of jewellery were also stolen. A Garda investigation is under way and it is believed that two men are being held for questioning.

1. Which verbs convey the **violence** of the attack?
2. Write a report (of similar length), using the **same** verbs but placing the attack in a **different situation**, and changing the details accordingly.

The Exam; Poetry

Exercise 3.

Read the poem carefully and then answer the questions which follow.

The House at Night

1. *Some stealthy spider is weaving round my bed*
   and mice are nibbling the curtains overhead.
   Weird footsteps make the floorboards crack,
   the staircase creaks,
   chill draughts thrill down my back
   from some forgotten window out of sight
   this is the house at night.

2. *There's a whispering on the landing*
   where a creepy tropic plant is standing,
   and the coatrack in the hall
   lets fall a scarf – a long, soft fall:
   a snake's loose coils that rapidly grow tight
   this is the house at night.

3. *From the distant kitchen come the notes of dripping taps*
   plink-plonking secret codes
   I cannot get the meaning of: a sudden
   icy shudder – the refrigerator groans – a hidden
   oven, cooling, ticks in rustling ember-light
   this is the house at night.

4. *But even stranger is my own tense breathing*
   as I lie here speechless looking at the ceiling
   that seems to swim all round like falling snow.
   I can hear my eyelids batting gently, slow
   then quick as heartbeats as I freeze with fright
   at something in the mirror shining bright
   has someone left the telly on all night?
   No, thank heaven, it's all right,
   it's only the moon's pale, spooky light
   touching my tangled sheets with chalky white
   yes, this is the house at night.

James Kirkup

Watch Your Language!

1. Concentrate on the **verbs** in this poem. Underline each one. You should find twenty-four (excluding 'is').

2. 'Chill draughts **thrill** down my back'. What do you think the verb 'thrill' means here? Look up a thesaurus to find other words for thrill, and a dictionary for other meanings.

3. Comment on the verb '**groans**' in the image 'the refrigerator groans' in Verse 3. What exactly is it describing, do you think?

4. Choose **ten** to **fifteen verbs** from this poem and write **a.** a poem, **b.** a descriptive paragraph, or **c.** a piece of dialogue of your own. Try not to repeat a verb. Include also some **movement, sound** and **talking verbs** from this unit.

Unit 7

Grappling with Grammar

The Past Tense 2

The final two past tenses to be considered are **the past perfect simple** (**had** done) and the **past perfect continuous** (**had been** doing).

Stage 1

The past perfect simple

Example   John **had worked** in Cork, before he **came** to Dublin.

In this example, two actions occurred in the past, one **before** the other. The first action is in the past perfect simple ('had worked'), the second in the past simple ('came'). The past perfect tense is especially important when you want to stress that one event **finished** before another began in the past. This tense is very useful when you are writing a story. It makes it clear to the reader when exactly things happened in relation to each other in the **past**.

Example   He **had visited** [1] his aunt in Portlaoise, (where he had **lived** [2] as a child) before he **left** [3] for the States.

As you can see, the **final** action is in the **past simple** tense.

N.B.! There are **two** situations when it is best to use the **past simple** instead of the **past perfect simple**.

1.   When the second action happens as a **result** of the first.

Example   When Sorcha **arrived**, we **opened** a bottle of wine.

2.   When there is a **sequence of events** in a story, in the past.

Example   When the alarm went off, the burglar **panicked** [1]. He **raced** [2] out the door and **fell** [3] over a motorbike outside, and a policeman promptly **arrested** [4] him.

Exercise 1. Complete these sentences with the **past perfect simple** of the verbs in brackets.

> (Example) Sheila returned to Ireland after twenty years in the States, to find that many things _____ (change). **had changed**

1. Her best friend, Mary, was no longer there. She _____ (go) away.
2. Most of her family were no longer there, either. They _____ (leave) many years before.
3. The local hotel was no longer open. It _____ (close) down in 1985.
4. Dr. Harris was no longer alive. He _____ (die) six months before.
5. She didn't recognise the town. It _____ (change) completely.

Exercise 2. Enlarge on the skeleton notes in the brackets, as in the following example, using the **past perfect simple tense**.

> (Example) Susan didn't want to come to the cinema with us.
> (She/already/see/film/twice)
> She **had** already **seen** the film twice.

1. Mam wasn't at home when I arrived. (She/just/go/out)
2. We arrived at the pitch late. (The match/already/begin)
3. Donna wasn't hungry when I rang. (She/just/finish/her fifth doughnut!)
4. Mick invited Tina to dinner last Saturday, but she couldn't go. (She/already/arrange/go out with/someone else)
5. I was really delighted to see Maura again. (I/not/see/her/for years)

Stage 2

The past perfect continuous

Now look at this sentence:

> (Example) They **had been** playing for half an hour when there was a terrible thunderstorm and the match was stopped.

We use the **past perfect continuous** to say **how long** something had been going on **before** something else happened. This may also refer to **habitual** actions in the past that had been going on for some time.

> (Example) Joan **had been** smoking for twenty years before she finally saw sense.

Exercise 1. Read the following situations and then follow each one with a **sentence** in the **past perfect continuous** tense, according to the skeleton notes provided.

> **Example**   Teresa was very tired, so she went to bed much earlier than usual.
> (She/study/hard/all day)
> She **had been studying** hard all day.

Your turn!

1. The two boys came home, one with a black eye and the other a cut lip. (They/fight/in the schoolyard)

2. When Mr. Butler walked into the room, it was empty, but there was a distinct smell of cigarette smoke. (Some students/smoke/there during lunchbreak)

3. When Paula came back from a session on the sunbed, she looked very red. (She/lie/under it/for too long)

4. I arranged to meet Peter in a café, but after a while, I realised that I had come to the wrong one! (I/wait there/for twenty minutes) before I realised my mistake.

5. Donna woke up terrified in the middle of the night because she didn't know where she was. (She/dream/about a giant-sized doughnut) which had taken over the world!

Exercise 2.   Answer the following questions with a sentence in **the past perfect continuous** form.

> **Example**   What had you been doing before you had the crash?
> I **had been talking** to my girlfriend on my mobile phone.

You may use your imagination in your answers to these questions, as there are many possibilities.

1. Where had she been working before she came to Galway?
2. Who had he been speaking to before the accident?
3. How long had they been playing before rain stopped play?
4. Why had you been thinking about it for so long?
5. What had you been doing before you started this unit?

Stage 3

Exercise 1.   Do you remember Donna? She's the one who has popped up in a number of the exercises in this unit! She is addicted to doughnuts! Read this mini-saga about her, and identify each past tense as you read. You will find examples of all six past tenses from this unit and Unit 6.

1. Donna **ate** ten doughnuts yesterday. (Tense: _____)
2. Donna **has** eaten doughnuts every day since she was a kid. (Tense: _____)
3. She **was eating** her fifth doughnut at about six o'clock when her boyfriend, Paul, rang. (Tense: _____)

4. 'Donna? It's me, Paul. **Have** you **been eating** doughnuts again all day?!' he asked. (Tense: _____)

5. 'Who? Me?!' said Donna, guiltily, stuffing a sixth doughnut behind a cushion on the sofa. 'No, way, Paul! I'm giving them up, honest. I **had eaten** just one little one before you rang but only one. I swear!' (Tense: _____)

6. Paul sighed. He **had heard** it all before. (Tense: _____)

7. 'I don't believe you, Donna! You sound like you're stuffing your face this very minute! Come on. Own up! Just how many doughnuts **had you been eating** before I rang?!' (Tense: _____)

Exercise 2.   Did you spot all of the six tenses in Exercise 1? Good! Now, answer the following questions about Donna in the same tense as the question. Be very careful with the wording.

> (Example)   What do you think Donna **did** the moment she put the phone down?
> I think she **ate** the sixth doughnut hidden behind the cushion on the sofa. (past simple)

Now you do it.
1. What **did** she do **after** she ate the sixth doughnut?
2. What **has she done** so many times already?
3. What **was she doing** when her Mum and Dad came home from work?
4. What **has she been doing** since she was a little girl?
5. What **had she done** just before Paul rang?
6. What **had she been doing** all day?

The Exam; Reading

Exercise 3.

Here are some short extracts of the type used in the **Reading** and **Fiction** sections of the Junior Cert. exam papers. **Identify the tenses** of the verbs in bold, and then answer the questions which follow. Write **a complete sentence** in **the same tense** as the question, in each case.

1. He **had been** a tall man. From feet to neck **covered** a long space. His head **lay** beside him. When she **pushed back** the leaves and layers of earth and debris Moya **saw that** he'd had large white teeth, all of them cracked or broken, long fingers, and very big bones. All his **clothes had rotted away** except some threads of blue denim from his overalls. The buckles of the overalls **had turned green**.
    a.   Had he been a small man?
    b.   Where did his head lie?
    c.   What had his teeth been like?
    d.   What had happened to his clothes?

2. The bull **seemed** to take no notice of me as I **edged** my way into the stable. He just **turned** with awesome slowness and **made his way** into the stall. There Harry **dropped** the rope over Monty's horns and **tied** it tightly to a huge iron bar in the wall outside. I **opened** the door of his stall and as I **passed along** his massive body I **sensed** the terrible power of this animal. I **ran** my fingers along its massive neck to find the vein from which I would take the blood. The skin was hard and leathery and it would take a good jab to pierce it. The bull **stiffened** but **did not move** as I **plunged** the needle in and with relief I **saw** the blood flowing into the syringe. I **was withdrawing** the needle and thinking how simple the job was after all when everything **started to happen**. The bull **gave** a tremendous roar and **whipped** his head around at me with incredible speed.

    a. Just **one** past tense features in this extract (except for 'was withdrawing'). Identify this tense.
    b. How did the bull react as the vet edged his way into the stable?
    c. What did Harry do?
    d. What did the vet do with the needle?
    e. 'I **was withdrawing** the needle.' Which past tense is this?

3. The trend towards co-education **has gathered pace** this century as women **have fought** for equal rights and opportunities. The vast majority of schools in England are now mixed and **it has long been thought** correct to say that co-education is right for everyone. However, this argument is unjust to good single-sex schools. Changes **have been made**, especially in the last couple of decades, to face up to weaknesses in the system. Girls' schools, for example, **have made** great strides in ensuring that a broad choice of subjects is available, including a wider range of sciences, design and technology, information technology and sports.

    a. Identify the past tense of the verbs in bold in this text.
    b. What has gathered pace this century?
    c. What have women fought for?
    d. Has it always been thought that co-education is correct for everyone?
    e. What changes have been made in girls' schools, for example?

Summary – verbs in the past tense

Examples	Tense
1. I **wrote** to Paul **last week**.	Past simple
2. I **was waiting** for Nora for two hours.	Past continuous
3. I **have** just **moved** house.	Present perfect simple
4. I **have been** dreaming of this house for years.	Present perfect continuous
5. I **had read** the book before I saw the film.	Past perfect simple
6. I **had been** looking forward to this trip for a long time, before it happened.	Past perfect continuous

N.B.! When you understand and practise the past tenses, your expression will become clearer, more precise and more varied. Students often use only the past simple or the present tense in their writing, and these mixed together wrongly most of the time! Try to avoid 'would' when describing past actions, even **habitual** ones. It becomes repetitive and boring. Use it once to introduce a memory, for example, and then continue in the **past simple**, the **past continuous**, or the **past perfect** forms. This will result in much better writing. Watch those tenses!

Punctuation Please!

Dashes and Hyphens — -

Question   What's the difference between a dash and a hyphen?

Answer   Good question! Both are written as short lines, and they look alike, but the dash is **longer** than the hyphen.

Example   Dash: You know what will happen – you'll lose your way.
Hyphen: This is very up-to-date information.

They each have different uses, too. Let's deal with the dash first.

Stage 1

Dash

Uses

1. A single dash marks a **sharp break** in a sentence.

    Example   Books, copies, notes – he threw them all in the bin.

2. Two dashes can be used in order to **provide extra information**.

    Example   Come to me after class – don't forget your French copy – and I'll try to explain the bit you've missed.

3. Dashes can be used **instead of brackets** ( ) to enclose words giving extra information. They give **more emphasis** to the words between them than brackets do.

    Example   Shoes – which must be brown – will be worn at all times.

4. Dashes are used to introduce a **comment** or an **explanation**.

    Example   a. (comment) Soccer star David Beckham has been transferred for a record fee – €35 million. (comment)
    b. I sell vegetables – carrots, peas, broccoli, anything. (explanation)

    In Example (b) the dash explains what kind of vegetables.

5. A dash shows a **break in speech**.

    Example   a. Sheila picked up the knife and screamed: 'Get out of here or I'll kill you, you –'
    b. 'Really, now you ask me,' said Alice, very much confused, 'I don't think –' 'Then you shouldn't talk,' said the Hatter. (Lewis Carroll, *Alice in Wonderland*)

6. A dash may be used to add an **element of surprise**, an **unexpected turn of thought**, or a **witticism**.

    Example   'There is always an easy solution to every human problem – neat, plausible and wrong.' (H. L. Mencken)

7. A longer dash (called a 3-em dash) may be used to indicate a word or part of a word that's been left out, often because it's coarse or rude.

    Example   'You're a d——— fool!'

Finally . . . be careful how you use dashes. They are often used as excuses for bad punctuation. Students sometimes put them between two words when they should use either a comma, colon or semi-colon. Dashes should be used **sparingly**.

Let's exercise them.

Watch Your Language!

Exercise 1. Rewrite the following sentences inserting either one or two dashes in the correct place in each one, as appropriate.

1. He thought Paris was the most beautiful city in the world until he saw Florence.
2. The Mayor launched the new lifeboat which slid gracefully into the water and crashed into another boat.
3. I have made some plans not very detailed ones for the trip to Rome.
4. I appreciate your offer will you really manage without it?
5. You must handwrite your essay typing will not do and hand it up tomorrow.
6. Put the baby to bed don't forget her bottle and I'll ring later to check how she is.
7. As Tom charged out the door, Mr. Brown roared after him: 'Don't forget your But his words were drowned out by Tom's motorbike.
8. We were happy to eat *pâté de foie gras* we changed our minds when Ian told us how the geese were force-fed.
9. There are thirty students in my class ten of them are girls.
10. Mary burst into the loo to tell her mate the news only to realise she was in the gents toilet.

Exercise 2. Add one or two dashes and any necessary **commas** to these sentences.

1. The 1798 commemoration ceremony the biggest event ever held in the town was attended by over two thousand people.
2. Joe Mullery was fined for having six adults and two children in his mini three in the front three in the back one child on the floor in the front one child lying across the window.
3. My grandmother the one who died before I was born travelled all over Europe and America.
4. Many countries Ireland was one of them did not qualify for the World Cup in 1998.
5. Complete this application don't forget to sign it and post it off quickly.
6. Peggy was quite happy to share a room with Denise until she heard about her pet snake sharing it too.
7. We had to wait two hours for the train cows had wandered on to the track at Arklow.
8. The class is divided on this issue half agree with the uniform half don't.
9. Sunscreen sunglasses sunhat she left them all behind on the bed.
10. Tennis star Pete Sampras once had his hands insured for a colossal sum $3 million.

Stage 2 ─────────────────────────────

Hyphen

Our hyphens are in a mess.

E. Whitaker-Wilson, *How to Punctuate*

Uses

1. A hyphen is used to join two words together. This changes the meaning of **both** words. These are then known as **compound** words.

> **Example**
> | side + show | = | side-show |
> | seat + belt | = | seat-belt |
> | jelly + babies | = | jelly-babies |

2. A hyphen is used to mark the division of words at the end of a line **in print**. The break should be a **syllabic** one.

> **Example** 'sing-' (at the **end** of one line) followed by 'ing' (at the **beginning** of the next line)

However, in **handwriting**, this use should be avoided altogether.

3. Combinations of **three words** divided by **two** hyphens are quite common in English.

> **Example** brother-in-law, commander-in-chief, up-to-date, Stratford-upon-Avon

4. A hyphen is used to break up:
   a. telephone numbers (046-28351)
   b. account numbers (Acc. No. 3030-6145-2332)
   c. continuous numbers in street addresses and pages (10-15 St. Stephen's Green, pages 138-155)

5. Hyphens are used in **compound adjectives** before nouns.

> **Example** a light-blue shirt, a well-known politician

6. Hyphens help to avoid confusion in the **spelling** of some words.

> **Example** mis-spell, hair-raising, hitch-hike, stock-still, stage-struck

7. Hyphens help to avoid mispronunciation:

> **Example** co-operate, pre-eminent, co-ordinate

8. Hyphens always feature with certain Latin prefixes:

> **Example** ex-champion, non-smoker, sub-committee, vice-captain

Finally . . . as with dashes, the hyphen should be used with care.

> *The hyphen is not an ornament but an aid to being understood, and should be*

employed only when it is needed for that purpose.

H. W. Fowler, *A Dictionary of Modern English Usage*

Let's exercise it.

Exercise 1.   Match a word from List A and one from List B to form a **compound word**, requiring a **hyphen**, for List C. Write out the newly formed words – **with hyphens**, of course!

List A	List B	List C (with hyphens)
spirit	off	_____
cross	hearted	_____
audio	fiction	_____
sky	west	_____
half	blank	_____
law	level	_____
non	examine	_____
south	visual	_____
play	abiding	_____
point	high	_____

Exercise 2.   Write at least three compound words that require a **hyphen** for each of the following 'starter' words. Consult your **dictionary** if you get stuck.

(**Example**)   1. cross-reference   2. cross-check   3. cross-country

1. cross- _____   _____   _____
2. self- _____   _____   _____
3. pro- _____   _____   _____
4. all- _____   _____   _____
5. semi- _____   _____   _____
6. off-_____   _____   _____

Stage 3

Dashes and hyphens

Exercise 1.   Insert the following **hyphenated** compound words into the sentences below.

back-breaking   mouth-watering
hair-raising   heart-breaking
heart-warming

1. He found that picking grapes for seven hours was _____ work.
2. It was _____ to get the letter from home, saying they missed her.
3. Taking the roller coaster ride on 'Space Mountain' was a _____ experience.
4. Although we were on a diet, we couldn't resist the chocolate cake – it looked so _____.
5. It was _____ to watch the little girl crying over her broken dolly.

Exercise 2. Now write ten sentences of your own, using the five compound words from Exercise 1, plus the following compounds and the stimulus words provided in brackets:

1. all-round (athlete)
2. Anglo-Irish (Agreement)
3. cross-examination (witness)
4. free-range (hens)
5. hitch-hike (Cork)
6. fifty-fifty (the Lotto)
7. law-abiding (citizen)
8. North-South (relations)
9. play-off (match)
10. post-war (Europe)

The Exam; Reading, personal writing

Exercise 3.

1. In his books, the Irish writer Roddy Doyle uses **dashes** instead of quotation marks when writing **dialogue**. Read the following extract from his Booker Prize award-winning novel *Paddy Clarke Ha Ha Ha* **and comment briefly on his use of dashes**. For example, do you think the dialogue is easier to read with dashes rather than quotation marks? If so, **why** is this?

We loved marching. We could feel the boards hopping under us. We put so much effort into slamming our feet down that we couldn't keep in time. She made us do this a couple of times a day, when she said we were looking lazy.

While we marched this time Miss Watkins read the proclamation.

– Irishmen and Irishwomen: In the name of God and of the dead generations from which she receives her old tradition of nationhood, Ireland, through us, summons her children to her flag and strikes for her freedom.

She had to stop. It wasn't proper marching any more. She hit the blackboard.

– *Suígí síos*.

She looked annoyed and disappointed.

Kevin put his hand up.

– Miss?

– *Sea*?

– Paddy Clarke said his granda's Thomas Clarke on the tea-towel, Miss.

– Did he now?

– Yes, Miss.

– Patrick Clarke.

– Yes, Miss.

– Stand up till we see you.

It took ages for me to get out of my desk.

– Your grandfather is Thomas Clarke?

I smiled.

– Is he?

– Yes, Miss.

– This man here?

She pointed at Thomas Clarke in one of the corners of the tea-towel. He looked like a granda.

– Yes, Miss.

– Where does he live, tell us?

– Clontarf, Miss.

– Where?

– Clontarf, Miss.

– Come up here to me, Patrick Clarke.

The only noise was me on the floorboards.

She pointed to a bit of writing under Thomas Clarke's head.

– Read that for us, Patrick Clarke.

– Ex – eh – executed by the British on 3 May, 1916.

– What does Executed mean, Dermot Grimes who's picking his nose and doesn't think I can see him?

– Kilt, Miss.

– That's right. And this is your grandfather who lives in Clontarf, is it, Patrick Clarke?

– Yes, Miss.

I pretended to look at the picture again.

– I'll ask you again, Patrick Clarke. Is this man your grandfather?

– No, Miss.

She gave me three on each hand.

2. Try writing a short piece of dialogue of your own using **dashes** for punctuation, instead of quotation marks. It should be about the same length as the extract above and based on one of the following situations:
    ●   a row with one or both of your parents over a night out
    ●   a discussion of a European Championship 2004 game
    ●   a disagreement over who should pay for something in a restaurant or shop
    ●   a situation involving conflict of some kind.

How Do You Spell . . .?

Double-letter Words 2

In this unit, you will be exercising double-letter words from 'm' to 't'.

1. Double 'm' and 'n' words

Double 'm'	Double 'n'
accommodate	annual
common	beginning
grammar	channel
immediately	innocence
recommend	tyranny

It would be useful to **underline** the double 'm' or 'n' of each word in the above list. This will remind you that there are two of them. These words are often misspelled.

Exercise 1.

1. Study the ten words above for five minutes in class. Remember it will be easier to learn these spellings because each word contains a **double** 'm' or 'n' and they are written in alphabetical order.

2. When the five minutes are up, your teacher will call out each word in the order in which you have learned them. Write them out, one underneath the other, in a list, being very careful with those **double** 'm's and 'n's!

3. Exchange your copy with the person next to you. You will now correct his/hers, and he/she will do likewise with yours. Please refer to the **original spelling list** when correcting each word.

4. Give **one** mark for each word spelled correctly, and a total mark out of ten.

5. If a word has been spelled **incorrectly**, cross it out and write the **correct** spelling of the word beside it, again checking from the original list.

6. Take back your own copy and write out any words you have spelled incorrectly, **five times** each.

Exercise 2.   Can you unjumble these words from your double 'm' and 'n' list?

1. LNHCANE
2. DMROMECNE
3. RAMGAMR
4. YEMILDEMIAT
5. NIBGNIENG

Exercise 3. Write **two** sentences each for the remaining **five** words, using the word in a **different** situation/context in each sentence.

> **Example** annual
>
> Sentence 1. 'I see Mrs. Flanagan is off on her **annual** holiday again.
>   That'll be her tenth, you know.'
> Sentence 2. The Dublin Fringe Festival is an **annual** event now.

2. Double 'p' words

appeal	approach
appear	opportunity
appearance	opposite
appetite	support
applied	supporter

This list should be quite easy to learn as the first six words begin with '**app**', the next two with '**opp**', and the final two with '**supp**'.

Exercise 1.

As for double 'm' and 'n' words.

Exercise 2.
Do you remember the **cloze-style** exercise **for double 'd' words in Unit 4?** Read the notes and instructions again, and do exactly the same with these words from the double 'p' list.

1. a. __earance
    b. app_____
    c. appear___
    d. _____ance
    e. _____

2. a. ____orter
    b. supp___er
    c. ____ort__
    d. _____er
    e. _____

3. a. ___etite
    b. app_____
    c. appet___
    d. _____ite
    e. _____

4. a. _____ity
    b. opp___unity
    c. ___ort_____
    d. opport_____
    e. _____

5. a. ___osite
    b. opp_____
    c. oppos___
    d. _____ite
    e. _____

Remember! This exercise is designed to help you to **spell** better. It is not a test in comprehension. It is simply a way of learning to spell a word **in stages**.

Exercise 3.
Using your imagination, write a series of **questions** and **answers** in dialogue form, using all ten double 'p' words from the list above, once only.

> **Example** 'Did Paula **approach** you about the job in Sales?'
> 'Yes, and I told her she'd have my full **support**'.

3. Double 'r' words

arrange	horrible
arrive	irritable
barrier	marriage
correspondence	quarrel
embarrass	terrible

The words **embarrass** and **marriage** are often misspelled. Underline that part of the word where the spelling error usually occurs:

- the 'ia' in marriage (often misspelled as 'ai'), and
- the **double 'r' and 's'** in embarrass.

Exercise 1.

As for double 'm' and 'n' words.

Exercise 2. Fill in the gaps in the following piece of dialogue with suitable words from the list of double 'r' words.

Mr. Dawson: Did we receive any _____ from that Sheridan man, Pamela?

Pamela: No, Sir. I did try to _____ a meeting with him, for next Wednesday, but he declined.

Mr. Dawson: Really! The cheek of the man! Is he deliberately trying to _____ me, in front of my colleagues?! Why is he creating this _____ between us, do you know?

Pamela: I've no idea, Sir.

Mr. Dawson: Well, let me know the moment any letters _____ in for me, will you?

Pamela: Of course, Sir.

(Exit Mr. Dawson. Phone rings.)

Pamela: Hello, Mr. Dawson's secretary speaking. Who's calling, please?

Mr. Sheridan: Hello, gorgeous! How's my favourite girl, then? Is that _____ old sod, Dawson, working you too hard again? Come away with me, my lovely. Ours could be a _____ made in heaven!

Pamela: Oh, Mr. Sheridan! You're a _____ man!

Mr. Sheridan: Yes, well, you've a _____ life with that bully. If you worked for me, I bet, we'd never have as much as one _____. Come on, Pamela. What do you say? Will you marry me?

The Exam; The drama continues

Exercise 3.

Continue the above dialogue, using **all ten** double 'r' words once again. Keep the same characters: Pamela, Mr. Dawson and Mr. Sheridan. You may, however, write the dialogue between just two of these characters, if you wish.

4. Double 's' words

discuss	message
essay	necessity
express	passenger
impossible	pressure
issue	scissors

Did you notice how **all** the above words have a **vowel letter** immediately in front of the double 's'? Underline these letters. It will help you to remember how to spell them.

Exercise 1.

As for double 'm' and 'n' words.

Exercise 2.

1. Having learned the spellings, can you **unjumble** these double 's' words?
     a. ENCSYISET   d. RSIOSCSS
     b. ILSPMOSEIB   e. SEPUSRER
     c. ESGSPNREA

2. Here are **synonyms** (words of similar meaning) of the remaining five double 's' words. Can you match them up?
     a. converse _____   d. concern _____
     b. convey _____   e. communication _____
     c. composition _____

    Use a thesaurus or a dictionary if you can't figure them out. All of them beginning with 'c' should help!

Exercise 3.
Now that you have your dictionary out (!), write an alphabetical list of double 's' words, beginning with 'a'. (If you've forgotten your dictionary, do this exercise for homework).

> **Example**   'a' for address
> 'b' for boss
> and so on

You can forget 'x', 'y' and 'z', but there is a 'w' word with 'ss' in it.

5. Double 't' words

attack	cottage
attempt	lettuce
attitude	matter
attractive	motto
battle	settlement

Notice that the first four words in this list begin with '**att**'. This is quite common for double 't' words. You will find a lot of '**att**' words in your dictionary. Note too how the double 't' in battle and matter is preceded by 'a' also.

Exercise 1.

As for double 'm' and 'n' words.

Exercise 2.

Here are some **definitions**, from the *Concise Oxford Dictionary*, of the words in the double 't' list. Place the correct word after each one.

1. a small simple house, especially in the country. _____
2. the act or an instance of settling. _____
3. seek to achieve or complete (a task or action). _____
4. a prolonged fight between large organised armed forces. _____
5. a composite plant, *Lactuca sativa*, with crisp edible leaves used in salads. _____
6. attracting or capable of attracting; interesting. _____
7. a sentence inscribed on some object and expressing an appropriate sentiment. _____
8. to act against with force, to seek to hurt or defeat. _____
9. a physical substance in general, as distinct from mind and spirit. _____
10. a settled opinion or way of thinking. _____

Exercise 3.

Now write one sentence of your own for each word in the double 't' list, in which the meaning/definition as given in Exercise 2 is **clear**. Words may have several meanings. I have given only one definition for each word. Look up the other possibilities in your own dictionary.

Summary – double-letter words (Units 4 and 7)

1. Remember the point I made at the beginning of Unit 4: 'One of the most common errors made in spelling double-letter words is to leave out one of the two letters.' Having exercised lots of this type of word, you should now be able to avoid making this error.

2. Make your own personal list of double-letter words – ones you frequently misspell – and practise writing them in simple, clear sentences.

3. Take a page of any short story or novel that you have read and **underline** any double-letter words you find. This will make you more aware of them, and reinforce the spelling at the same time.

4. Check your favourite magazine or newspaper for **headlines** using double-letter words, **advertisements** also.

5. Compose some shock headlines of your own, using double-letter words. For example: 'Embarrassment for Gary in *Eastenders*!'

Finally … watch that spelling!

Words at Work

Words with Attitude

Stage 1

Expressing your opinion: debates

In conversations with your friends, you constantly state your opinion or your attitude to all manner of things. It's easy in speech, isn't it? You don't have to worry about your grammar, punctuation, spelling or vocabulary. **In the exam, however, you are required to express yourself in writing.** You have to stop and really think about what you want to say. If you are asked to state your opinion or attitude, you can't simply reply (as you might in conversation) – 'That's stupid!' – and leave it at that. Explaining exactly **why** something is 'stupid' – if that is truly your opinion – requires more thought. You don't have a lot of time, so the arguments you make must be well chosen and clearly stated.

Here are some 'words with attitude' to get you started:

1. **Agreeing:**
   - I couldn't agree more with . . .
   - I am fully in agreement with . . .
   - It is a very good idea to . . .
   - I take your point.
   - It's certainly true that . . .
   - That's certainly an excellent point/idea . . .
   - The point about (topic) is extremely relevant . . .

2. **Disagreeing:**
   - I couldn't disagree more with . . .
   - I refuse to accept that . . .
   - I disagree entirely with . . .
   - On the contrary, I . . .
   - I don't accept the point that . . .
   - I must seriously question/dispute that point.
   - I'm afraid I think that's absolute rubbish/nonsense.

3. **Giving your own point of view:**
   - As far as I'm concerned . . .
   - I can see your point of view, but . . .
   - First of all I'd like to explain . . .
   - Let me explain why I feel this way.
   - It's quite clear to me that . . .
   - There can be no doubt/question that . . .
   - I'm certain/convinced that . . .
   - I do not dispute the fact that . . .
   - It's obvious that . . .
   - I feel very strongly that . . .
   - I think it is essential/necessary/important that I/we . . .

Make sure your opinion/attitude is argued sensibly, and not mere prejudice. If, for example, you were asked what could be done to reduce smoking among teenagers, it might not be too intelligent to reply: 'Shoot the tobacco manufacturers!' More reasoned arguments, supported by statistics for example, would make a better impression on the examiner.

Exercise 1.

Debating the issue; classroom activity

1. Your teacher will announce that the topic for class debate is that: **Teenagers are obsessed with themselves**.
2. He/she will first divide the class (by roll, perhaps) into **two** opposing sides. Side A – **proposing** the motion, i.e. **agreeing** with it, and Side B – **opposing** the motion, i.e. **disagreeing** with it.
3. Each half of the class must then nominate **three** students from their side to be their **team** and to debate the motion on their behalf.
4. Each side will then be given **five minutes** only to submit as many points as they can to their **three** debaters.
5. Your teacher will then call for silence, appoint a **timekeeper** from the class, and call upon Team A, Speaker 1 to propose the motion. Each team will have just **ten minutes in total** to debate their side of the argument, i.e.

Side A: proposing	Side B: opposing
Speaker 1 – max. 4 mins	Speaker 1 – max. 4 mins
Speaker 2 – max. 3 mins	Speaker 2 – max. 3 mins
Speaker 3 – max. 3 mins	Speaker 3 – max. 3 mins

Speaker 3 on each team must **sum up** for his/her side of the motion.

6. At the end of the debate, your teacher will call upon 'the house' to decide, by a show of hands, the outcome of the debate, i.e. the winning team.

N.B. The debaters must **use some or all of the 'words with attitude'** phrases from the introduction when making their points. Your teacher will monitor this.

The Exam; Personal writing

Exercise 2.

The motion for your next debate is that: **Irish people do not make foreigners welcome.** Write the speech you would make for **or** against the motion.
(Junior Cert. Higher level, 2003)

The Exam; Functional writing

Exercise 3.

(Junior Cert. Ordinary level, 2003)

Write out your argument for or against the motion that: **Footballers** or **Top Models** or **Pop Stars are paid too much.** You should be either totally **for** or totally **against** this motion. State clearly and convincingly the reasons for your opinion.

Stage 2

Sexism in words

Exercise 1.

Oral and/or written

Discuss this statement:

Almost from the moment you are born you are taught how to be a male or how to be a female . . . you were taught that being a boy is one thing, being a girl another. This is what is meant by sex-role stereotyping.

(C. Adams and R. Laurikietis, *The Gender Trap*, Book 1)

You might like to consider some of the following questions:

1. How do parents **dress** their children from babyhood on?
2. Do we use different **language** for boys and girls?
3. We give boys and girls different **toys**. Why?
4. Does our **education system** foster equality of the sexes?
5. Is it possible to avoid **sexism**?

Exercise 2.

Sexist	Neutral
chairman	chairperson
salesman	salesperson
air hostess	flight attendant
housewife	homemaker
actor/actress	actor
Mrs./Miss	Ms.
he . . .	he or she/they . . .

Make a table with the following headings: **Male Female Neutral**
Put the words below under the individual headings, depending on whether you think they apply to one heading more than another. Then write a brief comment on the choices you made for each heading.

beautiful	competitive	chatty	powerful
ambitious	kind	efficient	caring
quiet	nagging	strong	handsome
aggressive	confident	gentle	charming
shy	sympathetic	cry	confrontational
complaining	polite	rude	brutal
brave	argue	talk	discussion
gossip	weak		

Exercise 3.

Would you like to change sex for a day?

1. Take ten minutes to think about how you would spend the day as a member of the opposite sex. Make notes about what you would do and how you would behave. Would your personality change? How would it be affected? **Prepare a three-minute talk** on the imagined experience. Use the language of this unit when formulating your thoughts – not only the words from Exercise 2, but also the 'attitude' words and expressions from Stage 1.

2. **Comment on the caption** which accompanies this cartoon from an American magazine (*Collier's Weekly*) of 1903. 'What now little man?' How relevant is it to relations between the sexes today, at the start of the twenty-first century? Is this a good cartoon in your opinion? Give reasons to support your answer – using as many 'attitude' words as possible from this unit.

'What now little man?'

Stage 3

More formal words: job applications, CVs

Note: In conversation with our friends, we use informal, casual language and phrasing. However, when applying for a job, this is not appropriate. We must adopt a more formal style when we wish to present ourselves as serious and responsible candidates for a particular position. Look at this letter, written by 'Sloppy Sam', to a friend of his Dad's who runs a restaurant. Sam is looking for a holiday job.

Would you give Sam a job? I don't think so!

> Friday
>
> Howya Tony!
>
> Dad says there's a job going in your place. Can I have it? (Gis a job, yeh!!) I'm dead cool with most people and I'd say the bistro's a bit of a laugh. I'll give you a shout Tuesday to see what the story is. OK?
>
> Yours – whatever!
>
> Sam

Exercise 1. Sample letter of application

Here is a simple letter of the type that might give 'Sloppy Sam' a better chance of getting that job. I have left some blank spaces. Write out the letter into your copybook, **neatly** and very **carefully**, and fill in the blanks with words from the list below. Be especially careful with your **handwriting** and **spelling**!

> **awaiting, experience, apply, manager, advertised, cater, references, interests, interview, gained, position, faithfully, completed, available, principal**

2 Meadow Grove
Brookhaven
Blanchardstown
Dublin 15

28 June 2004

The Manager
Mac's Bistro
Bell Lane
Dublin 8

Dear Sir or Madam,
I wish to _____ for the _____ of temporary waiter, as _____ in the 'Dublin Herald' on 26 June.
    I am 15 years old, and have just _____ 3rd year in Brookhaven Community College, Blanchardstown. I have just taken the Junior Certificate examination. I am _____ the results.
    For the past year, I have had a part-time job in a local café, where I have _____ some _____ of working with the public. My _____ are: cookery, athletics and football. I am a member of my local youth club and I have helped to _____ for the members at club functions.
    I can supply _____ from the _____ of my school, Ms. A Brennan, and from the _____ of Clooney's Café, Mr. J Kelly. I am _____ for _____ at any time.
    I look forward to meeting you.
    Yours _____
    Samuel Hyland

Your Curriculum Vitae

Exercise 2.

Here is a sample Curriculum Vitae. The words come from the Latin, meaning the **'course of one's life'**. Make sure that you learn to spell these two words correctly.

A Curriculum Vitae (or **CV**) is a list of your **personal details, qualifications** and **experience**. **Layout** and **presentation** are very important. Remember that a good CV is your passport to a job interview.

Sample Curriculum Vitae

Personal details

Name	Anne Redmond
Address	Main Street, Charleville, Co. Cork
Telephone number	024-12345
Date of birth	14 August 1988
Place of birth	Cork

Educational record

Primary	1993–2001	Charleville National School
Secondary	2001–2004	Charleville Secondary School

Examination results

Junior Cert. June 2004

Subject	Higher level	Ordinary level
English	C	
Irish	C	
Maths	B	
French	B	
Home Economics	A	
Science		A
Geography		C
History		C

Work experience

Summer 2003 — General Services Ltd. Main St. Charleville — Duties: reception, secretarial, filing, switchboard

Achievements

Captain, Charleville Basketball Team
Class Prefect, 2003–2004
Assistant Manager, Charleville School Bank
Chairperson, Charleville Youth Club

Interests

Basketball, Swimming, Reading, Music

Referees

Mrs. Patricia Leahy, Office Manager,
General Services Ltd., Main Street, Charleville, Co Cork
Telephone: 024-21493
Miss Aisling Sullivan, Principal,
Charleville Secondary School, Charleville, Co. Cork
Telephone: 024-56508

Write out your own CV, in neat handwriting, into your copy. Then type it up on a computer. It will probably have a spell-check facility; however, this is not enough on its own! **Check your spellings in a dictionary**. This is really important if you want to impress a possible employer.

Sample covering letter

When you are applying for a job, you will need to write a short covering letter to accompany your CV. It should look like this.

> (your address)
>
> (date)
> The Manager (or name if you have it)
> (address)
>
> Dear Sir or Madam,
>
> I wish to apply for the position of (job) as advertised in (paper) on (date).
> I enclose a copy of my Curriculum Vitae, giving my personal details, educational record and work experience. I am available for interview at any time, and can be contacted at (phone number or address).
> Thank you for your consideration, and I look forward to meeting you.
> Yours faithfully,
> (name)

The Exam; Functional writing

Exercise 3.

Answer either (A) or (B)

A. Write a covering letter, enclosing a CV, in reply to the following advertisement:

Graham O'Sullivan

Due to expansion in Dublin City Centre,

Graham O'Sullivan Ltd. are recruiting

GENERAL ASSISTANTS

Full-Time & Part-Time
Positions Available
for our cafés
Competitive rates of pay.
Full training will be given.
Please ring **6767297** for further details or
send a copy of your CV to
14 Lr. Baggot Street, Dublin 2.

B. You need a **reference letter** from your Principal to secure a summer job. Write the letter you would like him or her to supply you with. The address you use should not be that of your actual school nor should you use your own name.

(Junior Cert. Higher level, 2001)

Unit 8

Grappling with Grammar

Prepositions and Conjunctions

Question What is a **preposition**?

Answer It is a word which:

1. links **nouns** and **pronouns** to the other words in a sentence.

Example Mary met her friend **at** the bus stop.

2. can be attached to an **adjective**.

Example 'good **at**': Donna is very good **at** sport.

3. can be attached to a **verb**.

Example 'climb **up**': I climbed **up** the hill in record time.

Question What is a **conjunction**?

Answer It is a word which links two parts of a sentence.

Example We ate fish **and** chips for weeks.

'And' is the most commonly used conjunction. Here are some more:

as, although, but, because, either, or, neither, nor, however, unless, until, that

Stage 1

Prepositions

Exercise 1.

Classroom activity, in pairs, oral

1. Decide who's A and who's B.

2. Your teacher will select pairs of students at random and call out a **preposition**, for example 'at'. Student A must compose the first half of a sentence, and Student B must then complete it, using the preposition 'at'.

> **Example** Student A: I'll meet you . . .
>
> Student B: . . . **at** the cinema!

3. A time limit of **twenty seconds** will apply each time. If a pair of students fails to complete the task in the set time, their turn passes to the next pair of students, and so on.

4. The pair of students which composes the most interesting/imaginative sentences with prepositions wins!

Exercise 2.

1. **Identify** and **underline** the prepositions in the following passage.

Sean O'Brien was very lonely and bored. He lived by himself in an old house on the edge of town and rarely spoke to anyone. Everyone thought he should have a pet for company, but the only animal he ever let into the house was a mangy mongrel with only one ear, which he christened 'Radar'. The first time he saw it, it snarled at him and Sean shouted back, 'Go on, then, you miserable one-eared mutt, get out of my yard!' To his surprise the dog immediately stopped snarling and slunk over to the corner of the house, where it sat eyeing him up from a safe distance. Mr. O'Brien stared at the dog for a while and finally said, 'Ah well, go on, then. You might as well stay, I suppose. But don't expect me to . . .'

2. Now write your own **ending** to this short tale (30–50 words). Use each of the following prepositions once only:

in, at, to, under, over, after, until, with, before, off

Exercise 3.

1. Choose any **preposition** from **Column B** which works with a word from **Column A** below.

2. Then compose a **complete sentence** for each one, which **concludes** with the words from **Column C.**

> **Example**   1. **Ashamed**: He was ashamed **of** himself for doubting her.

Column A	Column B	Column C
1. ashamed	on	everything you have done for us.
2. different	of	puzzles and word games.
3. good		football and garage music.
4. capable	from	himself for doubting her.
5. grateful	at	washing powders.
6. interested	for	everyone's safety in school.

7.	keen		Limerick and its history.
8.	responsible	to	what I had expected.
9.	similar		doing much better.
10.	allergic	in	the one we have at home.

N.B.! Different prepositions must be used after certain adjectives and verbs, depending on their context. Be careful with these, as they are often misused.

> **Example** bad **at**: He's **bad at** communication.
>
> bad **for**: Smoking is **bad for** you.

Exercise 4.

Write a **short** sentence for each of the following that clearly shows the difference in **meaning** and **usage** between the prepositions.

> **Example** good
>
> good at: She's good **at** maths.
>
> good with: He's good **with** kids
>
> good for: It's good **for** spots.

Now you do it!

1. good at: _____

  good with: _____

  good for: _____

2. familiar with: _____

  familiar to: _____

3. annoyed at: _____

  annoyed with: _____

  annoyed about: _____

4. decide to: _____

  decide on: _____

5. sensitive to: _____

  sensitive about: _____

6. disgusted at: _____

  disgusted with: _____

Stage 2

Conjunctions

Note: The words '**and**' and '**but**' are the most frequently used conjunctions, but there are others! Try to avoid overusing 'and' in particular, as the result is often a long, rambling sentence that merely confuses the reader.

Exercise 1. Link the situations in Column A to those in Column C, with a suitable **conjunction** from Column B. Write out the complete sentence each time, **underlining** the conjunctions as you write.

Column A	Column B	Column C
1. We got wet through	even though	I ate a huge lunch.
2. Our team seldom wins	so	ugly.
3. He never changes his mind	because	you're ready or not.
4. She's not giving in	or	it didn't matter because we won.
5. We often go to a disco	but	I can afford it.
6. Arnie is tall, dark	and	he's decided something.
7. I'm still hungry	unless	the other side is seriously bad.
8. Dad's leaving now, Sharon,	until	a club at the weekend.
9. I haven't got the money,	once	the others give up.
10. I run an expensive car	whether	sue me!

Exercise 2. Insert suitable conjunctions of your own into the spaces in this story:

Cormac and Elaine lived in the States _____ five years. _____ they were living there, Elaine had twins. She was attending university at the time, _____ it was difficult coping with the twins _____ study. _____ she had her degree, they decided to come home _____ both Cormac and Elaine felt they wanted to bring the kids up in Ireland. _____ they had _____ save a lot of money, they were happy. Elaine worked _____ a computer firm _____ Cormac _____ a building society.

Exercise 3. Use these ten conjunctions in the sentences below, as appropriate:

as far as, wherever, during, providing, as long as, as if, therefore, however, although, whereas

1. _____ I go, I seem to bump into my ex-boyfriend.
2. He looked _____ he'd seen a ghost.
3. You can borrow books from the library _____ you bring them back.
4. Where's Hannah? In class, _____ I know.
5. They really shouldn't talk _____ the concert.

6. Tom works really hard _____ Anne just couldn't be bothered.

7. _____ you're here, you may as well give me a hand.

8. There has been no rain for ages. _____ we have to be careful how much water we use. (Two sentences)

9. _____ I hated study, I decided to stay on at school.

10. There's no talking to him _____ hard I try.

The Exam; Personal writing, drama

Exercise 4.

Write **a short piece of dialogue** (one A4 page or two copybook pages) between **two characters**, which takes place **before**, **during** or **after** one of the following situations:

1. a family wedding
2. a confrontation of some kind
3. a visit to an elderly relation
4. a first date
5. a job interview

N.B.! Use as many **conjunctions** from Exercises 1–3 as possible but avoid **repeating** 'and' and 'but'!

Stage 3

Prepositions again

Look at these two sentences:

1. I'm interested in collecting posters. (gerund)
2. I'm interested in **posters**. (noun)

Certain prepositions can be followed by either a **verb** with 'ing' (the gerund) or by a **noun**. Here are the most common ones:

good at	tired of	bad at
responsible for	keen on	anxious about
fond of	capable of	afraid of
sick of		

Exercise 1.

Can you complete the following sentences with the gerund ('ing') **and** a noun, in each case?

> **Example** George is very good at:
> George is very good at play**ing** the concertina.
> George is very good at **Maths**.

		Gerund	Noun
1.	Rita is **keen on**	a. _____	b. _____
2.	Gráinne is **fond of**	a. _____	b. _____
3.	Tom is **afraid of**	a. _____	b. _____
4.	The principal is **responsible for**	a. _____	b. _____
5.	Sometimes, teenagers are **bad at**	a. _____	b. _____
6.	Mum is **anxious about**	a. _____	b. _____
7.	Horror films are **capable of**	a. _____	b. _____
8.	Irish people are **sick of**	a. _____	b. _____
9.	I'm really **tired of**	a. _____	b. _____

Exercise 2.

Verbs plus prepositions

Look at these two sentences:

1. He drank **in** the beauty of the scene.
2. He drank **to** his daughter's success.

Again, we see that **a change in preposition** results in **a change in meaning**.

Complete the following sentences with a suitable preposition after the verb, **according to the meaning**. Be very careful which one you choose (in, at, to, etc.). Don't just guess! Check your dictionary if you're not sure.

1. Burglars broke _____ their house.
2. Kevin broke _____ the champagne after the match.
3. They died _____ their beliefs.
4. Children in the Sudan are dying _____ starvation.
5. She's always comparing me _____ him.
6. Shakespeare compared her _____ 'a summer's day'.
7. David was leaning _____ the car.
8. Simon was leaning _____ David for support.
9. Uncle Shane provided _____ her in his will.
10. Tim provided his sister _____ a car.
11. Colm swore _____ the man for his bad driving.
12. She swore _____ the Bible she was telling the truth.
13. Susan was treated _____ her acne in Dublin.
14. Betty treated her friend _____ a meal.

The Exam; Functional writing

Exercise 3.

1. Read this letter to Shirley and **highlight or underline** all the prepositions and conjunctions.

2. Write a reply to Lovesick J. Verona in 120–180 words, giving your own advice to the correspondent. Use prepositions and conjunctions appropriately throughout your letter. Make good use of all those you've exercised in this unit!

Where does my duty lie?

Dear Shirley,

I am 13 and madly in love with the boy who lives in the villa next door.

Unfortunately, our parents don't get on, and mine have forbidden me to have any contact with him. The local vicar has agreed to marry us secretly, and I am on the point of agreeing to this, as my parents are insisting that I marry a friend of the family, whom I hate.

I would rather die than leave the man I love. What should I do? Should I give up family and home for him, or should I bend to my parents' wishes?

Lovesick J. Verona.

And finally . . . a joke!

Teacher: *What will you get if you use too many conjunctions, Peter?*
Peter: *Conjunctionitis, Sir!*

Punctuation Please!

Brackets, Blobs and Dots

Stage 1

Brackets ( )

Question   When do we use brackets (also called parentheses)?

Answer   1.   When adding **extra information**.

Example   The Second World War (**1939–45**) cost millions of lives.

2.   When inserting **an explanation**.

Example   Fiona (**Peter's boss**) is in London.

   3.   When giving **references**.

Example   A discussion of the key points is given below (**see p. 46**).

   4.   When enclosing optional words.

Example   There are many (**obvious**) problems.

In this example, the '**optional**' word means that the problems **may** or **may not** be obvious.

   5.   When explaining foreign words, especially Latin phrases:

Example   My attitude to life is *carpe diem* (seize the day).

Warning! Be wary of brackets. Many students use them to support badly written sentences. Instead of crossing out the entire sentence and starting over, they stick in a bracket or two, in order to sort out their thoughts. However, this often results in confused, misshapen expression, which looks dreadful and is difficult to read.

Example   Sandra (who didn't know it at the time) was being two-timed by Simon (who already had a girlfriend in Waterford) but nobody (not even her best friend) would tell her (poor Sandra!).

Here is how the above should read:

Example   Sandra didn't know it at the time, but Simon was two-timing her. He already had a girlfriend in Waterford but nobody (not even her best friend) would tell her.

The second version is clearer, and makes one long sentence into two more balanced ones. Using brackets once is quite acceptable. So the rule is: use brackets only where absolutely necessary or correct in terms of usage, as in Examples 1–5 in the introduction.

Exercise 1.   Insert appropriate **extra information** into the brackets in the following sentences:

1. During the Second World War (_____) Ireland remained neutral.
2. Mary McAleese (_____) is visiting the States at the moment.
3. Nobody (_____) would tell him. Poor Tom!
4. Cork (_____) is the capital of the South.
5. Brian Kerr (_____) is scouting for new players.
6. Mr. Mulvihill (_____) was busy putting up Fire Safety notices.
7. My Grandad used to always say *tempus fugit* (_____)
8. She (_____) re-vamped her image yet again for the film *Evita*.

9. So the students (_____) came up with a great idea.
10. Mark (_____) is leaving school.

Exercise 2. Insert brackets where **appropriate** in the following sentences:

1. Susie told me but I can't believe it that Mr. Mason is in love with Miss Breen.
2. The guard at least I think he was a guard told me I couldn't go in.
3. Arsenal will be without their key striker Dennis Bergkamp for the match against Chelsea today. Live on BBC1, 5.15.
4. For a discussion of the effect on the environment of pesticides see below Ch. 4, p. 73.
5. Chinese Foreign Minister Mr. Tang Jiaxuan said: 'There is no reason to shut the door to peace'. *The Irish Times*, Saturday 8 March 2003.

Exercise 3. Now write five sentences of your own, in which you insert brackets only once per sentence, in order to provide extra information or an optional word.

Stage 2

Blobs ●

Question When do we use blobs (also called bullet points)?

Answer Actually, there are no set rules here! One writer referred to this punctuation mark as 'the invasion of the blobs'. They are a fairly recent phenomenon, having 'invaded' newspapers some years ago. You'll now find them in magazines, advertisements and word-processing packages. Most books on punctuation don't mention them at all. But since they seem to be here to stay, you might as well learn how to use them!

Blobs are often used when giving **information** in short points, as in a list of items.

Example The town has many tourist attractions:
- stunning scenery
- a beautiful sandy beach
- a heritage centre
- a reputation for good craic.

Exercise 1.

1. Rewrite the following instruction and list of items with **one** colon (:) and **four** blobs.

If you intend eating corn-on-the-cob without getting butter all over your face, you'll need a large plate strong grips for the cob a very absorbent napkin equally messy friends.

2. Rewrite the following, deciding for yourself how many blobs are required (**one colon** is also necessary).

    Let me make some final comments about painting wash the brushes immediately after painting replace the lids tightly on the cans wash your hands thoroughly with spirit and soap don't lick the paint brushes wash the dog.

The Exam; Media studies

Exercise 2.

1. Here is an advertisement for the Ferrycarrig Hotel in Wexford. Can you rewrite the information contained in the ad into **seven blob points**? The first one is done for you.

    - Every luxurious bedroom and suite enjoys a spectacular view over the wonderful Slaney estuary.

Check out our views before you book your next break.

At the Ferrycarrig Hotel Wexford, every luxurious bedroom and suite enjoys a spectacular view over the wonderful Slaney estuary.

In addition we've a fabulous health and fitness club and golf on our clifftop course at St. Helen's Bay.

Our cuisine is as stunning as the views from both our beautifully appointed restaurants. Located just two hours from Dublin, it's our view that no other hotel can compare for your next break.

To find out more about our great Spring and Summer offers call us on 1890 51 61 71 now.

Ferrycarrig Hotel

The peace of Ireland you've been dreaming of.

---

2. Here is another advertisement for two hotels, which uses blobs to highlight points of information. This time, **rewrite one of these lists of blob points** in the form of a longer piece (as in the Ferrycarrig Hotel ad) expanding on the attractions of the hotel, in **full sentences**.

Sinnott
HOTELS

Connemara Coast
HOTEL ★★★★
Furbo, Galway
Tel. (091) 592108
- Breathtaking Views
- Grounds sweeping down to the shores of Galway Bay
- Leisure Centre
- Black & White Hotel Bar of the Year
- 10 mins. from Galway City

Connemara Gateway
HOTEL ★★★
Oughterard, Co Galway
Tel. (091) 552328
- Indoor heated pool and sauna
- Various walking and driving routes
- Cottage Style Bar
- Fishing & Golf nearby
- 20 mins. from Galway City

Stage 3

Dots . . .

Question When do we use dots (also called points of ellipsis)?

1. When we want to show that:

   a. words have been left out, as in a **quotation**, for example.

Example '. . . man, proud man,
Dress'd in a little brief authority, . . .'
(William Shakespeare)

   b. a **statement** is deliberately left **unfinished**.

Example Even before the match was half over, I thought, 'Well . . .'

2. In **advertising**, between short groups of words for emphasis (but this is not acceptable in more formal writing).

Example Don't hesitate . . . send for your free brochure today.

3. In textbooks, examination papers and business correspondence to indicate **words** to be filled in.

Example Textbook: Here are some sentence starters for letters:
   ● I am delighted to inform you that . . .
   ● I regret to inform you that . . .
   Exams: The four kinds of citrus fruits are . . .
   Business: Enclosed please find € . . . for . . . videos at € . . . each.

Rules:

1. Writers always use **three** dots. There is absolutely no reason for this number, but it has become standard practice.

2. A **full line** of dots indicates that a **whole paragraph** or more has been left out from a quoted passage. It may also show the omission of one or more **lines of poetry**.

Example I wandered lonely as a cloud . . . .
. . . . a host of golden daffodils.

3. Dots are always placed **inside** quotation marks, whether they fall at the beginning or end of the sentence.

> **Example**   Tom said, '. . . and let me assure you, I wouldn't have done that even if . . .'

Exercise 1.   Which words (indicated by dots) have been left out of these well-known quotations?

1. 'A four foot box . . . Year' (Seamus Heaney, 'Mid-term Break')
2. 'Romeo, Romeo . . . Romeo?' (William Shakespeare, *Romeo and Juliet*)
3. 'To be . . . question.' (William Shakespeare, *Hamlet*)
4. 'I am . . . world!' (Leonardo DiCaprio in *Titanic*)
5. A stitch . . . nine. (Proverb)
6. 'Ask not . . . for you, but what you . . . country.'
    (John Fitzgerald Kennedy, President of the USA)
7. All work . . . a dull boy. (Proverb)
8. 'I can resist . . . temptation.' (Oscar Wilde)
9. 'Nothing . . . you.' (song, sung by Sinead O'Connor)
10. A Mars a day . . . play. (Advertising slogan)

Exercise 2.   Write ten cliffhanger-style sentences, ending in three dots.

> **Example**   It was at that precise moment that I realised I could die . . .

The Exam; Reading

Exercise 3.

In exams, you are often asked to refer to, or quote from, a text. Students often make the error of quoting whole chunks of text, instead of employing dots to indicate the section being discussed. This is a useful tactic and a practical, time-saving device.

Read the following *Cosmo* magazine article on Dannii Minogue. Answer the questions below, employing dots and quotation marks to indicate the part of the text you wish to highlight.

So Dannii, your teens are a notorious time for feeling body conscious. How was it for you?

My younger teens were fine, but my latter teens were harder. I moved to Britain when I was 18 or 19. I wasn't fat but I wasn't skinny. Everyone knew Kylie and they'd

'People teased me for being fat'

It's hard to believe Dannii Minogue was ever criticised for her shape when she was a teen. She tells CG! how she refused to let people make her feel paranoid.

say like, 'You're fatter than her,' or, 'You're this, you're that, you're not like her,' and that was exactly true, I wasn't her. I was a completely different person. Most people would have taken it on board and probably developed anorexia and bulimia but thankfully I didn't.

Why do you think that was?

I started working when I was seven and I was surrounded by older people so I think I matured quicker. I realised everyone comes in different shapes and refused to let it get to me. I've always been true to myself and it's stood me in good stead. But when I turned 21 I lost all the weight. It just fell off.

Did people treat you differently?

It was interesting to see people's reactions to my weight loss. It was definitely a time when I realised who my real friends were. People wanted to hang out with me, but I wasn't going to fall for that because I was exactly the same person inside. A couple of years before they didn't want to know!

'Kylie was the rebellious one and I was the goody two shoes!'

Were you always fairly confident as a teen?

I guess I was, but I never thought about the whole body issue that much. I know people talk about how bad it is for kids these days with the intense pressure to be thin but for me, when I was in my early teens, it never felt that way. I never felt any pressure to look a certain way.

So you were always independent?

I was lucky in that I had parents who let me be myself. My friends felt more pressure from their parents telling them what they had to do with their lives. I was so lucky my parents supported me and let me do what my heart wanted me to do.

You had cool parents?

I think they were wise. My parents are like my friends and are still very much part of my life. I wasn't a rebellious child and I think it's because my parents never forced me into being something I wasn't. Kylie was the rebellious one because she was the oldest and was always testing the boundaries. I saw her go through it and learnt from it, and knew what the rules were. I was the goody two shoes, but people don't see us like that. They assume I'm the rebellious one and she's the goody goodie! CG

Cosmo, March 2003

1. How did Dannii feel about her weight as a teenager?
2. When she lost weight, how did people react to her weight loss?
3. According to Dannii, was she confident as a teen?
4. Describe her parents' attitude to her when she was a teenager.
5. How does she describe her relationship with her older sister, Kylie, at this time?

How Do You Spell . . .?

Silent-letter Words 2

In this unit you will be exercising silent-letter words from 'k' to 'w'.

1. Silent 'k' words

knack	knit
knapsack	knock
knee	knot
knife	know
knight	knowledge

Notice how all the above words begin with '**kn**', and except for 'knapsack' and 'knowledge', they are all words of **one syllable**.

The word '**know**' is often misspelled as '**now**', so watch that one! Again, **underline** the 'k' in each word. It will really help you to remember it.

Exercise 1.

1. Study the ten words above for five minutes in class. Remember it will be easier to learn these spellings because each word contains a **silent** 'k' and they are written in **alphabetical** order.

2. When the five minutes are up, your teacher will call out each word in the order in which you have learned them. Write them out, one underneath the other, in a list, being very careful with those **silent** 'k's!

3. Exchange your copy with the person next to you. You will now correct his/hers, and he/she will do likewise with yours. Please refer to the **original spelling list** when correcting each word.

4. Give **one** mark for each word spelled correctly, and a total mark out of ten.

5. If a word has been spelled **incorrectly**, cross it out and write the **correct** spelling of the word beside it, again checking from the original list.

6. Take back your own copy and write out any words **you** have spelled incorrectly, **five times** each.

Exercise 2.

1. Complete the pattern as shown in the example.

(Example)	knit	knits	knitted	knitting
a.	know	_____	_____ *	_____
b.	knock	_____	_____	_____
c.	knot	_____	_____	_____
d.	kneel	_____	_____ *	_____
e.	knead	_____	_____	_____

* Be careful with these two, they're **irregular**!

2. Write **one** question and **one** answer to that question, using the following silent 'k' words once only:

knife, knew, knack, knickers, knot, knick-knack, knight, knave, kneecap, knelt

(Example)	Q.	What's a **knave**?
	A.	Dunno. I wish I **knew**!

Compare your questions and answers with the student beside you. Give a mark out of ten for humour and originality!

Exercise 3. Supply the missing silent 'k' word for each of the following sentences – without referring to the original list. (Nos. 1, 3 and 4 have **slight** variations in spelling.)

1. In Home Economics class last week, Darren _____ over a whole pan of pancake batter.
2. He'd _____ you as soon as look at you!
3. 'Get _____!' he said, rudely.
4. Sheila hates _____. She prefers to buy jumpers in a shop.
5. It's common _____ that Ireland is a very popular holiday destination.
6. Colm did his _____ in, playing rugby.
7. Dad is my _____ in shining armour.
8. There's a real _____ to making a good Irish coffee.
9. Tom always _____ that Julie fancied him.
10. 'Oh no! I think I've left my _____ on the bus!'

Now, **check** your list to see if you've spelled the words correctly.

2. Silent 'l' words

balm	calf	chalk	could
calm	half	walk	should
			would

Notice that the above words are not written in alphabetical order, but in **three rhyming pairs** and **one trio of rhyming words**. This should make it easier to learn the spellings.

Exercise 1.

As for silent 'k' words.

Exercise 2.

1. Complete the rhyme:

   chalk,   walk,   t ———
   balm,   calm,   p ———

2. Write one sentence in which 'could', 'would' and 'should' are all used.

   (Example) 'If I **could** afford to go I **would**, as you **should** realise by now.'

3. Unjumble the following words from the silent 'l' list, and write them into the space provided:

   a. D U O W L _____   d. A H K L C _____
   b. L F A C _____   e. H L D S O U _____
   c. M L B A _____

The Exam; The drama continues

Exercise 3.

Write a short piece of **dialogue** between two characters in which each of the silent 'l' words is used just once and is underlined. Here is an opening question to get you started, but you may of course compose your own.

Pat: You're being very **calm** about this, aren't you?

3. Silent 'n' and 'p' words

Silent 'n'	Silent 'p'
autumn	cupboard
condemn	pneumonia
damn	psalm
hymn	psychic
solemn	receipt

1.   Notice that all the silent 'n' words have an '**m**' in front of them – so the ending is '**mn**'. Link the '**m**' and '**n**' together in your mind, and you should get the spelling right.

2.   Silent 'p' words are difficult to spell correctly, so learn these well. **Underline the '**p**'** in each word. '**Receipt**' and '**cupboard**' need special care, as they are often misspelled.

Exercise 1.

As for silent 'k' words.

Exercise 2.

1.   **Correct the spelling** in the following words, by replacing their silent '**n**' or '**p**' as appropriate.

colum	receit
sychology	neumatic
rasberry	salm
dam	solem
hym	condemed

2.   Now write one **negative** sentence for each correctly spelled world.

> (**Example**)   She **didn't** give me a **receipt**.

Quiz; what is it, then?

Exercise 3.

Here are **definitions** of some silent 'n' and 'p' words, taken from the *Concise Oxford Dictionary*. Can you identify them? (Your teacher may allow you to work on these in pairs, or give the exercise to you for homework as an individual challenge.)

   Clue: Most of them are from your list or Exercise 2. Learn the **spellings** as you are doing this exercise.

1. A bramble, Rubus idaeus, having usually red berries. _____
2. a fictitious name, especially one assumed by an author. _____
3. a skin disease marked by red scaly patches. _____
4. found guilty, convicted, assigned to something unwelcome or painful.
   _____
5. an upright cylindrical pillar often slightly tapering and usually supporting an arch, or standing alone as a monument. _____
6. considered to have occult powers, such as telepathy, clairvoyance, etc.
   _____
7. a large extinct flying bird-like reptile with a long slender head and neck. (Last seen in Jurassic Park!) _____
8. serious and dignified; accompanied by ceremony. _____
9. a song of praise, especially to God in Christian worship. _____
10. a recess or piece of furniture with a door and shelves, in which things are stored.
    _____

4. Silent 's' and 't' words

Silent 's'	Silent 't'	
aisle	bustle	listen
Carlisle*	castle	mistletoe
demesne**	christen	mortgage
island	fasten	thistle
isle	hustle	whistle

* A town in Cumbria, England.

** Pronounced: dem-aine.

1. There are very few silent 's' words, but they are often misspelled. The silent 't' words are more numerous. Did you notice that in six of the list words, the silent 't' is followed by '**le**'; in three of the words by '**en**', and **the odd man out is 'mortgage'**?
2. How do you say the word 'often' – pronouncing the 't' or not? Both ways are correct, but you must always remember to **spell** it with 't'!

Exercise 1.

As for silent 'k' words.

Exercise 2.   Answer the following questions with words from the silent 's' and 't' lists.

1. Which list word rhymes with 'bustle'? _____
2. Which list word rhymes with 'thistle'? _____
3. What do we kiss under at Christmas? _____
5. What does the bride walk up, to reach the altar? _____?
6. What is land attached to a mansion or estate called? _____

7.   What can we build from sand? _____

8.   What must we pay for twenty or twenty-five years, when we buy a house? _____

9.   What is the symbol of Scotland? _____

10. Can you complete the phrase, 'clean as a _____'?

The Exam; Media studies

Exercise 3.

Can you place **two or more** of the list words together with some words of your own, so that they make sense as the **title** or heading of a **newspaper or magazine article**?

> (**Example**)   Carlisle Castle: the legend unfolds
> Christmas hustle and bustle

Try to write ten titles/headings, or more if you can! Use your imagination, but remember to **spell** the list words correctly.

5. Silent 'u' words

biscuit	guest
building	guide
buoy	guitar
colour*	honour*
guarantee	labour*

* These words are often misspelled, because **American** English does not have a 'u' in them.

Lots of silent 'u' words begin with '**gu**', as do four of the above. Also, you will always find a '**u**' **after the letter** 'q', for example **queue**, **quest**.

Exercise 1.

As for silent 'k' words.

Exercise 2.

1.   Complete the pattern as shown in the example.

> (**Example**)   colour   colours   coloured   colouring

a.	guarantee	_____	_____	_____
b.	guide	_____	_____	_____
c.	honour	_____	_____	_____
d.	labour	_____	_____	_____
e.	build	_____	_____ *	_____

* Be careful! An irregular one.

2. Write **one** question and **one** answer for each of the remaining five words on the list, using the **same** word in both question and answer.

> **Example**   'Which **biscuits** do you prefer, Monica?'
> 'Oh, I like chocolate **biscuits**, Tom.'

Exercise 3. Use your **dictionary** to find the words defined below. **They all begin with 'gu'.** Write them into the spaces provided, being very careful with the **spelling**.

1. a dish of mashed avocado pears mixed with chopped onion, tomatoes, chilli peppers and seasoning. _____
2. to watch over and defend or protect from harm. _____
3. a defender, protector, or keeper. _____
4. a small tropical American tree, bearing an edible pale yellow fruit with pink juicy flesh. _____
5. a breed of dairy cattle from an island of this name. _____
6. a member of a small independently acting (usually political) group taking part in irregular fighting against larger forces. _____
7. to estimate without calculation or measurement, or on the basis of inadequate data. _____
8. A book of information about a place for visitors, tourists etc. _____
9. a machine with a heavy knife-blade sliding vertically in grooves, used for beheading. _____
10. culpable of, or responsible for, a wrong. _____

6. Silent 'w' words

wrap	wrinkle
wreck	wrist
wren	write
wrestle	writing
wriggle	wrong

Notice that each word begins with '**wr**', and the sound is 'r'. Just remember to put the 'w' in front! Underline the 'w' in each word. Keep it **visible**, so you don't forget it, when learning the spellings.

Exercise 1.

As for silent 'k' words.

Exercise 2.

1. Which five words from the above list are hidden in the boxes? Each word is in two parts. Spell out the completed word, and write it into the space beside the boxes.

K L E	I N G
G G L E	W R
W R I T	W R
A P	W R I N
O N G	W R I

1. _____

2. _____

3. _____

4. _____

5. _____

2. Now make your own boxes for the remaining five words in the list. Swop copies with your neighbour. Give yourselves a time limit of one minute to figure out the words, and to **write them out**. The one who finishes first, and whose words are **spelled correctly**, wins!

The Exam; Media studies

Exercise 3.   Write ten funny or shocking **newspaper headlines**, or ten **captions/ catchphrases** advertising a product or service using the silent 'w' words from your list.

> (**Example**)   'Wriggle that bum for charity!'

Words at Work

Words at Play: Puns, Proverbs and Quotable Quotes

Pun fun

What's made from custard and jelly, stands in the middle of Paris and wobbles?
The Trifle Tower.

What do French kids eat for breakfast?
Huit heures bix.

What do cats eat for breakfast?
Mice Crispies.

Watch Your Language!

Which cake wanted to rule the world?

Attila the Bun.

Teacher: What does illegal mean?

Dick: A sick bird of prey.

Jokes are a good place to start, because many of them depend on **puns** – the use of words that **sound** the same, but have different meanings. We often say that 'puns' are words that **play** on two or more meanings. The word 'pun' itself dates from the seventeenth century, and may have come from the now obsolete word, 'pundrigion', meaning 'a fanciful formation'. The jokes above are certainly that!

Exercise 1. Here are some 'school' jokes. Can you **identify and explain** the pun in each one?

Joke 1. Teacher: 'I wish you'd pay a little more attention. Peter!'

Peter: 'I'm paying as little as I can, Sir.'

Joke 2. Teacher: 'If we breathe oxygen during the day, Tracy, what do we breathe at night?'

Tracy: 'Nitrogen, Miss.'

Joke 3. Richard: 'Here Liam, why do the other lads in the team call me Cinderella?'

Liam: ''Cause you keep running away from the ball!'

Joke 4. Teacher: 'Right, class. What's the difference between lightening and electricity?'

Class: 'You don't get bills for lightening, Miss!'

Joke 5. Teacher: 'What's the formula for water, Marie?'

Marie: 'Em . . . em . . . H, I, J, K, L, M, N, O, Miss.'

Teacher: 'That's ridiculous, Marie! Where did you get that answer from?'

Marie: 'Paul, Miss. He said it was H to O.'

Exercise 2.

1. The titles of these books all relate to the **names** of their authors. Match each title to its most **suitable** author, from the box below.

> (**Example**) *The Burglar* by Robin Banks
>
> **a.** *Asking Questions* by _____
>
> **b.** *Punctuality Please* by _____
>
> **c.** *Songs for Assembly* by _____
>
> **d.** *Cliff Walks* by _____
>
> **e.** *Feet First* by _____
>
> **f.** *Greeting your Class* by _____

O. Wye, T. O. Proudfoot, A. L. Wayslate, L. O. Kidz, Hal E. Looyah, Lee Anne Dover

2. Now invent some funny titles of your own for the following authors.

> **Example** | Mary Higginbottom, **Mystery at Rear End**
>> a. Eva Brick _____
>> b. Luke Warm _____
>> c. L. R. Driver _____
>> d. Mona Lott _____
>> e. I. Basham _____

Exercise 3. Complete these sentences by adding a person's name from the list below. Your answers must reflect the use of a pun. Say the names **aloud** before you make your choice.

Abigail, Jack, Ernest, Isobel, Bridget, Robin, Herman, Carol, Frank, Rose

1. 'Can you help me change this wheel?' asked _____.
2. 'Zat is my voman!' yelled _____.
3. 'I burgle banks,' said _____.
4. 'Ring me at six,' said _____.
5. 'Are you really serious about this?' asked _____.
6. 'It'll be windy tonight,' remarked _____.
7. 'I cross that river every day,' said _____.
8. 'He's a real thorn in my side moaned _____.
9. 'Are you being totally honest with me?' Asked _____.
10. 'I love all those old Christmas hymns, don't you?' said _____.

Stage 2

Puns in newspapers and advertising

Newspaper headlines frequently use puns to catch the reader's attention.

> **Example** | 1. The Budget: A Matter of Life and Debt
>> 2. Smoking Bill comes under fire
>> 3. Zidane the Man!
>> 4. France for the Coup!

Exercise 1. Explain each of the puns in the **four** examples above.

Exercise 2. Here are some examples of **alliterative** puns from newspapers.

N.B.! These all have the **same letter** at the beginning of two or more words, for example, Sonia and shines.

1. SONIA SHINES BY THE LEE
2. CHILE CON-CARNAGE
3. BUZZING BELFAST
4. HENMAN IN A HURRY
5. The Beauty of Bali

    a. What does the word '**shines**' refer to in No. 1? How does it relate to Sonia O'Sullivan?

    b. What does the word '**carnage**' mean in No. 2? How might it relate to the word '**Chile**'? What type of situation or event might it refer to?

    c. Could No. 3 be from a Northern Ireland tourism promotion? If so, what might '**buzzing**' mean in this context?

    d. Who is Henman? Why is he in a hurry? (clue: Tennis)

The Exam; Media studies

Exercise 3.

Note: Political cartoons often parody (mock) the ruling political party of the day, as in this cartoon from *The Irish Times* (10 March 2003).

Examine this cartoon carefully and answer the following questions.

1. Is there anything about the cartoon that suggests to you that it might be a 'spoof' (fake) advertisement for a Harry Potter film?

2. What features of a **genuine** advertisement for a film can you identify in it?

3. Rewrite the text so that it reads like a **proper** advertisement for a Harry Potter movie.

N.B.! See the Media Studies section of the 2003 Higher level paper for a similar exercise.

Stage 3

Proverbs and quotable quotes

Proverbs

This cartoon is an example of a well-known **proverb**. No doubt you have quoted it many times yourself in order to persuade your parents that you're working too hard!

Proverbs are **sayings in common use that contain a widely accepted truth, or 'pearl' of wisdom.** There is an adjective – 'proverbial' – which is often used to describe someone or something that is as well known

All work and no play makes Jack a dull boy.

as a proverb, for example 'his proverbial honesty', or something that is typical, for example 'our proverbial summer weather!'

Exercise 1. Let's see how many you know! Complete these ten proverbs, in under two minutes. Your teacher will time you.

1. Too many cooks . . .
2. You can't have your cake . . .
3. Don't put all your eggs . . .
4. The family that prays together . . .
5. Birds of a feather . . .
6. Every cloud . . .
7. It's no use crying . . .
8. All's well that . . .
9. People in glasshouses . . .
10. Empty vessels . . .

Swop copies with your neighbour and correct each other's work. Your teacher will call out the endings. Award one mark for each correctly completed proverb. The student with the most marks is . . . a proverbial proverb person!

Exercise 2. Write a **short piece of dialogue** between two people in which each of these proverbs is used **once** only.

1. Blood is thicker than water.
2. Don't look a gift horse in the mouth.
3. Little children should be seen and not heard.
4. Never say die.
5. It never rains but it pours.

Note: Sometimes proverbs are **misquoted** and completed in a humorous way.

> **Example** 'Where there's a will, there's a way.' could become:
> 'Where there's a will, there's a **relative**.'
>   or
> 'He who hesitates is lost.' could become:
> 'He who hesitates is . . . **er** . . . **er**!'

Watch Your Language!

Exercise 3.

Individual or in pairs

Try completing these proverbs in a humorous way. (Your teacher might allow you to work in pairs on this, either in class or as an assignment to be completed in a few days, for example.) Your classmates and teacher will judge which student or students have produced the funniest proverb.

You can be as silly as you like as long as the two halves of your proverb **relate** to each other in some way – as with puns.

> (**Example**) A rolling stone . . . is an ageing rocker!

1. Many hands make . . .
2. A bird in the hand . . .
3. Better late . . .
4. Too many cooks . . .
5. There's no smoke . . .
6. When in Rome . . .
7. An apple a day . . .
8. Absence makes . . .
9. Great minds . . .
10. A rolling stone . . .

Quotable quotes

Quotations are extremely useful, especially when writing **essays**, preparing **debates/talks**, and **supporting** points being made in exercises or exams. When stuck for an opening (or a conclusion) to an essay, for example, a quotation can capture the key issue or mood of the piece. It will also focus the attention of the examiner on the point(s) being made.

Quotations need not always be taken from literature. **Songs, cartoons, jokes, magazines, advertisements, TV, billboards, witty remarks by famous people** – all are valid.

And finally . . . some quotable quotes.

Here are some that you might like, followed by some suggestions on how you might use them for exam practice.

1. *People ought to be one of two things, young or old. No – what's the use of fooling? People ought to be one of two things, young or dead.*

   Dorothy Parker (American wit in the 1930s)

Suggestions:

● **Debate**: 'Youth is wasted on the young' or 'Ageism is rampant among the young' or 'Young people despise the old'

● **Personal writing** (Junior Cert. Ordinary level, 2003): 'Life can't really be enjoyed until you leave school'

2. *'Four be the things I'd been better without. Love, curiosity, freckles, and doubt.'*

Suggestions:

- **Debate:** 'Teenagers are obsessed with image'
- **Personal writing** (Junior Cert. Higher level, 1998): You have been asked to write a humorous article or essay for the school magazine and have been given the freedom to choose your own title. Write out the article/essay you would submit.

3.   *The name's Bond – James Bond. Licensed to, er, thrill.*

Magazine

Suggestions:

- **Debate:** 'It's still a man's world'
- **Essay:** 'Bores'
- **Magazine article:** 'Boring males **or** females I have known'

4.   *I'm an instant star, just add water and stir.*

David Bowie (singer)

Suggestions:

- **Debate:** 'Pop idols are not real. They're custom-made machines.'
- **Personal Writing:** (Junior Cert. Higher level, 2003): 'I wish I could live that day again'
- **Magazine article:** 'Stars in their eyes' – Interview with 'Girls Aloud'

5.   *Macho does not prove mucho.*

Zsa Zsa Gabor (actress)

Suggestions:

- **Debate:** 'Macho males do not impress' **or** 'It's still a man's world'

6.   *No one's free – even the birds are chained to the sky.*

Bob Dylan (singer)

Suggestions:

- **Personal Writing:** 'What freedom means to me'
- **Newspaper article:** 'Prisoners of conscience, Amnesty International'
- **Poem** inspired by this quote.

7.   *Twas in a restaurant they met,*
      Romeo and Juliet,
      He had no cash to pay the debt,
      So Romeo'd while Juliet.

Vernon Naismith (American wit)

Suggestions:

- **Class debate:** 'The relevance of Shakespeare today'
- A four-line funny **poem** about **another** two characters from a Shakespearean play, or any play.

8.   *All books are either dreams or swords: you can cut, or you can drug, with words.*
                    Amy Lowell (poet, 1874–1925)

Suggestions:
- **Personal Writing**: 'The power of the leabhar'
- **Debate**: 'Literature is a load of dead people in books'
- **Poem**: Write eight or ten lines entitled '**WORDWARP**' or anything to do with words.

9.   *I wish I'd been a mixed infant.*
                    Brendan Behan (*The Hostage*, Act 2)

Suggestions:
- **Debate**: 'Co-education is best'
- **Personal Writing**: 'Memories of primary school' or 'My funniest childhood memory'
- **Personal Writing**: (Junior Cert. Ordinary level, 2003): Write a story which at some point includes the sentence: 'I was only messing – honestly!'

10.   *Keep violence in the mind. Where it belongs.*
                    Brian Aldiss (writer)
                    (from *Barefoot in the Head*, 1969 – last two lines of concluding poem 'Charteris')

Suggestions:
- **Debate**: 'Violence in society is out of control'
- **Poem**: 'Violence in my head' (8–10 lines)
- **Personal Writing**: 'The many faces of violence today'
- **School magazine article**: 'Violence in our schools' – what can **we** do about it? (Student's perspective)

Unit 9

Grappling with Grammar

Reported Speech

Question) What is reported speech?

Answer) It is **direct speech**, (someone's actual words) being **commented on** or **reported** by someone else.

Example) 'It's only a joke!' (direct speech) said Anne.

Anne said that it was only a joke. (reported speech)

Study these examples. Note the changes in **tense** from direct speech to reported speech.

Direct speech	**Reported speech**
1. 'I love chips!' said Dave	Dave said (that) he loved chips.
2. 'I am eating curry chips at the moment.'	He said (that) he was eating curry chips at that moment.
3. 'I have already eaten three bags.'	He said he had already eaten three bags.
4. 'I ate three bags yesterday, too!'	He said he had eaten three bags the day before too.
5. 'I will eat more for my dinner.'	He said he would eat more for his dinner.
6. 'I can eat more chips than anybody!'	He said he could eat more chips than anybody.
7. 'I may just eat chips until I burst!'	He said he might just eat chips until he burst.

Did you notice how:

- 'I' in direct speech becomes **he/she** in reported speech?
- the '**time adverbials**' also change? For example, '**yesterday**' changes to '**the day before**'.

Time adverbials

Direct speech	Reported speech
today	that day
this afternoon	that afternoon
this evening	that evening
tonight	that night
tomorrow	the following/next day
yesterday	the day before
now	then, at that time
last night	the night before
last week, year, etc.	the week, year, etc. before
next week, year, etc.	the following week, year, etc.
two weeks **ago**	two weeks **before**/previously

Although you may use these correctly in speech, it's very easy to become careless with them in your writing. The result is sloppy, unclear reporting. The **Functional Writing** and **Media** sections of the Junior Cert. paper often ask you to write **letters** or **reports**, so it is important to exercise reported speech.

Stage 1

Exercise 1.

Oral, in pairs

1. Choose a partner. Decide who's A and who's B.
2. Your teacher will select pairs of students at random and call out a **direct speech** statement, followed by a **name**.

> (**Example**) 'Sheila lives in Cork.' **Thomas.**

3. A and B then confer, and A replies: '**Thomas said** that Sheila **lived** in Cork.' You will be given just fifteen seconds to compose your reported speech sentence.
4. Student B in each pair **writes down** all the reported statements.

Expect to hear direct speech statements in a range of tenses from **present simple** ('lives') to **present continuous** ('is living') to **future** ('will live'), as well as a variety of verbs **and** time adverbials!

Exercise 2.   Put the following statements into reported speech.

> **Example**   'I'm really tired at the moment,' Karen said.
>   Karen said that she was really tired at the/that moment.

1.   'I'm really fed up at the moment,' Karen said.

   _____

2.   'I'm going to have my eyebrows shaved,' Bobby said.

   _____

3.   'I've seen that film four times,' Roy said.

   _____

4.   'I can't go. Auntie Marge is coming to tea tomorrow,' Rita explained.

   _____

5.   'We're coming home tomorrow,' the girls said.

   _____

6.   'I will start working really seriously tomorrow,' Mary promised.

   _____

7.   'We may never return,' the aliens said.

   _____

8.   'I can always finish it next week,' Joe said.

   _____

9.   'I've done everything I can,' explained the doctor.

   _____

10.   'We've finished our work, Miss,' the students said.

   _____

Exercise 3.

1.   Compose five **direct speech** statements in three minutes.
2.   Exchange your copy with another student. Write out each other's examples, in **reported speech**. Don't forget to change the **time adverbial** too!
3.   Swop copies again, and **correct** each other's work. Check with your teacher if you're unsure about any of them. Keep your statements simple – no hidden traps!

> **Example**   Student A: 'I'm going to town today.'
>   Student B: Tom said he was going to town that day.

Stage 2

Reported questions

In reported questions, the **word order** changes, as well as the tense.

> **Example** Direct: 'When **does** the bus leave?'
> Reported: **She asked me** when the bus **left.**
> Direct: 'When **did** the bus **leave?**'
> Reported: **She asked me** when the bus **had left.**

Exercise 1. Put the following questions into reported speech, introducing each statement with: '**He** asked me if . . .' or '**She** asked me if . . .', depending on the context. Change the **time adverbials** as required, **also**.

1. 'Do you like Bon Jovi?' Mark asked.

    _____

2. 'Are you meeting Paul this weekend?' Katy asked.

    _____

3. 'Have you heard about Dick and Shauna?' Tina asked.

    _____

4. 'Will you go over this Geography with me tomorrow?' Tom asked.

    _____

5. 'Can you mind the baby next week?' Mum asked.

    _____

6. 'Have you thought about my idea?' Sarah asked.

    _____

7. 'Did he really hate me?' Sorcha asked.

    _____

8. 'What will you buy with the money?' Gerard asked.

    _____

9. 'Have you finished the exercise?' the teacher asked.

    _____

The Exam; Functional writing

Exercise 2.

Here are some questions you might be asked in a **job interview**. **Report** the questions back to a friend. Begin each one with 'She asked me . . .'. Remember! **The word order** (syntax) will change also.

> **Example** 'How old **are** you?'
> **She asked me** how old I was.

1. Where do you live?

    _____

2. How much experience do you have?

    _____

3. What have you done before?

    _____

4. How much do you earn at your present job?

    _____

5. Why are you interested in this work?

    _____

6. What are your grades like in English?

    _____

7. Can you work at weekends?

    _____

8. Do you use our products?

    _____

9. What do you know about our firm?

    _____

10. When will your exams be finished?

    _____

Exercise 3.   A rather nosy woman at the bus stop asked Rhona these questions:

1. Has the 39 bus already gone?
2. Where do you live?
3. How long have you been at your school?
4. Do you like it there?
5. Are the teachers nice?
6. Do you get much homework?
7. Have you seen that film *Phone Booth*?
8. Is there a young man in your life?
9. Did you colour your hair yourself?
10. Will you be here again tomorrow?

Rhona was telling her Mum about the woman later that evening. Write out Rhona's reporting of the woman's questions. Begin like this:

First, **she asked me if** the 39 bus . . .

Stage 3

Reported commands, warnings and advice

Commands, warnings and advice can be reported in the following way:

1. **Command:**   'Lock the door, please.'
   Reported: She **told me to lock** the door.
2. **Warning:**   'Cigarettes can kill you.'
   Reported: The doctor **warned me that** cigarettes **could** kill me.
3. **Advice:**   'See your doctor, if the symptoms persist, Mr. Murphy.'
   Reported: The chemist **advised him to** see his doctor if the symptoms **persisted**.

Reporting verbs for commands, warnings and advice are:

> **order, command, forbid, remind, tell, warn, advise**

Exercise 1.   Here are ten examples of commands, warnings and advice in direct speech. Write them in **reported speech**. Use the reporting verbs from the list above and the examples.

> (**Example**)   'Do your homework!' (mum)
>   Mum **told** me to do my homework.

1. 'Stay out of trouble this time, son.' (the police)

   _____

2. 'Take some pain-killers every four hours.' (doctor)

   _____

3. 'Be more careful with your money.' (horoscope)

   _____

4. 'Wash those hands immediately!' (Dad)

   _____

5. 'Stay away from that place.' (friend)

   _____

6. 'Don't take any risks on Saturday.' (horoscope)

   _____

7. 'Use a dictionary to check your spellings.' (author of this book!)

   _____

8. 'Don't snack between meals.' (dietician)

   _____

9. Stop writing now!' (teacher)

   _____

10. 'I forbid you to use that kind of language, Jack!' (Mam)

   _____

The Exam; Functional writing

Exercise 2.

Question 1 on the Junior Cert. Higher level paper, 1998 reads:

'A letter has appeared in a daily newspaper claiming that "teenagers nowadays have no moral standards". Write a letter of reply in which you respond to the charge.'

Here are some of the comments one imagines may have been made in the letter of complaint:

1. Teenagers nowadays don't care about authority.
2. They are extremely selfish and immature.
3. They drink and smoke with no thought of the consequences.
4. They are irresponsible and bad-mannered.

Write your reply, using **reported speech**.

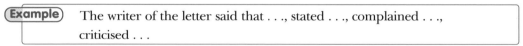

(**Example**) The writer of the letter said that . . ., stated . . ., complained . . ., criticised . . .

Try not to use emotive language. Be objective and answer the imagined criticisms one by one, in clearly expressed points.

The Exam; Poetry

Exercise 3.

Read the following poem, and then answer the questions which follow, in **reported speech**.

What the Doctor Said

He said it doesn't look good
he said it looks bad in fact real bad
he said I counted thirty-two of them on one lung before
I quit counting them
I said I'm glad I wouldn't want to know
about any more being there than that
he said are you a religious man do you kneel down
in forest groves and let yourself ask for help
when you come to a waterfall
mist blowing against your face and arms
do you stop and ask for understanding at these moments
I said not yet but I intend to start today
he said I'm real sorry he said

I wish I had some other kind of news to give you
I said Amen and he said something else
I didn't catch and not knowing what else to do
and not wanting him to have to repeat it
and me to have to fully digest it
I just looked at him
for a minute and he looked back it was then
I jumped up and shook hands with this man who'd just given me
something no one else on earth had ever given me
I may even have thanked him habit being so strong

Raymond Carver

1.   What did the doctor say about one lung?
2.   What was the patient's response to this?
3.   What three questions did the doctor ask him then?
4.   What did the patient say in reply?
5.   Was the doctor sorry for him? What did he say **exactly**?
6.   What did the patient say after he heard the bad news?
7.   What did he say the doctor had just given him?
8.   What do you think the poet meant in the **last line** of the poem? Begin with: 'I think he was saying that . . .'

Punctuation Please!

All of It: Challenge Time!

In Units 1–8, you exercised the following punctuation marks:

Unit 1. capital letters and full stops
Unit 2. commas
Unit 3. semi-colons and colons
Unit 4. question marks and exclamation marks
Unit 5. apostrophes
Unit 6. quotation marks
Unit 7. dashes and hyphens
Unit 8. brackets, blobs and dots

Expect quite challenging exercises in this 'Test Yourself' unit. A variety of punctuation marks will be required each time. If you are unsure about how to use any of the above, it would be wise to revisit the individual unit before attempting these exercises. This is 'proof of the pudding' time, so good luck!

Exercise 1.

1. Punctuate the following extract from *Angela's Ashes* by Frank McCourt. I have removed all the **capital letters**, **commas** and **full stops**.

    cyril benson dances he has medals hanging from his shoulders to his kneecaps he wins contests all over ireland and he looks lovely in his saffron kilt he's a credit to his mother and he gets his name in the paper all the time and you can be sure he brings home the odd few pounds you don't see him roaming the streets kicking everything in sight till the toes hang out of his boots oh no he's a good boy dancing for his poor mother

    mam wets an old towel and scrubs my face till it stings she wraps the towel around her finger and sticks it in my ears and claims there's enough wax there to grow potatoes she wets my hair to make it lie down she tells me shut up and stop whinging that these dancing lessons will cost her sixpence every saturday which i could have earned bringing bill galvin his dinner and god knows she can barely afford it i try to tell her ah mam sure you don't have to send me to dancing school when you could be smoking a nice woodbine and having a cup of tea but she says oh aren't you clever you're going to dance if i have to give up the fags forever

    if my pals see my mother dragging me through the street to an irish dancing class i'll be disgraced entirely they think it's all right to dance and pretend you're fred astaire because you can jump all over the screen with ginger rogers there is no ginger rogers in irish dancing and you can't jump all over you stand straight up and down and keep your arms against yourself and kick your legs up and around and never smile my uncle pa keating said irish dancers look like they have steel rods up their arses but i can't say that to mam she'd kill me.

2. Although the writer has chosen **not** to use **quotation marks**, are there places in this extract where they could have been used? Identify those sections and say why or why not you think quotation marks should have been used.

Exercise 2.   Punctuate the following edited extract from *Three Men in a Boat*, by Jerome K. Jerome. You will need to insert: **capital letters, full stops, commas, semi-colons, colons, quotation marks** and **question marks**.

we pulled out the maps and discussed plans we arranged to start on the following saturday from kingston harris and i would go down in the morning and take the boat up to chertsey and george who would not be able to get away from the city till the afternoon (george goes to sleep at a bank from ten to four each day except saturdays when they wake him up and put him outside at two) would meet us there

should we camp out or sleep at inns

george and i were for camping out we said it would be so wild and free so patriarchal like

harris said how about when it rains

you can never rouse harris there is no poetry about harris – no wild yearning for the unattainable harris never weeps he knows not why if harris's eyes fill with tears you can bet it is because harris has been eating raw onions or has put too much worcester over his chop

if you were to stand at night by the seashore with harris and say hark do you not hear is it but the mermaids singing deep below the waving waters or sad spirits chanting dirges for white corpses held by seaweed harris would take you by the arm and say i know what it is old man you've got a chill now you come along with me i know a place round the corner here where you can get a drop of the finest scotch whisky you ever tasted – put you right in less than no time

harris always does know a place round the corner where you can get something brilliant in the drinking line i believe that if you met harris up in paradise (supposing such a thing likely) he would immediately greet you with so glad you've come old fellow i've found a nice place round the corner here where you can get some really first-class nectar

in the present instance however as regarded the camping out his practical view of the matter came as a very timely hint camping out in rainy weather is not pleasant rainwater is the chief article of diet at supper the bread is two-thirds rainwater the beefsteak-pie is exceedingly rich in it and the jam and the butter and the salt and the coffee have all combined with it to make soup

after supper you find your tobacco is damp and you cannot smoke luckily you have a bottle of the stuff that cheers and inebriates if taken in proper quantity and this restores to you sufficient interest in life to induce you to go to bed

The Exam; Other drama

Exercise 3.

The following is an extract from the Other Drama section of the Junior Cert. Higher level paper, 2001. It is from the play *A Night Out* by Harold Pinter. **Punctuate it**. You will need to insert: **capital letters, full stops, commas, question marks, exclamation marks (2), apostrophes, dots, brackets** and **colons** after 'Albert' and 'Mother' each time. When you have finished the exercise, **correct it from your own set of exam papers**.

In the extract, **Albert** is talking to his **mother**.

Albert	mr ryans leaving you know ryan hes leaving the firm hes been there years so mr kings giving a sort of party for him at his house well not exactly a party not a party just a few you know anyway were all invited ive got to go everyone else is going ive got to go i don't want to go but ive got to go
Mother	(bewildered sitting) well i dont know
Albert	(with his arm round her) i wont be late i dont want to go id much rather stay with you
Mother	would you
Albert	you know i would who wants to go to mr kings party
Mother	we were going to have our game of cards
Albert	well we cant have our game of cards
	(*Pause*)
Mother	put the bulb in grandmas room albert
Albert	ive told you im not going down to the cellar in my white shirt theres no light in the cellar either ill be pitch black in five minutes looking for those bulbs
Mother	i told you to put a light in the cellar i told you yesterday
Albert	well i cant do it now
Mother	if we had a light in the cellar youd be able to see where those bulbs were you dont expect me to go down to the cellar
Albert	i dont know why we keep bulbs in the cellar
	(*Pause*)
Mother	your father would turn in his grave if he heard you raise your voice to me youre all ive got albert i want you to remember that i haven't got anyone else i want you i want you to bear that in mind

Albert   im sorry i raised my voice

(*mumbling*) ive got to go

(*he goes to the door*)

Mother (*following*) albert

Exercise 4.

Punctuation

Read the following article on Irish women and equality. I have removed **eight blobs** (bullet points) from the text. Can you replace them? (Remember that one of the major functions of blobs is to **highlight** the most important points.)

Some shocking new statistics have shown that equality is much more a myth than reality in Irish society today

We may believe that Irish women have come a long way and are intellectually liberated and economically accomplished, but figures show that we are deeply disadvantaged on almost every level. We are still excluded from 'serious' decision-making and until women and men share power equally in this country, we won't have a true democracy.

Our political representation in the Dail for starters ranks 59th out of 120 internationally – lower than certain Asian and sub-Saharan states we give state aid to. We are below the European and American average. We are also grossly excluded from other decision-making functions – only 3% of managing directors, 9% of secretary generals in the Civil Service, and 7% of High Court judges are women. The facts make stark reading:

Only 13% of those elected to the Dail are women up from 12% 10 years ago, which means it will take 370 years for the percentage of women in the Dail to reach 50%.

The percentage of women appointed to the cabinet in this government had declined by 7% while the percentage of female ministers of state has dropped by 11%. 10 counties have no woman TD. Only 1% of the Seanad are women. Only 15% of elected councillors are women.

This percentage has not risen since 1991. The percentage of women appointed to state boards rarely reached 40% although this has been an official government target since 1991. The Central Bank and Bord na gCon have no women on their boards. Bord Gais has only one women member while the ESB, Bord na Mona and Bord Failte have only two women board members each.

Woman's Way (4 February 2003)

Exercise 5. Note how **brackets** are used in this 'Top 10 Singles' chart from *The Irish Times*, 13 March 2003.

Compose your own 'Top 10 Singles' chart using **brackets** and other punctuation marks, e.g. capital letters. Copy the **layout** of this chart as closely as possible, and insert a photo of your favourite group/singer for visual impact.

TOP 10 SINGLES

1	(1)	**Beautiful** Christina Aguilera (*RCA*)	6	(10)	**Cry Me a River** Justin Timberlake (*Jive*)
2	(2)	**All the Things She Said** t.A.T.u. (*Interscope*)	7	(9)	**Big Yellow Taxi** Counting Crows ft V Carlton (*Geffen*)
3	(-)	**Sing for the Moment** Busted (*Universal*)	8	(8)	**If You're Not the One** Daniel Bedingfield (*Polydor*)
4	(3)	**Years 3000** Busted (*Universal*)	9	(-)	**Sound of the Underground** Girls Aloud (*Polydor*)
5	(4)	**Lose Yourself** Eminem (*Interscope*)	10	(6)	**Stole** Kelly Rowland (*Columbia*)

And finally . . .

Exercise 6.

Punctuate the following article from the *Sunday Independent*. Write it out, in paragraphs, as in the printed piece. You will find occasion to use **all of the punctuation marks** you've practised so far, plus **dashes** and **hyphens**.

SO YOU THINK YOU'RE FUNNY

ciara dwyer falls for channel 4s latest irish comic recruit graham norton

i saw him on stage in edinburgh it was love at first sight he is graham norton camp comedian

he was wearing a persil-white suit his brown eyes twinkled and he had the most divine beauty spot he swished onto the stage divilment written all over him do you like the suit he started it was skin-tight and spotless then he gave us that look a sideways glance a bulging of the eyes and a raised eyebrow all at once we howled

in nortons world its the little frivolous things that count he took off his jacket folded the arms together and hung it on the microphone stand a tidy stage is a happy stage we loved him

he singles out nora from the audience a middle-aged grey-haired woman wearing glasses nora looked a bit like a civil servant or someones mother at least

graham norton is the sort who can sanitise a curse word the sort who can be as camp as michael barrymore julian clary and kenneth williams in one and still be good clean fun

nora was not offended

with his gaudy kittycat phone norton collected messages from the advertisement he had placed in a singles column he ordered a pizza and when the delivery man appeared graham leered at his leathers whats your name norton asked neil the leathered one replied what a lovely name norton squealed that look was back

norton didnt do anything extraordinary on stage but his ordinary world was very funny

graham nortons new comedy show so graham norton started on channel 4 last friday night its supposed to be chat showish norton revealed weve come up with other things and now theres less room for guests

born in dublin and brought up in bandon graham studied speech and drama in london most of us know him as noel the youth worker priest in father ted but the boy has brains when ned sherrin was on holidays norton hosted radio four's loose ends no mean feat

now we venture into grahams world every friday the show wont be about issues of world importance unless its in a very superficial way it sounds like a line out of noel cowards private lives lets be superficial and pity the poor philosophers lets blow trumpets and squeakers and enjoy the party as much as we can coward would be mad about the norton boy

How Do You Spell . . .?

Confusing Words: Homonyms and Homophones

 Question   What's the difference between a **homonym** and a **homophone**?

Answer   Good question! It is very easy to confuse these two, but there is a real difference. Read the following definitions:

• A **homonym** (from two Greek words: **homo**, meaning 'same', and **nym**, meaning 'name') is a word with the **same spelling** as another word, **but with a different meaning**.

Watch Your Language!

> **Example**   coach: **a.** Tom is a football **coach**.
>
>   **b.** We hired a **coach** for the school tour.

●   A **homophone** (from two Greek words: **homo**, meaning 'same', and **phone**, meaning 'sound') is a word which has the **same sound** as another word, but a **different spelling** and a **different meaning**. Warning! These are the ones that cause the most confusion with spelling.

> **Example**   meet: I'll **meet** you at six.
>
>   meat: She doesn't eat **meat**.

Stage 1

Homonyms

Pupil: What's the orchestra reading, Miss?

Teacher: The score.

Pupil: Really?! Who won?

Exercise 1.   Write **two short sentences** for each of the following pairs of words that clearly show the difference in meaning between them:

> **Example**   The **bank** of the river overflowed.
>
>   The **bank** will loan you the money.

1. bank (of a river)   bank (for borrowing money)
2. arms (body)   arms (weapons)
3. bark (sound)   bark (of a tree)
4. fine (OK)   fine (money paid)
5. jam (for eating)   jam (traffic)

Exercise 2.

A.   Homonyms can be **nouns** or **verbs**.

> **Example**   Dad cut the wood with his electric **saw**. (noun)
>
>   I **saw** him doing it. (verb)

1. Write ten **sentences** using each of the words below as a noun **and** as a verb.

> **Example**   That **tie** is awful!
>
>   Don't **tie** it so tight!

     tie, lie, catch, coach, ground

B.   Homonyms can also be **adjectives**

2. Write five **questions** using each of the words below as adjectives.

     light, fine, utter, sound, fair

(**Example**) Plain: Is she really such a **plain** girl?

Note: You will find many examples of homonyms in your **dictionary**. They are usually indicated by a small number (1, 2, 3) to how the different meanings of the word.

(**Example**) **lock** (1): tuft of hair; **lock** (2): fastening of door or drawer; **lock** (3): part of a canal shut off for boats; **lock** (4): wrestling, a hold that keeps an opponent's limb fixed; etc.

Exercise 3.

1. Consult your dictionary and find **two** more meanings for each of these homonyms:

    a. **club**:   (i)   organisation
                  (ii) _____
                  (iii) _____

    b. **fair**:   (i)   just
                  (ii) _____
                  (iii) _____

    c. **break**:   (i)   separate into pieces, under a blow or strain
                  (ii) _____
                  (iii) _____

    d. **nerve**:   (i)   fibres in the body, carrying messages
                  (ii) _____
                  (iii) _____

    e. **see**:   (i)   perceive with the eyes
                  (ii) _____
                  (iii) _____

2. Write one sentence per word for each of the above homonyms, in which the word is used **twice** – but with a different **meaning in the second half of the sentence.**

(**Example**) see: I can **see** you've put a lot of work into this sculpture, but I don't quite **see** what it's all about.

Stage 2

Homophones

'Grate Sail! Bye Now! Everything Going Cheep!'

Although homophones can cause problems in spelling, they can also lead to some funny jokes, so let's start with a bit of fun! Here are some homophone jokes:

What do you give an elephant for stress?

Trunkquilizers

Watch Your Language!

Where did Sir Lancelot study?

At **knight** school!

Where are the Great **Plains**?

At the great airport!

Exercise 1. Here are some homophone jokes. As you can see from the examples, the joke is based on a **deliberate misspelling** of a key word in each one. Underline or highlight the word spelled incorrectly in each joke, and then write **the correct spelling** in a bracket beside it.

> **Example** What happened to the man who stole the car?
>
> He was taken into **custardy**. (custody)

1. What kind of ears does a train have? Enginears.

2. Why did the egg go to the Antarctic? Because he was an eggsplorer.

3. Knock! Knock!

   Who's there?

   Leopold.

   Leopold who?

   Leopold more votes than you in the election.

4. Where did Sir Lancelot get his education?

   Knight school.

5. Knock! Knock!

   Who's there?

   Carrie.

   Carrie who?

   Carrie my gear for me, will you?

6. Mr. Smith: 'Peter, how many legs has a horse'

   Peter: 'Six, Sir.'

   Mr. Smith: 'Six?!'

   Peter: 'Yes, Sir. Forelegs at the front and two at the back.'

7. Knock! Knock!

   Who's there?

   Hildegarde.

   Hildegarde who?

   Hildegardes the goal when we play hockey.

8. Mrs. Brown: 'What position does your Sean play in the football team?'

   Mrs. Murphy: 'Oh, a very important one! His brother says he's one of the drawbacks.

9. Teacher: 'Anita, what is the unit we use to measure electrical power?'

   Anita: 'The what, Sir?'

   Teacher: 'Absolutely right! Well done, Anita.'

10. Teacher: 'Which children's author wrote his books in a shed at the bottom of his garden?'

    Student: 'Roald Dahlia, Miss!'

Exercise 2.

(The serious bit!)

1. Sort these twenty words into ten pairs of homophones:

(**Example**) coarse, course

			pairs	
coarse	knot	1.	_____	_____
meet	cellar	2.	_____	_____
not	herd	3.	_____	_____
write	principle	4.	_____	_____
seller	thought	5.	_____	_____
heard	loose	6.	_____	_____
principal	aloud	7.	_____	_____
taught	course	8.	_____	_____
lose	meat	9.	_____	_____
allowed	right	10.	_____	_____

2. Now write **one sentence** for each pair, in which both words are shown to have separate **meanings** and **spellings**.

(**Example**) **not/knot** 'That's **not** the right **knot**, I'm afraid,' said the scout master.

Exercise 3.

Complete these sentences, choosing the correct spelling from the words in brackets, according to its meaning in the context of the sentence.

1. The _____ (principle, principal) actor was killed off in the last _____ (scene, seen) of the play.

2. He _____ (knows, nose) I only want some _____ (piece, peace).

3. If you don't _____ (practice, practise) you won't win _____ (there, their) scholarship.

4. It's a _____ (waste, waist) of time trying to make myself _____ (herd, heard) over you lot!

5. The Special Olympics afforded some amazing _____ (sites, sights) as the _____ (hole, whole) of Ireland turned out to greet the participants.

6. The kids _____ (through, threw) stones at passing cars, and at people on bicycles _____ (two, too).

7. We can _____ (here, hear) them from _____ (here, hear).

8. Denise _____ (past, passed) me _____ (by, bye) on the street.

9. I can't _____ (bare, bear) the _____ (thought, taught) of him leaving.
10. Dr. Ross has _____ (grate, great) _____ (patients, patience) with his _____ (patients, patience)!

Stage 3

Near homophones

In a pair of near homophones the sound is not **exactly** the same in both words but is so close that it is still easy to misspell them.

> (**Example**)   accept/except, affect/effect

Exercise 1.   Here are some more. Write short sentences to show the **clear** difference in meaning between each pair of near homophones. Use your **dictionary**. Be very careful with the **spelling** of the words in each case.

1. immigrant: _____
   emigrant: _____
2. formally: _____
   formerly: _____
3. border: _____
   boarder: _____
4. personal: _____
   personnel: _____
5. weather: _____
   whether: _____
6. breath: _____
   breathe: _____
7. bought: _____
   brought: _____
8. desert: _____
   dessert: _____
9. envelop: _____
   envelope: _____
10. angle: _____
    angel: _____

Exercise 2.   **Draw a line down the centre of your copy or A4 notepad**. Write the word **Homonyms** on the left and the word **Homophones** on the right. Underneath these headings, write out all the homonyms and homophones you have read and exercised in this unit. Think of it as a **spelling** exercise and be really careful.

- With the **homonym** list, write the **meaning** in brackets beside each word – as they are all **spelled the same**, remember!

> **Example**   bear (1) (Paddington); bear (2) (carry); bear (3) (put up with)

- With the **homophone** list, be extra careful with the **spelling** as it is **not the same**! Write the **meaning** also, in a bracket beside each word.

> **Example**   taught (past of 'to teach'); thought (past of 'to think')

This exercise will concentrate your mind on these confusing and often confused words!

Exercise 3.

Spot the spelling error!

Here are some extracts from an American article entitled 'The World According to Student Bloopers' (an American colloquialism for errors). The author – a history teacher – pasted together a 'history' of the world from student spelling bloopers, collected by teachers throughout the USA.

1. Read it carefully, and **underline or highlight** all the bloopers.
2. When you have finished laughing, go back and reread the passage, inserting the **correct spelling** for each blooper.

The inhabitants of Ancient Egypt were called mummys. They lived in the Sarah Dessert and travelled by camelot. They built the Pramids; they are a range of mountains between France and Spain.

The Bible is full of interesting caricatures. In the Book of Guinnesses, Adam and Eve were created from an apple tree. One of Jacob's sons, Joseph, gave refuse to the Israelites.

Without the Greeks we wouldn't have history. They had myths. A myth is a female moth. Homer wrote the Iliad and the Oddity. Socrates was a famous Greek teacher who went a round giving people advise. They killed him. Socrates died from an overdose of wedlock. In the Olympic Games, Greeks ran races, jumped, hurled biscuits and threw the java.

Then came the Middle Ages. King Arthur lived in the age of shivery. In midevil times most of the people were alliterate.

During the Renaissance, Martin Luther dyed a horrible death, being excommunicated by a bull. It was the age of grate inventions. Sir Walter Rally invented cigarettes. Sir Francis Drake circumcised the world with a 100-foot clipper.

The government of England was a limited mockery. Queen Elizabeth's navvy went out and defeated the Spanish Armadillo.

The greatest writer of the Renaissance was William Shakespear. He lived at Winsor with his Mary wives, riting tragedees, comedees, and errors. Romeo and Juliet are an example of a heroic couplet. Miguel Cervantes was writing at the same time as Shakespear. He wrote Donkey Hote. The next great otter was John Milton. He wrote Paradise Lost. Then his wife died and he wrote Paradise Regained . . . (to be continued).

Words at Work

Word Mix

1. **Using your dictionary**
2. **Foreign words and phrases**
3. **Malapropisms and misprints**

Stage 1

Using your dictionary

Neither is a dictionary a bad book to read. There is no cant in it, no excess of explanation, and it is full of suggestion – the raw material of possible poems and histories.

Ralph Waldo Emerson

If you want to improve your word power, you must develop a serious relationship with your dictionary! Invest in a good one, like the *Concise Oxford Dictionary*, or the *Concise Oxford School Dictionary* (the Irish edition).

You must then learn how to use it, so that you can find a word quickly. Dictionaries can be intimidating, but once you understand **alphabetical order** and the various **symbols** which accompany each word, you will have few difficulties. Let's begin.

Alphabetical order

'If I could write the alphabet, I'd put 'U' and 'I' together.'

You will be familiar with the term 'alphabetical order' because you can see its use in textbooks, telephone directories, address books, record stores, etc. It is a very useful way of locating items quickly. Words in your dictionary are also in alphabetical order, of course. It's easy enough to find the word 'abacus', for example, as it's on page 1 of most dictionaries! However, finding the word '**amusement**' means you have to work your way through from '**ab**' to '**am**', and then through all the '**ama**'s, '**amb**'s, etc. until you get to '**amu**'. This is not as tedious as it sounds. **At the top of each page in a dictionary** there are two words in bold black letters. These are **index words**. They are the **first** and last words on that page, and will help you locate your word more quickly.

Exercise 1.

Alphabetical order

With the help of your dictionary, arrange these words in **strict** alphabetical order; from 1–20. Begin with **1. Abacus**

abbey	bargain	crash	deer
abacus	baby	comb	dear
acrobat	breathe	cloud	dual
acting	blaze	clothes	dryer
altogether	buyer	cynical	disk

Exercise 2.

Alphabetical order, in pairs

Create your own exercise for **another** pair of students, by composing **four lists of five words each**, as in Exercise 1. Select your words from the letters 'e' to 'w' from your dictionary.

1. Time limit of **ten minutes** to select and write up the lists – with the order of the words in each list **mixed up**.
2. Swop copies with another pair of students.
3. Rearrange **their** words in strict alphabetical order, in ten minutes.
4. Take back your own copy and **check** the word order in your dictionary. Time limit of ten minutes also.
5. The pair of students who finish **first** are the winners.

Understanding your dictionary's symbols and letters

Study these dictionary entries. The numbers 1–8 represent the various parts of the entry, as follows:

1. headword (leisure, wage, proportionate)
2. phonetic script (leisure/leʒə(r))
3. definition (meaning)
4. countable
5. 'n' means 'noun' (part of speech), 'adj' – adjective, etc.
6. cross-reference (➝ fee (1) pay salary)
7. the same as (=)
8. example of **use** of the word

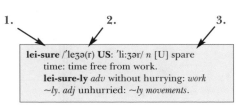

lei·sure /ˈleʒə(r) **US**: ˈliːʒər/ *n* [U] spare
time: time free from work.
lei·sure·ly *adv* without hurrying: *work
~ly*. *adj* unhurried: *~ly movements*.

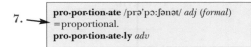

7. ➝

pro·por·tion·ate /prəˈpɔːʃənət/ *adj* (*formal*)
=proportional.
pro·por·tion·ate·ly *adv*

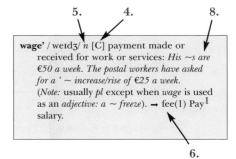

wage' / weɪdʒ/ *n* [C] payment made or
received for work or services: *His ~s are
€50 a week. The postal workers have asked
for a ' ~ increase/rise of €25 a week.*
(*Note:* usually *pl* except when *wage* is used
as an *adjective: a ~ freeze*). ➝ fee(1) Pay[1]
salary.

6.

Watch Your Language!

Exercise 3.

Symbols and letters

Select any **five** words from your own dictionary, and **identify the various parts of the entry** in each case, using some or all of the reference words 1–8 from page 225.

> **Example** student (from *The Concise Oxford Dictionary*, page 1210)
>
> 1. **student**   = headword
> 2. stju:d(ə)nt   = phonetic script
> 3. n.   = noun
> 4. a person who is studying esp. at university or another place of higher education   = definition

Exercise 4.   As you saw with '**n**' for noun, dictionaries use abbreviations in order to save space; these are generally listed **at the front of your dictionary**. Find out what each of these abbreviations means, and write out the **full word** in the space provided.

1.	adj.	_____	21.	masc. _____
2.	adv.	_____	22.	metaph. _____
3.	aux.	_____	23.	mod. _____
4.	Bibl.	_____	24.	n. _____
5.	Ch. Church_____		25.	neg. _____
6.	colloq.	_____	26.	obj. _____
7.	compar.	_____	27.	opp. _____
8.	conj.	_____	28.	perh. perhaps_____
9.	demons.adj._____		29.	pl. _____
10.	demons.pron. _____		30.	prep. _____
11.	esp.	_____	31.	pron. _____
12.	ex.	_____	32.	pronunc._____
13.	exc. except_____		33.	ref. _____
14.	F.	_____	34.	rel. _____
15.	f.	_____	35.	rel.pron._____
16.	fem.	_____	36.	sing. _____
17.	gen.	_____	37.	sl. _____
18.	incl.	_____	38.	superl. _____
19.	infin.	_____	39.	syn. synonym_____
20.	irreg.	_____	40.	v. _____

And finally . . .

> *The dictionary is the only place where success comes before work.*
>
> (anonymous)

Stage 2

Foreign words and phrases

At least **eighty per cent** of English words are borrowed from other languages, the main ones being Latin and French. Other contributors are Italian, German, Greek and Spanish. Even some Russian words are widely used today! Here is a list of words and phrases in common use in English, numbered 1–100, under their particular language heading. How many of them do you understand?

Latin

1. ad infinitum
2. ad nauseam
3. agenda
4. alias
5. alma mater
6. alter ego
7. circa
8. crux
9. curriculum
10. et cetera (etc.)
11. gratis
12. in camera
13. in memoriam
14. memorabilia
15. nota bene (N.B.)
16. opus
17. per annum
18. per capita
19. per se
20. post mortem
21. re
22. requiem
23. status quo
24. thesaurus
25. ultra
26. verbatim
27. versus
28. vice versa

French

29. avant-garde
30. bistro
31. blancmange
32. blasé
33. cartel
34. chef
35. chez
36. chic
37. clique
38. connoisseur
39. coup d'état
40. crèche
41. critique
42. cul-de-sac
43. déjà vu
44. dossier
45. en masse
46. fait accompli
47. faux pas
48. gaffe
49. genre
50. grand prix
51. haute couture
52. macabre
53. né(e)
54. par excellence
55. résumé
56. sabotage
57. séance
58. tête-à-tête
59. vis-à-vis

Italian

60. alfresco
61. bravo
62. confetti
63. diva
64. gala
65. gusto
66. influenza
67. maestro
68. mafia
69. manifesto
70. marina
71. stanza
72. studio
73. tempo

Greek

74. diaspora
75. dogma
76. ethos
77. eureka!
78. logos
79. phobia
80. trauma

Spanish

81. bonanza
82. don
83. fiesta
84. hacienda
85. hombre
86. incommunicado
87. junta
88. machismo
89. macho
90. paella
91. patio
92. sombrero

German

93. kaput
94. poltergeist
95. rucksack/ knapsack
96. wanderlust

Russian

97. glasnost
98. intelligentsia
99. pogrom
100. sputnik

Watch Your Language!

Exercise 1. Fill in the blanks in the following sentences with a **foreign word or phrase** from the list.

1. Richard made a terrible _____ when he asked Sandra how Greg was. Didn't he know they'd split up?
2. Preserving the _____ seems to be all he cares about.
3. The mad general came to power after a violent and bloody _____.
4. He never stops talking about football. He goes on and on about it _____.
5. I'd like to talk to you tomorrow, Carmel, _____ the proposed changes in the uniform.
6. It's a little difficult to eat _____ in this weather!
7. Maiphil was delighted to hear that her _____ had been chosen as the venue for the Christmas party.
8. Ciarán had a very interesting _____ with his six-year-old son last week, on the subject of women.
9. Ex-President Mary Robinson was very fond of talking about the Irish _____.
10. We'll have to buy a new hoover. This one is definitely _____.
11. Paul and Laura really believed they had a _____ in their house.
12. I'll never go there again! The whole thing was a dreadful _____.
13. Don't bother trying to get any sense out of him. He's strictly _____.
14. This time next week Sharon will be sitting in her Spanish hacienda eating _____.
15. Students abandoned their classes _____ when they heard that Colin Farrell was in the Principal's office!

Exercise 2.

Group work, class of thirty

The class will divide into five groups of six students per group. The **sixth student** in each group will report back to the teacher and class on the group's work. This is what you must do.

1. Group One will work with the words numbered 1–20
    Group Two with words numbered 21–40
    Group Three with words numbered 41–60
    Group Four with words numbered 61–80 and
    Group Five with words numbered 81–100.
    (Each group has twenty words.)
2. Everyone in each group reads **all** the words they have been assigned. They must then **make a list** of those they understand and their meanings. (ten minutes)
3. They should consult their dictionaries for those they **don't** understand, and write out their meanings, also. (ten minutes)
4. Each group of six will select **five words or phrases** from their list, and compose **a short sentence for each one** that clearly shows its meaning and usage. (five minutes)

5. Student 6 from each group reads out the group's five sentences to the whole class. (five minutes)

Exercise 3. Write a short piece of dialogue, **or** a humorous poem, **or** a report, which uses each of the following foreign words or phrases just once.

Chez Maurice	kitsch	crux	bravo	confetti
post mortem	tempo	machismo	incognito	trauma

Stage 3

Malapropisms and misprints

Question What's a malapropism?

Answer There is a play by Richard Brinsley Sheridan called *The Rivals*, in which there is a character called **Mrs. Malaprop**. She constantly **confuses** and misuses words which look and sound alike.

Example '**Illiterate him**, I say, quite from your memory.'
'Illiterate' should be '**Obliterate**'!

The **intention is humorous**, of course, and this kind of amusing error is called a 'malapropism'.

   Students often make mistakes like this too, but they're more commonly known as 'howlers' or 'bloopers' (American). See Exercise 3, page 223, for these.

   You can have great fun with malapropisms and increase your word store at the same time. There is a strong element of **punning**, as with Unit 8.

Exercise 1. In pairs, or from one student to the next around the class.
Used as a game, malapropisms can be spoken by one player to another, who has to guess the **correct** word or phrase.

Example Student A: Correct the malapropism in this sentence: 'You must keep your nose to the tombstone.'

Student B: It should be '**grindstone**'.
Correct this malapropism: 'She had an operation on her foot and it went sceptic.'

Student A: It should be '**septic**'.
Correct this malapropism . . .

Now you do it, identify and **correct** the malapropism in each of the following sayings:

1. Let the cat out of the sack.
2. Take the bull by the thorns.
3. To kill two birds with one spoon.
4. To be at a loose bend.
5. To feel under the feather.
6. To stick your leg out.
7. To scare on thin ice.
8. To put your food in it.
9. Like a red bag to a bull.
10. Like a mare with a sore head.
11. Look before you bleep.
12. The early nerd catches the worm.
13. A friend in Meath is a friend indeed.
14. Out of the frying ham into the fire.
15. Don't put all your veg in one basket.

N.B.! The student (or students) who produces the funniest malapropism gets a huge round of applause!

Exercise 2.

The story continues . . .

Do you remember 'The World According to Student Bloopers'? (page 223) Here is the next extract. Identify the 'bloopers' by underlining them as they occur, **and write what you believe is the correct word** over each one.

> Christopher Columbine was a great narrigator who discovered America while cursing about the Atlantic. Later, the Pilgrims crossed the ocean, and this was known as the Pilgrim's Process.
>
> They were met by Indian squabs carrying their porpoises on their backs. During the Revolutionary Wars the colonists won the mane war and no longer had to pay for taxis.
>
> Benjamin Franklin and Thomas Jefferson were two singers of the Declaration of Independence. Franklin died in 1790 and is still dead.
>
> Under the American Constitution, the people enjoyed the right to bare arms.
>
> Abraham Lincoln became America's greatest Precedent. He was born in a log cabin which he built with his own hands. He said 'In onion there is strength.'
>
> The Clue Clux Clan lynched negroes and other citizens. It claimed to represent law and odour. One night in 1865, Lincoln went to the theatre and got shot in his seat by one of the actors in a moving picture . . . (to be continued).

The Exam; Media studies

Exercise 3.

Finally, here are some **newspaper misprints** or **malapropisms**. They happen all the time! Underline the misprint in each sentence, and **write the correct word** in the space provided.

1. The accused had blond hair with a curly fridge. _____
2. For sale: Three bra electric fire. Mint condition. €20. _____
3. To give flavour to this dish, add a teaspoonful of curry powder, a small pinch of cinnamon and a couple of gloves. _____
4. Mr. and Mrs. O'Brien announce the forthcoming marriage of their daughter, Gretta, to Mr. Mark Greene. The couple will exchange cows on May 23rd. _____
5. John Morris, playing the role of Dr. Ross, has a terrific bedpan manner which is often funny. _____
6. Red settee puppies for sale. Good pedigree. _____
7. The suspect walks with a distinct limp and has a speed impediment. _____
8. The old couple on the fourth floor found the stars too much for them. _____
9. The holiday includes all food, wind, drinks and leisure activities. _____
10. The Phoenix Park is a conversation area and cannot be zoned for housing. _____

Unit 10

Bringing It All Together

Grammar, Vocabulary, Spelling

With the exception of **punctuation** (tested in Unit 9), this last unit aims to challenge your knowledge of all the language skills you have been exercising throughout this book: grammar, spelling and vocabulary. How well have you understood and exercised them? Let's find out!

Grammar: proper nouns

Exercise 1.

1. Read the following magazine article on the diary of Zlata Filopovic. Make a **list** of all the proper nouns in the article under the following headings: **People, Places, Dates**.

2. Comment on the title of the article, 'Child of War', using some proper nouns from your list.

3. Summarise the events recorded in her diary for the dates of Saturday 2 May and Thursday 7 May, in just **three** points, using proper nouns where appropriate.

N.B.! Don't forget to use **capital letters** for all proper nouns!

CHILD OF WAR

The Diary of Zlata Filopovic

In late 1991, Zlata Filopovic, 10, a Bosnian girl, started a diary of her life in Sarajevo. It soon became a chronicle of horrors. Over the next two years, as the city came under intensifying attack, Zlata grew from an innocent child into a wise teenager. She compared herself to Anne Frank, the Dutch Jewish girl who was killed by the Nazis and who left behind a moving account of her life in hiding.

FRIDAY, 27th September 1991

I'm home from school and I'm really tired. It's been a hard week. Tomorrow is Saturday and I can sleep as long as I like. LONG LIVE SATURDAYS! Tomorrow night, I'm 'busy'. Tomorrow is Ivana Varunek's birthday party. I received an invitation today.

THURSDAY, 5th MARCH 1992

Oh God! Things are heating up in Sarajevo. On Sunday a small group of armed civilians (as they say on television) killed a wedding guest and wounded a priest. On Monday the whole city was full of barricades. We didn't even have bread.

MONDAY, 30th MARCH 1992

Hey Diary! You know what I think? Since Anne Frank called her diary Kitty, maybe I could give you a name too. What about: ASFALTINA, SEFIKA, MIMMY or something else???

I'm thinking, thinking … I've decided. I'm going to call you MIMMY.

All right, then. Let's start.

Dear Mimmy,

It's almost mid-term. We're studying for our tests. Tomorrow we're supposed to go to a classical music concert at the Skenderija Hall.

SUNDAY, 5th April 1992
Dear Mimmy,

I'm trying to concentrate so I can do my homework, but I simply can't. Something is going on in town. You can hear gunfire from the hills.

SATURDAY, 2nd MAY 1992
Dear Mimmy,

Today was truly, absolutely the worst day ever in Sarajevo. The shooting started around noon. Mommy and I moved into the hall. Daddy was in his office, under our apartment, at the time. We told him on the intercom to run quickly to the downstairs lobby where we'd meet him. The gunfire was getting worse and we couldn't get over the wall to our neighbours, the Bobars, so we ran to our own cellar.

THURSDAY, 7th MAY 1992
Dear Mimmy,

I was almost positive the war would stop, but today … Today a shell fell on the park in front of my house, the park where I used to play and sit with my friends. A lot of people were hurt. AND NINA IS DEAD. A piece of shrapnel lodged in her brain. She was such a sweet, nice little girl.

MONDAY, 29th June 1992
Dear Mimmy,

BOREDOM!!! SHOOTING!!! SHELLING!!! PEOPLE BEING KILLED!!! DESPAIR!!! HUNGER!!! MISERY!!! FEAR!!!

That's my life! The life of an innocent 11-year-old schoolgirl. A schoolgirl without a school, without the fun and excitement of school. A child without games, without friends, without the sun, without birds, without nature, without fruit, without chocolate or sweets, with just a little powdered milk. In short, a child without a childhood.

Grammar: abstract nouns

Exercise 2.

1. Fill in the blanks in the following sentences with an appropriate **abstract noun**. The **first letter** of each noun has been supplied as a clue.

    a.   S_____ kills. (traffic slogan)

    b.   All's fair in L_____ and W_____.

    c.   'F_____'s just another word for nothing left to lose' (line from a song)

    d.   The problem with Roy in Coronation Street is that he has absolutely no sense of h_____.

    e.   P_____ is a virtue. (saying)

    f.   B_____ is in the eye of the beholder. (saying)

    g.   I can resist everything except T_____. (Oscar Wilde)

    h.   T_____ is stranger than fiction. (saying)

    i.   John just couldn't hide his d_____ at losing the match.

    j.   Schooldays are the best days of your l_____!

2. Can you name the **seven deadly sins**? They are all abstract nouns. Here's the first letter for each one:

    P_____   G_____   L_____

    E_____   Gl_____   J_____

    S_____

The Exam; Personal writing

3. Choose **one** of the seven deadly sins and write a **short story** or **essay** based on it.

Grammar: nouns, adjectives, verbs

Exercise 3.

1. Here is an extract from the Fiction section of the Junior Cert. Higher level paper, 1998. **Identify the nouns, adjectives and verbs** in bold and write them under their correct headings in the table below. There are eighteen of each. The extract (in edited form) is taken from the novel *Reading in the Dark* by Seamus Deane.

    The narrator, who grew up in a Nationalist family in Northern Ireland in the 1940s, as a child shared a room with his brothers, the eldest of whom is called Liam. In the extract the boy recalls the first novel he ever read.

    The **first novel** I **read** had a **green** hardboard **cover** and was two hundred and sixteen pages long. It was called *The Shan van Vocht*, a **phonetic rendering** of an **Irish phrase** meaning The Poor Old Woman, a **traditional** name for **Ireland**. It was about the great **rebellion** of 1798, the **source** of almost half the songs we **sang** around the August bonfires on the Feast of the Assumption. In the **opening** pages, people **were talking** in **whispers** about the **dangers** of the rebellion as they sat around a **great** open-hearth fire on a **wild** night of **winter** rain and **squall**. I read and re-read the opening many times. Outside was the bad weather; inside was the fire, **implied** danger, a love **relationship**. There was something **exquisite** in this **blend**, as I **lay** in bed reading while my brothers **slept** and **shifted** under the light that **shone** on their eyelids and made their **dreams different**. The **heroine** was called Ann, and the hero was Robert. She was too good for him. When they **whispered**, she did all the **interesting** talking. He just kept on about dying and **remembering** her always, even when she was there in front of him with her **dark** hair and her deep golden-brown eyes and her **olive** skin. So I **talked** to her instead and **told** her how **beautiful** she was and how I wouldn't go out on the rebellion at all but just sit there and whisper in her ear and let her know that now was forever and not some time in the future when the **shooting** and the **hacking** would be over, when what was left of life would be spent **listening** to the night wind **wailing** on graveyards and **empty** hillsides.

'For Christ's sake, put off that light. You're not even **reading**, you blank gom.'

And Liam would turn over, **driving** his knees up into my back and **muttering** curses under his breath. I'd switch off the light, get back in bed, and lie there, the book still open, re-imagining all I had read, the various ways the plot might **unravel**, the novel **opening** into **endless possibilities** in the **dark**.

Nouns (18)	Adjectives (18)	Verbs (18)
novel	first	read

2. Sentence building

Now choose **a** noun, **an** adjective and **a** verb from the table that would work well together in a single sentence. Write **ten sentences** in all, using different words from the table each time.

> (**Example**) Ireland (noun), wild (adjective), told (verb)
>
> The old people **told** stories about the **wild** untamed landscape of Celtic **Ireland**.

Grammar: adjectives
The Exam; Fiction

Exercise 4.

Read the following extract from the Fiction section of the Junior Cert. Higher level paper, 2002. Focus on the writer's use of **adjectives** in the text, and answer the questions which follow:

> She closed the door. I looked up and held my breath.
>
> 'I am Miss McDwyer. I will be teaching here for a while.'
>
> I glanced outside. It had stopped raining.
>
> 'This is my first year teaching,' her quiet voice told us as she smiled across the room.
>
> That was her first fatal mistake. Even as she said it I saw the boys' deadpan eyes brighten. Their set mouths curved into smiles. She spoke of the course, of the books we would study, of the things we would do. I was interested. To my utmost surprise, I was interested in English.
>
> 'We will begin tomorrow' she said. 'We have a lot to get through.'
>
> Sometimes when she spoke she stumbled on her words. Self-consciously she kept tucking a curl behind her ear. The boys' eyes sparkled wickedly. They were like tigers watching their prey. Soon they would move in for the kill.
>
> We started the next day. Miss McDwyer was early for class. She was full of enthusiasm. So much so, we thought she would burst.
>
> 'We will start with a short story.' There was a lot of moaning and groaning. 'It's called "Old House" and is written by James Brown.'
>
> There was uproar. James Brown must be the most boring, dull writer in the history of mankind. Even his name was boring.
>
> She beamed. 'You will be surprised what you will find in a short story.'
>
> Laughter filled the room. What could possibly be found in a short story?
>
> She was right. We were surprised. There were hidden meanings behind the words, secret messages buried within masked symbols, found only after much uncovering. It was almost as if we were lost in a maze and trying to work our way out. I was so absorbed in my work I did not hear the bell gong drearily throughout the school. Already I was looking forward to the next class.
>
> We started another short story. 'This is called "The Windows of Wonder" and was written by Bryan McMahon,' she informed us. 'Now you can really see the art of the short story.'

I set about it with zest. Nothing was ordinary any more. Everything glinted and shimmered. The words were no longer black and white. They were yellow and purple and red, wavering and contracting, pacing and dancing. Something ignited me.

From 'Miss McDwyer', a short story by Cathy Toft

1. Underline or highlight the adjectives used to describe Miss McDwyer. What do they tell us about the kind of person she is?

2. 'This was her first **fatal** mistake.' To what does the adjective 'fatal' refer? Is it a good choice of adjective for the situation? Explain. (two or three sentences)

3. '**deadpan** eyes . . .' '**set** mouths . . . What do these adjectives tell us about the boys in the class?

4. 'The words were no longer **black** and **white**. They were **yellow** and **purple** and **red** . . .' Comment on the writer's use of colour adjectives in her description of words.

Grammar: nouns, adjectives, verbs

The Exam; Poetry

Exercise 5.

Read this poem carefully, and then answer the questions which follow. The poem is taken from *The School That I'd Like*, edited by Edward Bishen.

Step with Me into a Future School

I'll show you around.
Even at a glance you've found
Things very different and strange.
– Where are the clouds of white dust
From the scraping chalk?
Nobody sits on wooden chairs, at wooden desks,
Listening to teachers talk.
The framed blackboard is nowhere to be seen.
Everything is clean.
The rooms are bright,
And large, and wide, and very light.

No one minds what we wear.
Clothes aren't considered important,
So usually our feet are bare.
No one minds about anything much, really.

There is no whisper
Of engraved desks, arranged in ranks.
Or uniforms.
How could you bear
The drabness? Didn't you care
That each child was an echo
Of his neighbour?

We study at school for three days each week.
For the last hour of the third day
We hold discussions, in groups.
We talk on many things,
From religion to politics,
To our own personal problems.
We discuss human relationships,
And we look back, and see
What happened when knowledge gave man power.
Then we realize the importance
Of wisdom, as well.
– These discussions are led
By a student who is studying
For A.O.Es.
(Those are the Advanced Oral Exams.
When a pupil has taken one,
He writes a thesis on their improvement.
Not many people are bright enough
To take them all. I won't be.
You have to be really clever, you see.)

It is a good school.
Hard work, sometimes,
But people always lend
A hand.
I can depend on someone
To help me understand.
There is so much to learn
That I will only touch the edge of it –
And simply sift the sand.

– If I had a good brain
I would dig really deep, and learn.
But I am not shaped for that.
I have as much to give
As the bright ones.
I know how to live
Even if I never reach second in command.
I have my purpose, too.
If we were all brilliant,
Who would be the crew?

There is a lot for me to do
To prepare me for whatever is in store.
But although I am a student and I learn,
I am not preparing for life.
I am alive now.
Learning is the start of something stretching before me,
And my heart
Says it will be great.
But I can wait.
This present learning tense suits me all right,
Although I'm not too bright.

Melanie, 14

Watch Your Language!

1. Underline all the **nouns**, **verbs** and **adjectives** in the **first two verses** of this poem (as far as 'neighbour?'), and then write them out in three lists under the headings below. Remember that '**is**', '**are**' and '**aren't**' are verbs too! You should have twenty-one verbs (some are repeated), twenty-three nouns and eighteen adjectives (one is repeated).

Nouns (18)	Adjectives (18)	Verbs (18)

2. **Sentence building**

    Select examples of each part of speech from your list that you feel would work well together, and make ten sentences – one noun, verb and adjective per sentence.

    > (**Example**) She couldn't **bear** (verb) the **drabness** (noun) of her **large** (adjective) flat any longer.

3. **Reading comprehension**

    Read from the line *There is so much to learn* in stanza 3 to the end of the poem. Try to summarise in your own words what Melanie is saying about school, and her own present and future. Quote from the poem to support your thoughts, and refer to earlier verses if you wish. (100–120 words)

Grammar: past tenses

Exercise 6.

Write a story based on the following notes. Each section (1–5) represents a **paragraph** in your story, but you may write up to eight sentences per paragraph. Use the past tenses (simple, continuous, present perfect simple and continuous, past perfect simple and continuous) throughout. If in doubt about these, revisit Units 6 and 7 before you begin.

1. Last summer/Brenda and Paul/first holiday abroad, with their three children Sarah, Alan and Stewart.

2. First problem/plane delayed eight hours/sleep at airport. Middle of August/very hot/thousands of people. Paul suffers/claustrophobia. Alan ill. Not/good beginning to the holiday.

3. Plane overbooked/Paul and Brenda/different parts of plane. Brenda in smoking part with kids even though allergic to smoke. Kids/terrified/flying.

4. Get to holiday destination/local representative for travel agent very bad English/hotel dirty/miles from beach. Brenda terrified of rats/one night sees rat in bathroom. Paul gets food poisoning/very ill. Stewart/sunburn and food poisoning.

5. Really angry/extra charges/not mentioned in brochure. Decide never/go to that resort again. Sue travel company/return home.

Grammar: reported speech

The Exam; Other drama

Exercise 7.

(Other Drama, Junior Cert. Higher level, 2002)

The following extract (in edited form) is taken from *Educating Rita* by Willy Russell. Read the extract and then answer the question which follows.

Background to the extract:

As an adult learner, Rita is attending university to study literature. She is a housewife and also works as a hairdresser. She studies at home and comes to college on a regular basis to meet her literature tutor, Frank.

Frank enters carrying a briefcase and a pile of essays. He takes sandwiches and an apple from his briefcase and puts them on his desk and then goes to the window ledge and dumps the essays and briefcase. He sits in a swivel chair, switches on the radio, opens the packet of sandwiches, takes a bite and then picks up a book and starts reading.

Rita bursts through the door out of breath.

Frank: What are you doing here? (*He looks at his watch*) It's Thursday, you . . .

Rita: (*moving over to the desk quickly*) I know I shouldn't be here, it's me dinner hour, but listen, I've gorra tell someone, have y' got a few minutes, can y' spare . . . ?

Frank: (*alarmed*) My God, what is it?

Rita: I had to come an' tell y', Frank, last night, I went to the theatre! A proper one, a professional theatre.

Frank gets up and switches off the radio and then returns to the swivel chair

Frank: (*sighing*) For God's sake, you had me worried, I thought it was something serious.

Rita: No, listen, it was. I went out an' got me ticket, it was Shakespeare, I thought it was gonna be dead borin' . . .

Frank: Then why did you go in the first place?

Rita: I wanted to find out. But listen, it wasn't borin', it was bleedin' great, honest, ogh, it done me in, it was fantastic. I'm gonna do an essay on it.

Frank: (*smiling*) Come on, which one was it?

> *Rita moves up right centre*

Rita: '. . . Out, out, brief candle!

Life's but a walking shadow, a poor player

That struts and frets his hour upon the stage

And then is heard no more. It is a tale

Told by an idiot, full of sound and fury

Signifying nothing.'

Frank: (*deliberately*) Ah, 'Romeo and Juliet'.

Rita: (*moving towards Frank*) Tch. Frank! Be serious. I learnt that today from the book. (*She produces a copy of 'Macbeth'*) Look, I went out an' bought the book. Isn't it great? What I couldn't get over is how excitin' it was.

> *Frank puts his feet up on the desk*

Rita: Wasn't his wife a cow, eh? An' that fantastic bit where he meets Macduff an' he thinks he's all invincible. I was on the edge of me seat at that bit. I wanted to shout out an' tell Macbeth, warn him.

Frank: You didn't, did you?

Rita: Nah. Y' can't do that in a theatre, can y'? It was dead good. It was like a thriller.

Frank: Yes. You'll have to go and see more.

Rita: I'm goin' to. Macbeth's a tragedy isn't it?

> *Frank nods*

Rita: Right. (*She smiles at Frank and he smiles back at her*) Well I just – I just had to tell someone who'd understand.

Frank: I'm honoured that you chose me.

Rita: (*moving towards the door*) Well, I better get back. I've left a customer with a perm lotion. If I don't get a move on there'll be another tragedy.

Imagine that you are Rita **reporting** this conversation with Frank, to her husband later in the day, **or** to the customer with the perm. Begin like this:

> 'Frank first asked me what I **was doing** there, that it **was** Thursday. I said I **knew** I shouldn't be there, that it **was** me dinner hour, but that I had to tell someone, so I **asked him if** he **had** a few minutes to spare …'

N.B.! Check back to the rules governing **reported speech**, in Unit 9, if you are unsure about a tense change. For the use of the **past tense** check Units 6 and 7.

Grammar: verbs
The Exam; Poetry

Exercise 8.

Read this poem carefully and then answer the questions which follow.

I Am Tired of the Wind

I am tired of the wind leaning against me,
    Let it lean somewhere else!
On a brick wall that is too insensible to care,
    Or the trees on the common.

Why should it shove me and elbow me?
    It is too familiar!
I will lure it to the cliff edge, then jump aside
    For it to plunge over.

There! Now it screams down, flailing the sea;
    Smashes on rocks.
Grass does not stir across fields, smoke blur above chimneys.
    Oh, but suddenly I am afraid!

If the wind is a God's breath and I've murdered the wind,
    Will not that dead giant
More terrible then than in his platinum waking day
    Snort gustily in my dreams?

John Smith

1. Underline all the **verbs** in this poem. Write them out in a list in your copy.

2. How does the poet feel about the wind in the first two verses? Why? Support your answer by reference or quotation.

3. 'Oh, but suddenly I am afraid!' Why is he afraid? Explore the images in the last verse for your answer.

4. What is your favourite image of the wind from this poem? Explain your choice in a few sentences (20–30 words).

Vocabulary: using your dictionary

Exercise 9.

1. Use your dictionary to check the meaning of these words **as they are used here**.

> **(Example)** My phone isn't **working**. – act or operate correctly or successfully.

    a. The young girls **careered** down the corridor at breakneck speed.

    b. Mr. O'Brien **trained** the clematis against the wall.

    c. Our Art teacher is on six months' **leave**, travelling in India.

    d. The business is looking for a young person with **drive** and energy.

    e. She's a **retiring** sort of person.

    f. Not everybody agreed with the idea **adopted**.

2. Write six sentences of your own in which each of the words in bold above is used in a different situation with a **different meaning**. Use your dictionary.

Vocabulary: using a thesaurus

Exercise 10.

Here are five entries from the *Bloomsbury English Thesaurus*. Choose three synonyms from each headword, and write **one** sentence per synonym, which clearly illustrates its particular usage and meaning.

> **(Example)** Headword:
>
> **certain**   Three synonyms: positive, confident, convinced
> 1. I'm **positive** it arrived on time.
> 2. Susan is **confident** she will succeed.
> 3. Terry is **convinced** that he's right about Sean.

Now, you do it!

beautiful *adj* charming, comely, fair, fine, exquisite, handsome, lovely, pretty.

beginning *n* arising, commencement, dawn, emergence, inauguration, inception, initiation, opening, outset, start, rise; origin, source.

funny *adj* amusing, comic, comical, diverting, droll, facetious, farcical, humorous, jocose, jocular, laughable, ludicrous, sportive, witty; curious, odd, queer, strange. * *n* jest, joke; cartoon, comic.

certain *adj* absolute, incontestable, incontrovertible, indisputable, indubitable, positive, inevitable, undeniable, undisputed, unquestionable, unquestioned; assured, confident, convinced, sure, undoubting; infallible, never-failing, unfailing; actual, existing, real; constant, determinate, fixed, settled, stated.

furious *adj* angry, fierce, frantic, frenzied, fuming, infuriated, mad, raging, violent, wild; boisterous, fierce, impetuous, stormy, tempest-uous, tumultuous, turbulent, vehement.

Vocabulary: idioms

Exercise 11.

Study the photograph and text below. Then answer the questions which follow.

Back to his roots

A DUTCH soccer fan has decided to blow the final whistle on his football following career.

In a bit of a stew after Holland's 2-2 draw with their Group E rivals Mexico, he has decided to pack it all in and follow the gentleman's sport of rugby.

Apparently envious of those rugged chaps and their cauliflower ears, he decided to go a little better and, in a move reminiscent of Royal Ascot, he festooned his lobes with a few carrots.

And that, he told our intrepid reporter, was the root of his problem.

1. What does the idiom 'Back to his roots' mean in the context of the photograph and the text?
2. What does it **usually** mean? Write one sentence to illustrate its more general use.
3. There are five other idioms in the text. Can you identify them? Write a brief comment on the meaning and usage of each one, in the context of the article.
4. Do you find this photo funny? If so, explain **why** you do, in 30–50 words.

Vocabulary: puns
The Exam; Media studies

Exercise 12.

To pun or not to pun! Do you remember 'Words at Play', Unit 8? Study these three examples. Then answer the questions which follow each one.

A

Let's All Cold Hands
If your hands feel like this, you may be suffering from Raynaud's.

1. Where is the pun in the caption?
2. What is the original saying?
3. How effective is the picture in conveying the message? Comment.
4. What do you learn about Raynaud's disease from the picture and the text?

B

Oh baby, it's well Dunne!

'VALUE Club for Baby' has just been launched by Dunnes Stores.

It seems as though babies are the hippest thing as far as supermarket loyalty schemes are concerned. It's not long since Tesco launched a new loyalty card called 'Babyclub'

Extra

Value Club for Baby will provide extra benefits to Dunnes Stores VALUE club members (of whom there are over 700,000) who have children under three years old.

It will apparently provide a range of offers on a number of essential items.

1. Where is the pun in the headline?
2. How does it relate to the news story in the text?
3. How will customers who have children under three benefit from 'Value Club for baby'?

C

Can you compose a witty 'pun' for this picture that connects the image of the man and the book to the words 'World Book Day 23 April 1998'?

Vocabulary: alliteration
The Exam; Media studies

Exercise 13.

Here is an advertisement that uses alliteration very imaginatively.

1. Comment on the effectiveness of alliteration in this ad, in terms of selling its message to the consumer.
2. Make up your own alliterative phrases for the following items:
   - pears
   - a deodorant
   - the Hurling Final
   - a chocolate bar
   - a washing powder
   - a chicken dish
   - the Lotto
   - a sun holiday
   - a rock concert
   - a front-page newspaper headline

THE PLEASURE OF PEACHES.

THE TEMPTATION OF TRUFFLES.

THE JOY OF JELLYBEANS.

THE INDULGENCE OF ICE CREAM.

THE ECSTASY OF ECLAIRS.

THE BLISS OF A BANK HOLIDAY SPENT

IN THE FOOD HALLS AT HARRODS.

*This Bank Holiday Monday,
Harrods is open from 10am until 6pm.
So visit the Food Halls, our nineteen restaurants
or any of our 300 other departments.*

Vocabulary: similes

Exercise 14.

1. Underline the **similes** in the following passage.

    Susie walked into the principal's office, trembling like a leaf. She was as white as a ghost and terrified. Mr. Brown on the other hand was as cool as a cucumber. He indicated a chair, and told her to sit down. Susie's heart was as heavy as lead. She knew she was in trouble and Mr. Brown was as hard as nails – everyone knew that.

    'So, Susie . . .', Mr. Brown said, his arms folded over his chest. 'What's this I hear about you riding your bike like a maniac around the PE hall last Wednesday? The yard's not big enough for you, eh?' He glared at her, his eyes like ice, and Susie shook like a jelly.

    'I'm . . . I'm really sorry, Mr. Brown. It's my friend. She's as mad as a hatter and she dared me to do it. Honest, I'd never have done it otherwise. I'm as weak as a kitten where she's concerned. She's always making me do daft things. It'll never happen again, I swear!'

    'It had better not, young lady, or you'll be out of here as quick as a flash, do you hear?'

2. Now, **continue the story**. Include some similes from those you exercised in Unit 4. Be as inventive as you can.

The Exam; Personal writing
Media studies

Exercise 15.

Here is a compelling advertisement from the National Drugs Helpline. Make use of it in one of the following ways:

1. **Personal writing, dialogue**

    Write the conversation that takes place between two teenagers who have just read this advertisement. One of them has already experimented with ecstasy. The other has not.

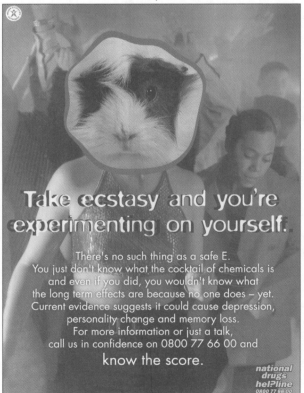

Take ecstasy and you're experimenting on yourself.

There's no such thing as a safe E.
You just don't know what the cocktail of chemicals is and even if you did, you wouldn't know what the long term effects are because no one does – yet. Current evidence suggests it could cause depression, personality change and memory loss.
For more information or just a talk, call us in confidence on 0800 77 66 00 and

know the score.

national
drugs
helpline
0800 77 66 00

2. **Personal writing, debate/talk**

Write out the arguments you would make for and against experimenting with drugs.

3. **Media studies, advertising**

   a. How do you interpret the central message of the ad (Take ecstasy and you're experimenting on yourself)?

   b. Does the picture shock or startle you in any way? Why? How effective is it in conveying the message?

   c. Examine the text. What is the **main** point being made?

The Exam; Functional writing: book reviews

Exercise 16.

The ancient force of Bealtaine blows on May Day, and fuses life into the scarecrow near Niamh and Daire Durkan's home. But Glasán isn't the only scarecrow to visit them. The Black One has also been awakened by the power of the Bealtaine winds ... Niamh and Daire find themselves drawn into a dangerous attempt to destroy the evil powers of Greyfang and Deathtooth. And the wolves of Morrigan are in waiting ...

'One of the year's most exciting books ... fast, tense and one I didn't want to finish.'
Sunday Independent

'One of the best of its kind for many a long day.'
Consumer Choice

'Riveting fantasy ... a fast-moving tale where no words are wasted. From the awakening of the scarecrow, Glasán, the story moves at an ever-increasing pace with strange incidents, frightening gatherings and terrifying sequences in rapid succession ... Absolutely brilliant ... exciting, funny and adventurous.'
Books Ireland

A magical tale of power and revenge – a blend of high adventure and ancient Irish myth – the first in the Giltspur series.

1. Read the **summary** of the plot of this book *The Battle Below Giltspur*, by Cormac MacRaois. Write a summary of the same length of **any** book you have read which impressed you.

2. **Write a letter** to the author of any text you have studied, telling him or her whether or not you enjoyed it, and explaining why. (Functional writing 3, Junior Cert. Higher level, 2002).

The Exam; Functional writing

Exercise 17.

Write a 'star profile' type article on one member of the band Blue for your school magazine **or** local newspaper.

Do your research. Find out as much as you can about the person before you write it. If you are not a fan of this group, pick an individual performer or group of your own choice. (200 words approx.)

The Exam; Media studies/debate

Exercise 18.

(Junior Cert. Higher level, 2002)

1. What point do you think is being made by this cartoon?
2. 'Young people watch too much television.' Make **three** points for **or** against this argument.
3. Based on your experience of Media Studies what advantages do you think television has over radio and print media?

The *Boston Globe* 1988. L.A. Times Syndicate

The Exam; Personal writing/debate

Exercise 19.

Read this article from *The Irish Times*, March 2003, and then answer the question that follows.

Over to you: Do you feel pressured to wear designer labels to school?

**Laura Jefferson,
Transition Year Student,
Dublin**

My school is an all-girls school. We wear a uniform most of the time. We have very few non-uniform days, but, when we do, it is like a fashion parade. Some people will actually go out and spend loads of money on the latest labels and styles just to impress the other students.

I think uniforms are worthwhile. They create a sense of equality amongst the students and, as a result, there is less stereotyping and we have fewer preconceptions of our fellow students.

Nonetheless, it is a real pity that we all have to wear the same clothes in order to stop people making judgments about us. It's a shame that we live in a world where we cannot be trusted to draw our conclusions from the way people behave, rather than how they appear.

I respect people who don't dress themselves from head to toe in labels. I can't relate to a walking advertisement. Even though I feel this way, I have still bought big-label brands myself and have fought with my own parents about clothing choices.

The pressure is on us all.

There is quite a mix of students from different backgrounds at my school. Many of the students who wear the latest gear are not from rich families. I wonder what kind of pressure their parents are under to pay for clothes when there is so little money coming in. These expensive clothes and runners are probably made by kids in Thailand who are desperately poor. Then they are bought by parents here who are not too well-off either and who can't really afford them.

The clothing companies are getting money from poor families on both sides of the world and all because some school bully says it should be so. What a ridiculous situation for us all.

Write a speech for **or against** the motion that **Peer Pressure dictates what we wear.**

The Exam; Personal writing
Exercise 20.

Peace at last . . . as the finishing touches are put to a mural
on the Shankill Road in Belfast.

Study this photograph, then write your reaction to it in the form of an **essay** or a **poem**, using some of the **hyphenated words** below, and the words 'New Life' as your title.

1. Anglo-Irish	13. hair-raising	25. pig-headed	37. small-minded
2. anti-climax	14. head-on	26. pigeon-hole	38. three-dimensional
3. anti-social	15. law-abiding	27. point-blank	39. two-dimensional
4. by-product	16. long-reaching	28. self-assured	40. warm-hearted
5. by-election	17. narrow-minded	29. self-centred	41. well-being
6. broad-minded	18. non-committal	30. self-confident	42. well-meaning
7. cine-camera	19. non-existent	31. self-conscious	
8. cold-blooded	20. non-stop	32. self-contained	
9. cold-hearted	21. North-South	33. sell-out	
10. counter-attack	22. old-fashioned	34. short-sighted	
11. cross-section	23. one-sided	35. single-handed	
12. go-between	24. pent-up	36. single-minded	

The Exam; Personal writing

Exercise 21.

Write a speech for or against the motion that:
Winning isn't Everything.

Spelling: prefixes

Exercise 22.

> re-, under-, over-, un-, mis-, dis-

Add one of the above **prefixes** to the verb in brackets in the sentences below, making any necessary changes to the spelling.

1. We were _____ (charge) for the wine.
2. The steak was so burnt, it was clearly _____ (cook).
3. I hate _____ (pack) my suitcase after the holidays.
4. You can always _____ (heat) it in the microwave.
5. He's wrong. He was obviously _____ (inform).
6. Don't _____ (estimate) him. He's very clever.
7. They _____ (connect) the electricity because they hadn't paid their bill in over a year.
8. Your essay is not good enough. It will have to be _____ (write).
9. The stain has completely _____ (appear).
10. Brian can neither tie nor _____ (tie) his shoelaces.

Spelling: suffixes

Exercise 23.

> -y, -ly, -like, -ful, -less

Make **adjectives** from these nouns, using one of the above suffixes.

1. coward _____
2. youth _____
3. fun _____
4. child _____
5. hope _____
6. success _____
7. filth _____
8. life _____
9. leisure _____
10. mind _____

Sentence building

Exercise 24.

Write ten sentences of your own, using each of the following **prefixes** and **suffixes** just once.

> re-, un-, mis-, dis-, over-, -ly, -ful, -less, -like, -y

Vary the type of sentence, that is, question, exclamation, negative, etc.

Spelling: silent-letter words

Exercise 25.

Do you remember those silent-letter words? Study these examples and then add **one more word** for each silent letter from the list below.

| (Example) | Silent 'b' – | after 'm', as in | lamb |
| | another word | | **thumb** |

1. Silent 'e' – at the end of a word, as in   late
   _____

2. Silent 'g' – before 'n', as in   gnat
   _____

3. Silent 'h' – at the beginning of a word, as in   honest
   _____

4. Silent 'gh' – at the end of a word, as in   neigh
   _____

5. Silent 'k' – before 'n', as in   knee
   _____

6. Silent 'l', as in   calf
   _____

7. Silent 'n', as in   solemn
   _____

8. Silent 'p', as in   physics
   _____

9. Silent 's', as in   aisle
   _____

10. Silent 'w', as in   wriggle
    _____

     sign, though, half, psychology, gate, autumn, wrong, hour, knot, island

Spelling traps! 'able' or 'ible'

Exercise 26.

'able/ible' words. Do you remember them? Here's the test!

Write the endings of these words, with either 'able' or 'ible'. Don't guess! Go back and learn them before doing the test if you need to.

1. sens____		6. fashion____	
2. cap____		7. soci____	
3. comfort____		8. gull____	
4. leg____		9. miser____	
5. respons____		10. account____	

Spelling: near homonyms

Exercise 27.

'accept' or 'except'? Do you remember? Here's the test!

Put the correct word in each space.

1. accept/except?
   a. We were all there _____ Sean.
   b. Please _____ my invitation.

2. affect/effect?
   a. The news of his death will _____ her badly.
   b. Your stupid insults will have no _____ on me!

3. quite/quiet?
   a. It's beautifully _____ in here, isn't it?
   b. You're _____ right, of course.

4. principal/principle?
   a. Sister Carmel is _____ of Loreto College, Swords.
   b. 'A _____'s a _____.' (Mary, in *Juno and the Paycock*, by Sean O'Casey)

5. lightning/lightening?
   a. Thunder and _____ really scare me.
   b. This room could do with _____ up.

Spelling: using your dictionary

Exercise 28.

One word or two, for example, 'Maybe' or 'May be'

Put the correct one in the spaces in these sentences. Don't guess! Check with your dictionary if you are not sure.

1. maybe/may be?
   a. I _____ late home this evening. Don't wait up.
   b. _____ she won't like it.

2. anyone/any one?
   a. Has _____ seen Colm?
   b. Which one do you want? _____, I don't mind.

3. into/in to?
   a. Have you been _____ see the dentist yet?
   b. He went _____ the staffroom five minutes ago.

4. sometimes/some times?
   a. _____ in my life have been difficult.
   b. Kids get fed up _____.

5. everyone/every one?
   a. Will _____ be there?
   b. Spots! I hate _____ of the little horrors!

And finally . . . confusing words

Exercise 29.

The last instalment of 'The World according to Student Bloopers!'

When you read it, you will see that it doesn't **always** make sense! Can you **rewrite** it so that it reads as a clear (if rather sketchy) version of these periods of history? Correct any **spelling errors** as you go. Have fun!

Meanwhile in Europe, the enlightenment was a reasonable time. Voltare invented electricity and also wrote a book called Candy. Gravity was invented by Isaac Walton. It is chiefly noticeable in the Autumn, when the apples are falling off the trees.

Bach was the most famous composer in the world and so was Handel. Handel was half German, half Italian, and half English. He was very large. Bach died from 1750 to the present. Beethoven wrote music even though he was deaf. He was deaf so he wrote loud music. He took long walks in the forest even when everyone was calling for him. Beethoven expired in 1827 and later died for this.

France was in a very serious state. The French Revolution was accomplished before it happened. The Marseillaise was the theme song of the French Revolution, and it catapulted into Napoleon. During the Napoleonic Wars, the crowned heads of Europe were trembling in their shoes. Then the Spanish gorillas camed down from the hills and nipped at Napoleon's flanks. Napoleon became ill with bladder problems and was very tense and unrestrained. He wanted an heir to inherit his power, but since Josephine was a baroness, she couldn't bear children.

The sun never set on the British Empire because the British Empire is in the East and the sun sets in the West. Queen Victoria was the longest queen. She sat on a thorn for 63 years. Her reclining years and finally the end of her life were exemplatory of a great personality. Her death was the final event which ended her reign.

The nineteenth century was a time of many great inventions and thoughts. The invention of the steam boat caused a network of rivers to spring up. Cyrus McCormick invented the McCormick raper, which did the work of a hundred men. Samuel Morse invented a code of telepathy. Louis Pasteur discovered a cure for rabbis. Charles Darwin was a naturalist who wrote the Organ of the Species. Madman Curie discovered radium. And Karl Marx became one of the Marx brothers.

The First World War, caused by the assignation of the Arch-Duck by a surf, ushered in a new error in the anals of human history.

Spelling – Most frequently misspelled words

Here is my own alphabetical list of frequently misspelled words. It is based on those my own students often misspell, and also includes some that colleagues in other subject areas have suggested. 'Science', apparently, is very often misspelled! Note that the words are spelled in syllables, for easy learning.

Follow this **procedure** for all the spellings on the list – a **letter** at a time perhaps:
1. Learn the spelling, of an 'A' word for example.
2. Cover it, and write the word (in pencil) in the 'Spell it' space.
3. Check to see if it's correct. If it isn't, rub it out and relearn it, before writing it again.
4. Write a short sentence with this word in it, in the space provided.

	Word	Spell it	Short sentence
A	ab-so-lute-ly	absolutely	You're absolutely right.
	ac-ci-den-tal-ly		
	a-cross		
	ad-ver-tise-ment		
	af-fect		
	al-read-y		
	al-ways		
	a-mong		
	a-mount		
	ap-pear-ance		
	ar-gu-ment		
	au-thor		
	au-tumn		
B	beau-ti-ful		
	be-gin-ning		
	be-lieve		
	bi-cy-cle		
	bor-ing		
	bril-liant		
	bro-chure		
	bud-get		
	bun-sen		
	bus-i-ness		

Word	Spell it	Short sentence
C cal-en-dar		
cam-paign		
can-celled		
ca-reer		
ca-tas-tro-phe		
cel-lo		
change-a-ble		
char-ac-ter		
choc-o-late		
christ-mas		
col-lege		
com-plete-ly		
con-cer-to		
con-science		
crit-i-cism		
crotch-et		
D def-i-nite-ly		
de-scribe		
de-scrip-tion		
de-ter-mined		
dis-ap-pear		
dis-ap-point-ed		
E e-con-om-ics		
ef-fect		
el-i-gi-ble		
em-bar-rass		
en-vi-ron-ment		
es-pe-cial-ly		
ex-ag-ger-ate		
ex-cept		
ex-cite-ment		
ex-haust-ed		
ex-hi-bi-tion		
ex-is-tence		
ex-pla-na-tion		
ex-traor-di-nary		

Word	Spell it	Short sentence
F fa-mil-iar		
fam-i-ly		
fas-ci-nat-ing		
fa-vour-ite		
Feb-ru-ary		
flu-o-res-cent		
for-eign		
for-tu-nate-ly		
for-ty		
friend		
fright-ened		
G gen-u-ine		
gor-geous		
gov-ern-ment		
grad-u-al-ly		
gram-mar		
grate-ful		
guar-an-tee		
guess		
gym-na-si-um		
H hand-ker-chief		
hand-some		
heard		
heav-i-ly		
heav-y		
hon-est-ly		
hor-ri-ble		
hos-pit-al		
hu-mor-ous		
hy-giene		
I im-me-di-ate-ly		
in-for-ma-tion		
in-no-cent		
in-tel-li-gent		
in-ter-est-ing		
in-vis-i-ble		
ir-rel-e-vant		

Word	Spell it	Short sentence
J jeal-ous		
jew-el-ry		
jour-ney		
judge-ment		
K kid-napped		
kin-der-gar-ten		
know-ledge		
L lab-o-ra-tory		
lei-sure		
li-a-bil-i-ty		
li-brar-y		
lis-ten		
lit-er-a-ture		
live-li-hood		
loose		
love-ly		
lux-u-ry		
M man-age-a-ble		
may-be		
men-tion		
mile-age		
mis-chie-vous		
mort-gage		
mov-able		
N nec-es-sar-y		
neigh-bour		
nei-ther		
niece		
nine-ty		
no-tice-able		
O o-be-di-ent		
oc-ca-sion-al-ly		
oc-curred		
op-in-ion		
op-por-tu-ni-ty		
op-po-site		
op-ti-mism		

Watch Your Language!

	Word	Spell it	Short sentence
P	par-al-lel		
	par-lia-ment		
	pas-sen-ger		
	per-suade		
	pleas-ant		
	po-et		
	pos-sess		
	pre-cious		
	prej-u-dice		
	priv-i-lege		
	pro-fes-sion		
	psy-chol-o-gy		
R	re-al-ise		
	re-al-ly		
	re-ceipt		
	re-cent		
	rec-og-nise		
	rec-om-mend		
	ref-er-ee		
	rel-e-vant		
	re-spon-si-ble		
	res-tau-rant		
	rhyme		
	rhythm		
	ri-dic-u-lous		
S	safe-ty		
	sand-wich		
	scene		
	scis-sors		
	sep-a-rate		
	sim-i-lar		
	sin-cere-ly		
	sol-dier		
	sol-emn		
	speech		
	sta-tis-tics		
	suf-fi-cient		

Word	Spell it	Short sentence
sug-gest		
sup-pose		
sure-ly		
sur-prise		
sus-pi-cious		
sym-me-try		
T tech-ni-cal		
tech-nique		
tem-per-a-ture		
tem-po-rar-y		
ter-ri-ble		
their		
the-o-ry		
tired		
to-mor-row		
trag-e-dy		
tri-umph		
twelfth		
U un-doubt-ed-ly		
u-nique		
use-ful		
u-su-al-ly		
V vac-u-um		
val-u-a-ble		
veg-et-able		
ve-hi-cle		
vi-cious		
vil-lain		
vol-ume		
W weath-er		
Wed-nes-day		
weird		
wheth-er		
wom-en		
wool-len		

Watch Your Language!

Word	Spell it	Short sentence
Y yacht		
yearn-ing		
yes-ter-day		
yield-ing		
yo-gurt		
young-ster		
Z za-ny		
zeal-ous		
zo-di-ac		
zon-ing		
zo-o-log-i-cal		
zo-ol-o-gist		
zo-ol-o-gy		

And absolutely finally . . . a joke!

Teacher: *How many letters are there in the Space Alphabet?*
Bright student: *24, Miss – E. T. went home!*